DATE DUE

Demco, Inc. 38-293

Too Late to Die Young

TOO LATE
TO DIE YOUNG

Nearly True Tales from a Life

Harriet McBryde Johnson

Henry Holt and Company · New York

Henry Holt and Company, LLC
Publishers since 1866
115 West 18th Street
New York, New York 10011

Henry Holt® is a registered trademark of
Henry Holt and Company, LLC.

Distributed in Canada by H. B. Fenn and Company Ltd.

Library of Congress Cataloging-in-Publication Data

Johnson, Harriet McBryde.
    Too late to die young / Harriet McBryde Johnson.—1st ed.
    p. cm.
    ISBN-13: 978-0-8050-7594-6
    ISBN-10: 0-8050-7594-1
    1. Johnson, Harriet McBryde. 2. People with disabilities—
United States—Biography. I. Title.

HV3013.J65A3 2005
362.196'748'0092—dc22
[B]   2004054007

Henry Holt books are available for special promotions and
premiums. For details contact: Director, Special Markets.

First Edition 2005

Designed by Victoria Hartman

Printed in the United States of America
1   3   5   7   9   10   8   6   4   2

For all of those
who let their stories cross mine,
especially
my Valentine

Contents

Preface

I have come to expect it. The glassy smile. The concerned gaze. The double take—sometimes hilarious—when I roll out to meet a client in my waiting room or show up someplace where someone like me is not expected. The discombobulation that comes in my wake.

It's not that I am ugly. It's more that people don't know how to look at me. The power wheelchair is enough to inspire gawking, but that's the least of it. Much more impressive is the impact on my body of more than four decades of a muscle-wasting disease. Now, in my midforties, I'm Karen Carpenter–thin, flesh mostly vanished, a jumble of bones in a floppy bag of skin. When, in childhood, my muscles got too weak to hold up my spine, I tried a brace for a while, but fortunately a skittish anesthesiologist said no to fusion, plates, and pins—all the apparatus that might have kept me straight. At age fifteen, I threw away the back brace and let my spine reshape itself into a deep twisty S-curve. Now my right side is two deep canyons. To keep myself upright, I lean forward, rest my rib cage on my lap, plant my elbows on rolled towels beside my knees. Since my backbone found its own natural shape, I've been entirely comfortable in my skin.

A few times in my life—I recall particularly one largely crip, largely lesbian cookout in Colorado—I've been looked at as a rare kind of beauty. There is also the bizarre fact that in Charleston, South Carolina, where I live, some people call me Good Luck Lady: they consider it propitious to cross my path when a hurricane is coming and to kiss my head on voting day. But most often the reactions are decidedly negative. People on the street have been moved to comment:

I admire you for being out; most people would give up.

God bless you! I'll pray for you.

You don't let the pain hold you back, do you?

If I had to live like you, I think I'd kill myself.

I used to try to explain that in fact I enjoy my life, that it's a great sensual pleasure to zoom by power chair on these delicious muggy streets, that I have no more reason to kill myself than most people. But it gets tedious. God didn't put me on this street to provide disability awareness training to everyone who happens by. In fact, no god put anyone anywhere for any reason, if you want to know.

But most people don't want to know. They think they know everything there is to know just by looking at me. That's how stereotypes work.

Because the world sets people with conspicuous disabilities apart as different, we become objects of fascination, curiosity, and analysis. We are read as avatars of misfortune and misery, stock figures in melodramas about courage and determination. The world wants our lives to fit into a few rigid narrative templates: how I conquered disability (and others can conquer their Bad Things!), how I adjusted to disability (and a positive attitude can move mountains!), how disability made me wise (you can only marvel and hope it never happens to you!), how disability brought me to Jesus (but redemption is waiting for you if only you pray).

For me, living a real life has meant resisting those formulaic narratives. Instead of letting the world turn me into a disability object, I have insisted on being a subject in the grammatical sense: not the passive "me" who is acted upon, but the active "I" who does things. I practice law and politics in Charleston, which I'll nominate as the most interesting small city in America. I travel. I find various odd adventures. I do my bit to help the disability rights movement change the world in fundamental ways.

And I tell stories. On one level, that's not unusual. Most Charleston people—rich and poor, black and white, young and old—tell stories as part of daily life. For any Charleston lawyer, any Southern lawyer for that matter, storytelling skill comes so close to being a job requirement that maybe it should be tested on the bar exam. Beyond that, for me, storytelling is a survival tool, a means of getting people to do what I want. I'm talking mainly about getting people to drive my van.

I don't drive, but work and politics frequently compel me to travel to Columbia. It's two hours each way on Interstate 26, a straight road through flat land, with many miles of pine trees, a few creeks, and one brown river. For Charleston people, it's not a glamor destination. We're still angry that a coterie of real estate developers moved the state capital up there in the early nineteenth century. We all know there is no heat on earth worse than the inside of a van that has been baking in a Columbia parking lot all day.

For all these reasons, Charlestonians don't line up to drive to Columbia and back. To get a driver, I have to offer some incentive. Living on a budget with unpredictable cash flow, I naturally prefer not to pay when I can help it. Therefore, I offer stories.

My tales are true, or nearly true, as true as memory allows. They evolve in telling. They shift focus and emphasis, depending on what the listener—an active participant in the story's creation—wants. There are questions, digressions, reactions. Easter lets me know when I've found a character's voice by raising her right hand with an emphatic "Thank you!" With Dave, it's silence that tells me the pacing is right; his habitual magpie-chatter stops. When Mike says, "Wait a minute, let me get this straight," he leads me to an angle I hadn't noticed. I may recount the same sequence of events over and over again, but each listener makes a new story. That's because storytelling itself is an activity, not an object. Stories are the closest we can come to shared experience.

Drawn from the particularities of life, driven by what-happens-next, my stories don't aim to satisfy the general curiosity about what it's like to live in a withered body like mine or feed the public appetite for inspirational pap. Like all stories, they are most fundamentally a chance to ride around inside another head and be reminded that being who we are and where we are, and doing what we're doing, is not the only possibility.

I offer here a collection of tales as I tell them in my van. These are the tales I most enjoy telling. They have a mix of themes and characters and incidents sufficient to get the van from downtown Charleston all the way to Pinopolis at least, and maybe to Manning.

Is there a point? Who am I to say? Philosophically, I think meaning is created by people in interaction, sorting things out together. This book doesn't have a tidy message. It isn't a tidy work. If I had the freedom of fiction writing, I'd cut the number of characters, but in truth my experience is crowded and over-populated; I rarely do anything alone. Events as they happen dictate which people appear, how long they stay, and what is or is not revealed about them. This is true even of the central

"Harriet" character. As she appears in these narratives, she is self-centered, smart, active, funny, argumentative, sociable, engaged, loving, vain, forgiving, and ready for adventure. At the same time, there are many things about her that are not revealed and many stories that are not told.

Of course I worry. Despite my fine talk, I am offering parts of me and of my life as objects for sale and consumption. As much as I resist, those dominant narrative templates may be imposed from without. All readers come with their own perspectives; inevitably, some will read through the filters of social expectations. In this medium, I can't adjust the tale as I go along, based on individual reactions. I must fix it once, knowing the conversations will move on without me.

But, as you'll see, I've had some experience with odd positions and with the surprises they bring. With luck, what follows will expand perspectives—yours and mine. If so, I will count it an adventure worth the undertaking.

1

Too Late to Die Young

I'm three or four years old. I'm sitting on the living room floor, playing with dolls. I look up at the TV and see a little boy. He's sitting on the floor, playing with toy soldiers. Then he's in Little League; he stumbles on his way to first base. He visits a doctor. His parents are sad. He's in a wheelchair. Then a bed. Then I see the toy soldiers. No boy. An unseen narrator says, "Little Billy's toy soldiers have lost their general." It's a commercial for the Muscular Dystrophy Association. As the narrator makes the pitch, a realization comes to me: I will die.

Is it really one of my earliest memories? Or was it manufactured by my imagination? I don't suppose it matters. Either way, it was my truth. It is my truth.

I'm a little girl who knows she will die, but I don't say anything; I don't want to distress my parents. Somehow, though, my mother realizes. "That boy," she tells me more than once, "has a different kind of muscular dystrophy. Girls don't get it." Maybe, I think, but he looks a lot like me. And pretty soon I see little girls on the telethon and hear that girls, too, have "killer diseases."

I don't know the word, but I figure my mother is in denial.

By the time I am five, I think of myself as a dying child. I've been sick a lot. There is some discussion before they decide to send me to kindergarten. I am glad they do.

When I die, I think, I might as well die a kindergartner.

✦

I'm in a courtroom at the defendant's table. I look up at the bench and hear the judge sentence me to death. A gasp rises from a faceless crowd. They're shocked, astonished. I'm not. I've known all along. There's no question of guilt or innocence, justice or injustice. It's simply a fact. It's hard to understand, but true. I will die.

How old am I when that dream first comes to me? Eight, I think.

The death sentence hangs over my childhood like a cloud. Beneath the cloud, I live a happy child's life. Why not? A daughter of graduate students who become teachers, I am well tended by a succession of black women. My sister, Beth, two years old when I arrive on the scene, generally tolerates me with good grace; three brothers come along for me to boss. The TV regularly brings me Dick Van Dyke, Andy Griffith, and Bullwinkle, and one person in a wheelchair, Dr. Gillespie, who fulminates and barks orders at handsome Dr. Kildare. I lay LPs on the turntable and soak up the sounds of Joan Baez and Los Hermanos de Vera Cruz. There are books with beautiful pictures. To try to fatten myself up, I get black beans and fried bananas. To fry my brain, *Alice in Wonderland*. All these things are great pleasures, then and now. But then and now, life has a certain edge. I know it will not last.

When I am thirteen, I read Orwell's *1984* and calculate how old I'll be then. No way, I think. I go to a "special" school and then a "normal" high school and study hard, but I have no fantasies of a future. I study because somewhere along the way I've developed a competitive streak and because studying, too, is a pleasure.

And besides, I think, when I die I might as well die educated.

✦

I'm watching an old Dracula movie on TV. I'm twelve, old enough to know this is cheesy pop culture, and yet it speaks to me. Like any preteen I pick up, without fully understanding, the latent sexual charge: the count's perverse seduction of the Englishman's fiancée is weird sex safely disguised as weird violence. But for me it's not only about strange passions under the moon, bats passing through tight cracks, moaning in canopy beds, or even all that neck-biting. For me, the best part is when Professor Van Helsing, the expert from Amsterdam, taps his pipe and explains, "They are called the Undead." The professor's presentation has the dull rationality of a graduate seminar. Dramatically, it's agony. But I love it. It gives meaning to the crashing ending, that moment when they drive the stake through Dracula's heart. For Dracula, there is no heaven or hell, no rebirth, no haunting. It's dust to dust and vanishing in the wind. Ah! Beautiful!

I've accepted the reality of death so early it's hard to imagine life without it. But figuring out what it means is another matter. I look to conventional religion and try to think of death as a one-way ticket to a perfect place. With a naturally legalistic mind and a smattering of Catholic doctrine, however, I conclude that the odds are against a straight shot to heaven, especially since Thought Crime counts. And anyway, who would want perfection, having known the gorgeous squalor of the Carolina Lowcountry?

There are mystical and occult alternatives. Hauntings, auras, and energy fields. Reincarnation. Time warps, parallel universes.

Returning to the Oversoul. But none satisfies me. It is Professor Van Helsing who speaks to the fundamental tragedy of refusing to die; it is Dracula's end that shows the way out.

And what of Dracula's bride? The feminist view is that she pays the price of breaking convention in a patriarchal society. For me, her story means something else. When the tale starts, she is beautiful, healthy, engaged to be married—normal in every way. But she, too, gets a stake in the heart. She shows that death is not only for people like me.

It comes in a slow dawning, this idea that death is for normal people, too. In childhood and youth, I am personally acquainted with only a few dead people, but there are lots of them around—they live in family stories. At our Thanksgiving table, my mother speaks of Great Aunt Harriet's dinner rolls, which always came out of the oven just as the family sat down to eat. Great Aunt Harriet died nearly twenty years before I was born; the black people who made those rolls, and timed them so perfectly, are dead, too. As we spoon out the oyster casserole, my grandmother tells how Uncle Oscar found a pearl in his oysters and set it in a gold tiepin. Then someone, maybe someone born after Uncle Oscar died, remarks that of course it happened to Uncle Oscar, because he was rich and drew more riches like a magnet.

So rich uncles and hospitable aunts die. I will die. It is only one more step to infer that everyone at our table will die, too. What amazes me is that the others seem oblivious. They seem to think that dying is only for the terminally ill, only for people like me.

I don't see myself as morbid or obsessed, but I think about death a lot. I know it isn't normal, but my relationship with death becomes part of me. I can handle it, even if normal people can't. I decide to be discreet, like Dracula, and live quietly among normal people. No need to trouble them with details. No need for them to know about the coffin I keep in the basement.

I start being vague about my medical diagnosis. Rather than owning this or that form of muscular dystrophy or this or that type of muscular atrophy, I say I have "a muscle disease." I don't want others to connect me with the dying people on the telethon. I figure if I let people peek in my basement, they'll jump to the wrong conclusion. They'll define me as one of the undead, an unnatural creature, not really alive but feeding on the lifeblood of others. Or, alternatively, they'll make me a pity object, one of Jerry's Kids—someone to make them grateful they are not like me. By setting me apart as a death totem, they can avoid looking in their own basements where their own coffins wait.

I know I am as alive as any of them, and they are as mortal as I. I am set apart not by any basic realities, but by perceptions—theirs and mine. They insist on dividing the world between the living and dying; I insist on both at the same time. Why not?

I study, play, work, find a place in a family and a community, and enjoy the many delights that continue to fall on me. As my body continues to deteriorate, my life looks more and more normal.

At twenty-five I leave the cozy comfort and familiar dysfunctionality of home and family to go to law school. I figure, I'll be twenty-seven when I finish; if I go now, I can probably practice for a couple of years.

By this time, the thought is almost subconscious: when I die, I might as well die a lawyer.

◆

I've just turned thirty. I've been lolling in bed for nearly three weeks; I say I've strained my neck, but really it's major depression. Just before my birthday, my mother had brain surgery; she's come through it beautifully, but I'm terrified to think I could actually outlive my parents. I'm put further adrift by the sudden death of the crazy German doctor who nursed me with pea soup and sausages when I refused to go to the hospital with pneumonia. Now I remember how he kept vigil at my bedside so my parents could sleep and then fell asleep himself. As I listened to his deep barrel-chested rumble, I imagined he was snoring in German. In the middle of the night, in the middle of a medical crisis, that snore made me smile and know again that life is a great gift, worth hanging on to. Now, in my depression, the memory makes me smile again. But then I sink back down.

Maybe "sink" is the wrong word; it feels more like "rising." It has that kind of intensity. Is this a midlife crisis? Should I now take stock? Deal with my disappointed expectations? My thoughts race by, but I manage to grab them and take a look. I find they are coherent. I'm bonkers, but rational. I know what's bothering me: my plan to die young hasn't worked out. I wonder, what would I have done differently if I'd known I would live so long? What do I do now? My thoughts take on the structure of a song, a song with too many verses. But there's a simple chorus, repeated over and over: it's too late to die young.

The time comes and I tell them my neck is better. I go back to work and all of life's routines, but some things have changed. I went in bed agnostic and have come out atheist. When the next medical crisis comes, I find I can hear the death sentence without dread. The lessons of Little Billy and his toy soldiers, of Dracula and his bride have gone from my head to a deeper place. I have taken death into my heart.

I decide to talk about the coffin in the basement. As an experiment, I confide to two nondisabled woman friends that I am genuinely surprised to be alive at age thirty.

"I had no idea," one says. "I've never thought of you that way."

"Absolutely not," the other agrees.

They refuse to believe I am under a death sentence. I am pleased my reticence has been so effective, but I also wonder if it will ever be possible to get real.

Then I reconsider my childhood death sentence and decide I have been the victim of a fraud. Sure, I am mortal. Yes, I will die. But I have never been terminally ill the way I was led to believe. I study the telethon and try to understand its peculiar power. It spews out the same old messages—"killer disease," "life ebbing away," "before it's too late." As I hear the death sentence pronounced on another generation of children, I wonder how many have actually been killed by the predictions. How many have suffered pneumonia without vigilant parents or a crazy German doctor with pea soup? How many have died for lack of a reason, when a reason was needed in the middle of the night, to hang on to life? Worst of all, how many have lived and died without learning to value their own lives?

I join the telethon protest and oppose physician-assisted suicide. I want people to know our culture is playing fast and loose with the facts. While anyone may die young, it's not something you can count on. You have to be prepared to survive.

Among allies in the disability rights movement, I start hearing things I don't expect. "We're not dying," some comrades say. "We're disabled, not terminally ill." Even in the movement, denial rules. It's not only nondisabled people who shy away from what's in the basement.

I decide to embrace the death sentence. No need to fear it; no need to hasten it. Mortality is something all people share, a unifying force. Every life, whether long or short, is a treasure of infinite value. These things are true, I figure, and it's my job to say so.

When I die, I might as well die honest.

✦

I'm thirty-nine. A man has come to my law office for a will. He has advanced AIDS. I start explaining the options: "When you die . . ." I'm horrified to realize I've dropped the polite circumlocutions and make a quick substitution. "When your will takes effect . . ."

I'm flustered. He looks at me with a wise, weary smile. "It's OK," he says. "I know what's going to happen. That's why I'm here."

He has unlocked the door. He knows about the coffin in the basement. We can get real.

"So explain what happens when I croak," he says.

By the time the final documents come off the printer, we're laughing so hard I wonder what the lawyer in the next office will think. "I can't tell you," he says, "how great it is to work with someone who can deal with this stuff without freaking out. Most people are so . . . compassionate."

We shake hands. "It's been my pleasure," I tell him. It really has.

Life still demands circumlocutions. Concealing my exact diagnosis—even officially from myself—remains the easiest way to deal with popular fears; I can't hope to bring everyone around to my way of thinking. Sometimes I wish I could do what they do, pretend that death is something that happens to other people. But denial is not an option now.

In youth, I accepted death as the end of all things. Now I know it is more. It is part of all we are, all there is. Wallace Stevens wrote:

> *Death is the mother of beauty, mystical*
> *Within whose burning bosom we devise*
> *Our earthly mothers, waiting, sleeplessly.*

An awareness of death fosters appreciation for the stuff of life. Those structures of material creation, webs of relationships, cultural institutions, language, thoughts, memories become marvelous. How extraordinary that they exist, yet are no more permanent than soap bubbles floating in the air! The author of Ecclesiastes said (in arguing a position very different from mine) that everything we undertake is striving after wind. In other translations it's rendered "a vexation of the spirit," but I like striving after wind. It seems a fine description for all the activity of humankind from the beginning to the end. Why do it? Why not?

Now I am unexpectedly middle-aged. In the last twenty years or so, I've lost most movement in my arms and in several fingers; in the last four years, I've lost the ability to swallow most solid foods and lost so much flesh that I am coming to look like the skeleton I will someday become. Yet, day by day, my physical deterioration has been slow, downright gentle. If the next twenty years are like the last, I'll be old. It certainly could happen.

Still, in my heart, the old death sentence remains in force. Sometimes the death-penalty dream comes back, just as I created it in childhood—the same anonymous judge, faceless spectators, nondescript Perry Mason–style courtroom. I wonder, why doesn't the dream story happen in one of the real courtrooms where I work? Why not use a real judge? How about a ghostly visit from the late J. B. "Bubba" Ness? Shouldn't attorney David Bruck be there beside me? He might get me off.

Why is it so plain? I'm not sure. Maybe it's sufficient to keep in my mind a plain truth: I will die.

Now the dream typically comes after a loss. It tells me that death remains mysterious. My mind continues to struggle with what it is, what it means. How can I imagine a world without me? How have I survived so many friends, so many family members, so many heroes? How many more losses will there be? Why can't Mel Brooks live forever? For someone so funny, even two thousand years wouldn't be enough! Death is natural, but not just. It is a random force of nature; survival is equally accidental.

Each loss is an occasion to remember that survival is a gift. I owe it to others to make good use of my time.

When I die, I might as well die alive.

◆

It's late October. Beth and I are coming home from Cuba, on layover in a Mexican airport. She gives me a poke: the Aeromexico counter is decorated with paper skeletons to celebrate the Day of the Dead. We wait in line and I contemplate the skeletons. Our plane might crash. Not likely, but possible. We get on the plane and experience the miracle of an uneventful flight. I remember those skeletons with joy.

I shouldn't care what happens to my bones. When I'm dead I'll be past caring. Yet I think about it sometimes. I like the way it is for wild things. It would be good to be swallowed up in a swamp, feed delicious crabs, nourish the fetid fertility of pluff mud. Over centuries the weight of earth and slow growth of roots could grind my bones to powder. My skeleton might give strength to the cyprus trees.

But I am not a wild creature. There are rules. The rules don't suit me. I don't want my body preserved by chemicals, sealed off in a box, set apart in a graveyard. A body, no longer living but artificially tied to a life that once was, becomes hideous. I don't want that.

Most of all, I don't want my name on a tombstone. It's enough to have my name recorded in dull public records with the names of generations of lawyers filing lawsuits and writing deeds and wills. Let my tale-telling family connect me with a few good stories. That way, Aunt Harriet, though dead, will have a place at the table.

Yet even in my family, memories will fade. I may be confused with the other Aunt Harriet, the one who served the hot rolls. Then, I'll be forgotten. Even ghosts must die to make room for new ones. That's fine. A little immortality—for a little while—is good enough. When the time comes, let my body and mind and memory vanish without a trace.

Between now and that time, there are things I want to do. While I have been expecting to die, my time has become filled with people and places and work and strange undertakings. I have become active and involved with a family and a community and a web of varied beloveds and a number of causes. My calendar is booked with deadlines and appointments and travel and meetings and occasions of celebration. I have stories to tell and retell and stories unfolding that I want to live out.

When I die, I might as well die striving after wind.

2

Hail to the Chief!

Well. I'll be damned if I'm going to turn myself wrong side out for the comfort and supposed security of that asshole."

The asshole in question is Ronald W. Reagan, the president of the United States. Normally, I call him the Asshole in Chief. That elicits outrage, and then I act contrite: "You're right, that was disrespectful—to a perfectly serviceable body part." Normally that's my riff, but my roommate, Norah, has heard it too many times, and even the first time, it made no impression on her. She's hard to outrage. Even now as I write this, after Alzheimer's transferred Ronnie from Teflon president to lamblike innocence and triggered a parallel process of public forgetfulness and forgiveness capped by a bicoastal state funeral, now that I'm old enough to remember with chagrin my youthful zeal for castigation, I suspect Norah—wherever she is—might not notice whether the word is Commander or Asshole. Hey, same difference.

I've just read a memo that was slipped under our door and flew into my path of travel when I blasted through with my power chair. It's crunched up with tire tracks by the time Norah gets in and hands it to me to read. Memo-reading is my main household chore. I'm a law student.

Norah is at the sink, furiously rewashing the dishes. "I see Little Miss Tidy has been here."

"Yes, Charlene's been here." Charlene's the nursing student who works for me. She's like the Anti-Norah. Wide-eyed, unfailingly sweet, tidy. Norah doesn't like the way Charlene washes dishes. I tell her to leave it alone for a minute. I tell her President Ronnie is paying a visit this Tuesday. He'll be speaking in the Horseshoe, right outside our door. The Secret Service says we are to vacate for the whole day.

The dish clattering stops and Norah says one word: "Goodness."

Under normal circumstances, Norah displays a mastery of colorful language that is impressive in an undergraduate; it's when she's really, really riled that she says things like goodness, heavens, and oh dear. Seeing her so upset has me taken aback, and, as I often do when confronted with raw emotion, I cool down. I shift into soothing mode. "Well, now, it's only a few hours, and probably we can get the time trimmed . . ."

"What are you talking about? I won't stand for it. This is America. I've lived under martial law!"

She's from New England. Her mother strikes me as a bit controlling, and God knows I'm not the most democratic of roommates, but this is hardly a police state.

"Several years ago," she explains, "we traveled behind the Iron Curtain. Something happened. I swore I'd never submit to anything like that ever again."

This is news to me and I can't help wondering if it's for real. She tends to do this Woman with a Past shtick, as though other people don't have pasts, as though my own past as the biggest little dog in crip school and then as the culture-shocked lone crip in nondisabled high school and nearly lone crip in college doesn't count.

But if it's an act, it's utterly convincing. I don't need the details about what happened behind the Iron Curtain. All right, we can fight for our rights. All right, I'll keep the Secret Service at bay—for Norah's sake.

◆

All this is happening in the fall of 1983, a time when we are a little skittish—and ought to be more skittish—about the coming of Big Brother to steal away our civil liberties. I've known Norah since the previous winter. At that time, my roommate was a pale and conscientious law student named Marie. Marie grew up without TV and seemed to be making up for lost trash with constant devotion to *Fantasy Island, Remington Steele,* and *Love Boat.* She was also devoted to her long-distance fiancé. Every day, without fail, she got a card in the mail from him and taped it to the wall over her bed. By the end of the semester, her side of the large bedroom we shared was a brain-numbing jumble of cute animals, dramatic sunsets, romantic landscapes, whimsical cartoons, and flowers! flowers! flowers! My zone stood in Spartan contrast. The only thing over my bed was the Karl Marx poster that my mother bought from the Young Communist League of Paris and gave to me because she thought a girl in student housing ought to have a big picture of a man over her bed. I wasn't sure a man who had just celebrated the hundredth anniversary of his death was exactly right, but I appreciated the thought.

Marie was a quiet and considerate roommate, but sometimes I needed relief. I hired Norah as my Anti-Marie.

There was also serious business at hand. I had advertised for a couple of morning personal assistants—we called them attendants then—to come early a few days a week and give me my breakfast, a bedpan, and a bath, and get me dressed. Norah was

a journalism student. Her resume gave no indications of any desire to serve humanity or help people and she had no hospital or
nursing home experience. I thought she might be exactly what
I was looking for.

She shows up for her interview in tight black jeans and a ruf-
fled off-shoulder polyester knit fuchsia top with black polka
dots. Although jarring on the preppy campus of the University
of South Carolina, the get-up does show off Norah's black hair,
ivory skin, and square shoulders. "I put this look together myself," she says. "Don't you think it's perfect for a South Carolina
video arcade hostess?" I guess so. She is dressed for her other job.

If the costume is Daisy Yokum, the persona is Bette Midler.
I have my doubts, but Norah doesn't bat an eye about bedpan
duties, says a job that's done by eight-forty each morning will
be perfect, and seems excited about riding the six A.M. bus with
all the other maids. She passes the lifting test, following my exact verbal instructions to put me in the bed and back in my
chair. I decide to put her on the schedule for a couple of hours,
see how she does, and expand her duties as tolerated.

Norah proves to be reliable, competent, and highly entertain-
ing. She is also in need of money; her parents hold her on a tight
leash. She becomes my primary PA. Marie is responsible only for
night duties. At the end of the year, Marie decides to transfer to
a law school close to her devoted, and Norah is the natural suc-
cessor roommate. It is time for me to meet her parents.

Other parents in this situation have expressed serious concerns. Can darling daughter handle the responsibility? Will
rooming with a disabled person deprive her of a positive college
experience? Will she be marked by my stigma? Could my odd-
ity rub off? Norah's parents are unequivocally positive. To be
sure, I give them, and Norah, some stern talk. Norah will be expected home at eleven every night. She will stay in after I go to
bed, sober enough to evacuate me in case of fire. She will not

break any laws in my presence. The more I talk, the more the parents like it. They agree to cover Norah's full share of the rent, up front, and so cheerfully that I'm tempted to ask them to advance mine, too. I worry that Norah might have second thoughts about rooming with a responsible adult, but the apartment is in a gracious Georgian building in the heart of the old campus and comes with built-in paycheck opportunities.

I hector University Housing until they paint over the tape marks Marie left for us to remember her boyfriend by. We move Karl Marx to the front room, right above the sofa. Within a week, my junk mail mysteriously includes a tracing on a paper napkin of Oral Roberts's miracle-making hands. "Touch them to your re-frigerator," the mailing says, "if you want food. Touch them to your wallet if you want money. Touch them anywhere you have a need." While Norah makes the required vulgar jokes about touching where she has a need, I speculate about who might have put me on Oral Roberts's mailing list. Beth, my sister, who has a fine taste for kitsch? Hans, my crazy German doctor, who recently presented me with a magical charm against the evil eye? Geneva, my maid at home, who sincerely believes in the power of prayer? Some wag from the law school? Could be anyone.

Because it is such a good conversation piece, we tack the tracing of Oral's hands to the wall in a place of honor, over the sofa, right beside Karl. For the spot over my bed, I get a new poster from the traveling museum show on Alexander the Great. Another big picture of a man. This man has been dead even longer than Karl and I don't care for his politics, but he is handsome.

My mother says that whenever you hang up your pictures, that's when a place starts to feel like home. I don't feel entirely at home except back in Charleston, but these rooms in Colum-bia are at least home away from home. Norah is right. Who are the Secret Service, to take over our home?

✦

The memo says if we have questions or concerns, we should call our residence hall advisor. Calling the residence hall advisor is one of my minor household chores.

"Hi, this is Harriet Johnson."

"Sure! In Rutledge Chapel!"

"Tenement thirteen." I live beside the chapel, not in it, and the official address has a grim Dickensian ring I like. "I got this interesting memo and it said to call you with any questions or concerns."

"Sure! Isn't it exciting! They're building a platform right there, right in front of your building."

"Well, why do they want us out of the building all that time?"

"OK! For security! I think they're going to do a thorough search and then maybe set up some kind of command center or whatever, to make sure the president is safe."

A search. I remember a tip I got in criminal procedure class just last week: don't consent. "OK, well here's the thing. I don't consent to a search of the premises or to any entry onto the premises for any purpose."

"Huh?"

"I don't want them to search my apartment or come in at all. Please tell them I say no."

"You can't say no."

"I think I can. I just did. Please just tell the powers-that-be what I said, and they can contact me to sort things out. I know this isn't within your authority." Nothing is within the residence hall advisor's authority; that's why calling her is only a minor household chore. I'm about to sign off when something occurs to me, something else I just learned in criminal procedure. "Please tell them, also, that my roommate withholds her consent. OK? Thanks a bunch!"

Professor Criminal and Constitution would be proud. He's a tough professor whose good opinion I value. I'm proud of myself, too. I know my stuff, as well I ought, being a second-year law student. No one is better at asserting rights than a 2-L. No one is better at anything worth doing than a 2-L. Second year is that golden time when you are past the terror of flunking out of law school and have not yet come into the terror of flunking the bar exam.

As a sharp 2-L, I know not to rely on oral communications. I know to put it in writing. I roll over to my Olivetti Praxis 35. It's one of the first electronic typewriters designed for home use; at about $800, it was a splurge when I got my first post-college paycheck, though much cheaper than the unattainable typewriter of my dreams, the IBM Selectric. It's sleek and sporty. With sixteen characters of memory and a lift-off correction ribbon, I can fix my typos as I go along without waiting for the Wite-Out to dry. The Olivetti is a modern miracle—when it's working. It's very often on the fritz, and because it's electronic, you can't look inside and figure out what's wrong and repair it with paper clips and rubber bands.

I turn it on and roll the paper in. So far so good. I let it warm up while I review the relevant documents: my apartment lease and the student handbook. My residence hall advisor calls back and tells me I'll be hearing from the acting dean for student affairs. I phone Mama. She's all for resisting the Secret Service occupation.

I bang out my first salvo, addressed to James Holderman, the president of the University:

> This is to inform you that we, the sole tenants and occupants of Tenement 13, apartment 1, do not consent to any entry upon or search of our rooms in connection with the Convocation on the Horseshoe this Tuesday.
>
> Under our lease agreement with the University and the

terms of Carolina Community, we have consented only to routine inspections by U.S.C. staff for the limited purpose of ensuring compliance with the University's health and safety regulations. We have never, and do not now, consent to any unwarranted entries by any other governmental agencies.

We understand and share your concern for the safety of the President and of the other dignitaries who will be on the Horseshoe that day. Consequently, we believe this type of event should be held in the Coliseum or other facility which can be secured without any impingement upon the privacy interests of students.

Not bad at all. Unwarranted. Impingement. Strong legal words. Norah and I sign. Tomorrow I'll get copies made at the Law Library and Norah and I will deliver the notice to President Holderman.

✦

"Where in the world did you get those clothes?" I ask Norah when we meet on the sidewalk in front of the president's office.

"Are they awful, or what?"

"Wow."

I can't believe what I'm seeing. A straight burgundy skirt, just above the knee. A white blouse with Peter Pan collar. Little stud earrings. Black pumps. Stockings.

"I have giant piles of this shit. My mother buys it for me."

I've done my best to look respectable. This morning, I had Charlene squeeze my twisty body into a neat shirtwaist dress and remove the JESSE JACKSON FOR PRESIDENT button from the floppy bag that hangs on the back of my chair. I wrapped my two long braids around the top of my head like the Scandinavian lady who advertises—what is it?—Folger's coffee? But I don't have it in me to pull off a look like Norah has now. It's the perfect conservative coed. It's—Marie.

Norah holds the door open and we go into the Presidential Outer Office. It is peopled by three young male student workers who look eerily like President Holderman himself and therefore eerily like Jim Bakker, by far the most famous of all the unsavory evangelists in the Carolinas. I explain our business and ask to see the president. After a short wait, we're directed to the acting dean of student affairs. I leave a copy of my written notice for the president with one of the moon-faced boys. It's almost like my first subpoena.

From his first warm handshake, the acting dean reveals that his title ought to be Acting Dean of Smoothing Over Difficulties. Lavishing upon us his undivided attention, he seems to value our opinions. He apologizes profusely for inconveniencing us, agrees that the Coliseum might be a better location, but explains they're stuck as elaborate plans have been worked on for weeks. "Thing is," he says soothingly, "the Secret Service is running the show."

I'm not soothed. "I hope you understand that's alarming to us. These are strangers! We don't feel right about having MEN we don't know going through our THINGS!" I may as well hit him with maidenly modesty and play the Magnolia Blossom Factor.

Even in mother-selected clothes, Norah doesn't have much of a Magnolia Blossom Factor, but she comes out with that Iron Curtain experience. The Dean of Smoothing Over is visibly moved. He will relay our concerns to the Secret Service liaison. He is certain they will be reasonable and respectful.

It's been a good meeting, and I haven't even raised the disability issues. Maybe I won't need to tell anyone that, because I can't sit on a toilet, barring me from my bedroom means no peeing for the duration.

✦

Norah tapes a copy of our written notice to our door. The student handbook tells us not to tape stuff to our doors, so I write in large letters: OFFICIAL NOTICE—DO NOT REMOVE.

I phone my sister and bring her up to date.

"So they'll all be right outside those big windows," she says. "Ronnie, Strom Thurmond, that idiot Republican dentist . . ."

"Yeah, our very own Energy Secretary, who knows all about drillin', heh-heh-heh."

"You ought to get Charlene to put plastic explosives in your tires. You want me to come down?"

"Beth! Don't be ridiculous! I have hard tires. No tubes."

"Really? Too bad."

"And anyway, I'd blow myself up, along with the rest of them."

"Yeah, but wouldn't it be cool? You gotta die sometime, right?"

"Well, that's true," I say. "And I've often wondered why assassinations don't happen more often than they do. I mean, they're impossible if you're worried about getting caught or killed, but if you don't mind, then it seems awfully easy. And as many people as there are who get themselves in prison or killed, looks like more of them would find a way to make it worthwhile."

In truth, we don't want to assassinate the Asshole in Chief or Senator Strom or Energy Secretary DDS. In truth, individual personalities don't matter; take one out, and another takes his place; violence invites more violence and a higher level of repression; real change means broad-based social transformation through nonviolent collective action. We know all that. We're only fooling around.

✦

The next day, Saturday, I venture over to Pizza Hut to eat lunch with friends and to feel them out about a possible demonstration in connection with Ronnie's visit. I'm not getting much solidarity. The law students are worried about their brilliant career prospects. Folks in my other major network—disabled students—are worried about fitting in on campus. I guess I understand, but I simply can't allow these buzzards to occupy my front yard without saying something about it.

On the way home, my vintage E&J power chair conks out. It's been happening a lot, so I have this down to a drill. I get a passerby to push me to the nearest safe house—a place where someone will help me use a phone. I phone Doug, a high school shop teacher now working on his master's. His grad school hobby is wheelchair repair. He takes care of all the chairs on campus, asking only for reimbursement for parts; he has been known to drive across town to save $2 on a pair of motor brushes. He says he'll grab his toolbox and go to my apartment.

I find someone else to push me home, and Doug sets me on my bed. Every time my chair conks, I go absolutely nuts. I can't do anything on my own. I'm stuck. Like a helpless cripple! Whatever plan I've made—and I've always made some plan— gets derailed. But the good news now is that my behind is very happy for this unexpected time out of the chair, happily recumbent, relieved of pressure.

While Doug works, I talk to Beth on the phone. "How's the conspiracy coming?" she asks.

"Fine."

"I have an idea. Before the Secret Service comes in, clean your apartment out. Have it all empty, except for a great big poster of Jodie Foster. Do it up like a shrine. Maybe use news clips about Hinckley."

"That's great. They'll have all the security forces so busy watching me that it might make things easier for the assassin."

"And let's hope someone shows up with more sense than Hinckley."

"Really," I say, "what was that guy thinking about, using a .22?"

Doug expresses only the mildest disapproval of the way Beth and I talk. Hey, girls just want to have fun. I'm grateful for his indulgence. I'm also grateful for the continuing gift of his mechanical skills and—maybe most of all—for the fact that he's never made the irritating suggestion that I get a new chair. He's probably guessed I don't have the money. Lots of people imagine all crips are like leprechauns, with a magic pot of gold to pay for all our stuff. I happen to have a grant for 3.5 hours per day of personal assistance, but otherwise I'm like any other law student, with no coverage whatsoever for equipment. Doug doesn't nose about such things. Instead, he says the E&J Premier is a great chair, the Model A of power chairs with nice simple motors and no unreliable, unrepairable electronic gizmos. It's a pleasure to work on. Of course, E&J doesn't support maintenance of the Premier, but you can use car parts and lawn mower parts and paper clips and rubber bands. I've been smart to keep it for so long.

Norah calls Doug L7. He is that square. I tell him he's one of those rare people who give Christians a good name. I invite him to come to my apartment Monday night for a sign-painting party. Maybe if I can get one group to make them, I can get another group to carry them.

✦

That night Norah and I wake up to what sounds like gunfire in our living room. If I could move, I'd hit the ground, but Norah jumps up to confront whatever it is. Firecrackers. They were pushed through the big crack under our door where all the memos come in. No doubt some Young Carolinian for America doesn't like the notice on our door.

◆

There's a new guy among the students hanging out in the Horseshoe. He's wearing jeans and a plaid shirt like half the guys on campus, but something's not right. The cut of his jeans is a bit Kingston Trio. He has steel gray hair and a hard brief-case he never puts down.

"Good evening, Mr. Phelps," Norah mutters.

She's been behaving very well, but it's time for me to caution her. "Keep your distance from that guy. Act like you haven't no-ticed him. Let him think he's blending in. For God's sake, don't ridicule him. Watch what you say."

"Yes, Mom."

The firecrackers during the night have left me a bit on edge. I don't like this new presence disturbing the Horseshoe's long settled equilibrium of green lawns, powerful old oaks, classical buildings, brick paths, and genuine college students.

◆

The Secret Service liaison says there will be no search.

"What will there be?" I ask.

"A dog-through and sweep."

It's clear he'd prefer not to tell Norah and me anything, but the Dean of Smoothing Over has brought us to his office for a meeting at the unusual time of seven P.M. on Sunday. A number of agents are here, but not Mr. Phelps. I guess he's back at the ranch, blending in.

"A dog-through and sweep?"

"We have a dog trained to detect explosives. We'll take the dog through the apartment, do a sweep, and leave."

"What if the dog—what does it do?—points?"

"It won't, unless explosives are present."

"But what if it does?"

The dean intervenes. "What I'm hearing is that this dog only points for explosives. He's not interested in your private things, or drugs—not that you young ladies are into drugs. He's not interested in anything but dynamite and so forth, so this won't be intrusive."

"But, suppose the dog reacts. Will there then be a search?"

"Yes," the liaison admits.

Bingo! Those 2-L cross-examining skills hit pay dirt. "Now, suppose," I continue, "some person or persons unknown placed lit firecrackers under our door in the middle of the night last night. Would the dog-through likely detect something like that as late as Tuesday?"

"Quite possibly. The dog has been trained to detect commonly used explosives from trace elements."

"And in that case, how would the search be conducted?"

"Its scope would depend on all the facts and circumstances."

The alarming thing is that these guys don't think this is funny. In my mind's eye, they're photographing everything in sight, shredding our mattresses, carting off our things in evidence bags. I don't want them in our apartment, and certainly not without being there to witness it.

"I'm sorry," I say, "but it sounds like a dog-through and sweep is a kind of search, and we're not consenting to a search."

We go back to the apartment and Beth phones again. After I give her a full report on the meeting, she has another idea: "Here's what you should do. Fill your apartment with wrapped packages.

All done up with bows and ribbons and lots of tape. Packages within packages. And inside each one—something ticking."

"Beth, that's probably a violation of federal law."

"But think how funny—"

"Not to these guys."

◆

On Monday morning, I roll four long blocks to the law school, reasonably confident that Doug's latest repair will keep me moving for a while. Once I make it there, I'm fine. Under this roof I have everything I need in a typical day: all my classes, the law library, phones, a place to eat the food I carry with me, a coffee machine, a microwave, and some eight hundred people to whom I am somewhat connected. There's always someone handy to hold a door open, get a book out of my bag, carry my coffee from the machine to a table, or open a yoghurt. The law librarians let me keep stuff on a low table in the reference section. When my chair conks, someone going the same way will give me a push. In this environment, I get along without paid help for most of my day. So do the four other law students in power chairs. In various ways, we return the favors, not necessarily one to one or quid pro quo, but to the community as a whole. I critique outlines and drafts, take care of the pro se nuts researching their own cases in the library, help make the classes interesting, and tell stories between classes. Through such contributions, I have earned my place as at least a little big dog in the law school community.

Over the weekend, some buzz has developed about my response to Ronnie's visit. With so many highly verbal, extremely sociable people cooped up with few serious responsibilities, this place is naturally gossip central.

Aphrodite, the law school student president, says someone has been asking about me.

"What did you tell them, Bebe?" She has to go by Bebe. Aphrodite fits her too well.

"I told them you're the kind of person who's read her lease and knows her rights."

I've had worse recommendations. I go into the law library and a small crowd gathers to hear my account of Mr. Phelps and the proposed dog-through and sweep.

Most of the students' politics are much more like Ronnie's than mine. A few John Birchers are disappointed that Reagan has failed to stand up to the left-wing steamroller that runs America. In our chats in the law school canteen, I've tried without much success to give them comfort: I tell them from first-hand knowledge that in Columbia, South Carolina, the left-wing steamroller has a hard time getting a quorum to conduct business. Now it seems they have grudging admiration for my temerity in defying federal authority and defending my home. I get only gentle ribbing.

"You can't say anything good about the president, can you?"

"No, that's not true. I can say something good about Ronnie and Nancy, too: they wear their clothes well." I tell how my sister has been calling every day with a new assassination plot.

Another worldy-wise 2-L interrupts. "You've been doing this on the phone in university housing? You know that phone is probably tapped. The university controls the whole system and the administration probably consented."

Now that I think of it, there has been a lot of clicking and static on the line. I've attributed it to the wilderness conditions of Beth's habitat in western North Carolina. But having encountered Mr. Phelps and the humorless liaison and all the rest of them, I can't be sure.

I realize I said no to the Secret Service without thinking about it too hard. It was simple: We don't like the guy; we don't want him in our front yard; we won't let his people in our room. No thanks. In this as in most things, I expect to either get what I want or not. I don't expect repercussions. I don't see myself as a target because at this stage of my life I don't see myself as much of a threat. I'm just a tiny wheelchair woman with a certain amount of mouth. Now I wonder if there's some reason that Norah and I are hanging out on this line by ourselves. It occurs to me that Ronnie is the head of the apparatus that is waging an illegal war against Nicaragua and dispatching the death squads in El Salvador. It's an apparatus that isn't always indulgent to people who say no.

I need backup. Time to crank up the left-wing steamroller. The student members of the radical National Lawyers Guild— all five—get a personal invitation: "Make signs for those who can't!" I've decided they'll help make the signs and the disabled students will carry them.

◆

Norah and I have been summoned to another meeting at five-fifteen. For both of us by this time, reality has moved in, to become a continuing disquieting presence, like Mr. Phelps right outside our door. It's unavoidable: Ronnie will be on the Horseshoe tomorrow. We can't keep him off. Given that he's coming, it's not in our power to keep the Secret Service out of our apartment. It doesn't matter what the Fourth Amendment says.

We tell the Dean of Smoothing Over and the Secret Service liaison that we won't agree to leave before they arrive. We'll wait for them at the apartment. However, once they show up, we won't interfere with a search and we'll leave as soon as the search is over and we'll stay away—if they'll agree to leave when we leave and stay out.

The Dean of Smoothing Over's face brightens. This looks to him like a reasonable compromise.

The Secret Service people don't see it that way. They agree to lock the door and not occupy our apartment, but they absolutely won't permit us to be present for the search. I'm frustrated. "I don't understand the reason."

"We don't want to jeopardize the safety of our agents by placing them in an untenable situation."

"Like Norah and I will take your armed agents hostage? Do you imagine that as a real possibility?"

"An explosive device could be set off."

"But surely I'd use a remote control. Why would I blow myself up? Your people are safer with me there!"

Oops. This is not helping. Time to end the meeting. However, the indefatigable Dean of Smoothing Over extracts a small concession from the feds: we can have our apartment until eleven A.M. After that, they say we must be out.

As we leave, the dean apparently wants us to leave happy about something, so he tells us disabled students and our attendants will get front-row seating for the president's speech. I say I hope we won't be arrested. The Bar Committee on Character and Fitness doesn't like an arrest record, even if acquired in a spirit of fun and in defense of civil liberties, and my brilliant career could be stopped before it starts. The dean makes no promises and he makes no threats. He repeats what he said at the outset: the Secret Service is running the show.

Back at the Horseshoe, we see Mr. Phelps and raise our hackles.

"I know," Norah says. "I'll watch what I say."

"And watch what you sing." Norah is an enthusiastic singer in piano-bar style, and not bad when she gets started on the right key. Her repertoire includes "The Internationale." She knows only snippets of the words and the tune is barely recognizable, but Mr. Phelps has probably been trained to detect the commonly sung Communist anthems from trace elements.

✦

"How do you like your Blenheim?" Norah asks my guests.

She can't believe my sign-painting party shopping list didn't include controlled substances. Partly because of social isolation during my teenage years, I've been drunk exactly once in my life; it was an accident and I didn't like it. Being sober in a crowd of drunks is an experience I get way too often nowadays. Therefore, all the drinks I offer are soft. Technically. I serve Blenheim Ginger Ale, specifically Old #3. Harder to score than pot, Blenheim is unobtainable in Columbia and only sporadically obtainable in Charleston; regular use requires a connection near the Pee Dee River, where it's made. Number 3 separates the sheep from the goats when it comes to hard drinkers of soft drinks. One sip is enough to make the uninitiated sheep fall flat. We tough old goats relish the big slow swallow and the Blenheim-induced hot flash that starts by cauterizing the throat, then shoots from the stomach straight into the marrow of your bones. Most people dilute Old #3 with lots of ice. I drink mine straight and unchilled. Although my parties are as dry as Rosalyn and Jimmy's Southern Baptist White House, no one can call me unsophisticated or pious.

Norah's off the clock but insists on bustling around like my servant. I've begged her to relax and hang out. No, she doesn't want to hang out with my friends. What's wrong with them? Nothing. They are wonderful, terrific, perfect friends—for me. She'll be the maid.

For the faint of heart, I offer mass-produced soft drinks. There's also salty, greasy party food. But it's poster board and markers that make a party an event.

A quad buddy and I are perched high in our chairs, watching the nondisabled guests and the hotshot para play on the floor. It's like a small child's birthday party before they all get cranky, everyone happily engaged in structured activities, sharing their markers, working cooperatively. The results are looking good.

HANDS OFF CENTRAL AMERICA. U.S. OUT OF EL SALVADOR. NO NUKES. PEOPLE NOT PROFITS. For the disability rights crowd: ACCESS FOR ALL. SAVE 504. And, to leave no one out: HI RON! WELCOME MR. PRESIDENT! $AVE $TUDENT LOAN$.

Norah has scored huge sheets of yellow paper for our two front windows. I've confirmed that the student handbook and lease agreement strictly prohibit affixing anything to the building's exterior but do not regulate what can be seen through the glass. Norah and I decide each of us will pick the slogan for one window. I want RON STEALS FROM THE POOR & GIVES TO THE MILITARY. Norah sticks closer to home: END MARTIAL LAW ON THE HORSESHOE! She wants a "no pigs allowed" graphic on hers. There's group discussion, sketching, countersketching, negotiation, consensus, and execution—resulting in a cute, fat piggy-bankish pig with a curly tail, surrounded by a circle bisected by a diagonal line.

◆

Charlene comes at six forty-five A.M. and gives me my toast and coffee in bed at seven. She tidies up while I eat. It's a normal beginning to what I expect will be a strange day.

When my coffee kicks in, Charlene knows I'm capable of high-level decision-making so she asks me what I want to wear. It can be tricky. My budget doesn't cover personnel for costume changes, so whatever I pick in the morning has to work for all events on the day's schedule. Today I will be locked out of my room for several hours, so it's all the more important to get it right. I've been wearing vestments of respectability for the encounters with the Secret Service, but at this point, I think the people who outfitted Mr. Phelps are unworthy to be objects of my fashion concern. I tell Charlene it'll be my favorite hippie dress, cotton gauze in rich burgundy and indigo paisley, shot through with multicolored metallic threads that miraculously don't make me itch. In this dress, so light and loose it's almost as comfortable as nakedness, I can't imagine being unhappy or stressed. No need for the Folger's coffee lady braid-coil; the two low-maintenance pigtails may look nerdy and juvenile but in my mind they're radical, Buffy Sainte-Marie. No need for stockings; strap sandals on my feet and I'm ready to roll.

As usual, I'm ready at eight-forty. I might as well buzz up to my nine o'clock class. My classmates try to bait Professor Criminal and Constitution into a discussion of the strengths and weaknesses of the government's potential case against me, but he doesn't bite. I'm glad. I'm in no mood to be the object of recreational hairsplitting in law school's hypothetical world. The minute class ends, my seatmate chucks my casebook in my bag and I shoot out. I need to get back to the apartment.

Before I make it outdoors, a student worker from the placement office chases me down. "There's been a cancellation and we have an interview for a Charleston summer clerkship for you today at one."

I answer without thinking even for a second. "OK. What the hell." I'm out the door and headed home as fast as this Model A of power chairs can carry me.

✦

I hit my remote buzzer to unlock my door and before I can bang through Norah has opened it. She's evidently posted herself on guard, ready for action. I start to launch into a typical 2-L lecture on how to behave in front of law enforcement, but Norah has better ideas than I do.

"We need to try not to do anything weird. Like don't buzz them in. I'll open the door, so they won't be nervous. We stay out of their space. Stay where we can see them and they can see us."

"Yeah," I say. "No sudden moves!" I've heard the line in so many B-movies and now it makes sense.

It's ten-fifteen. There's a light knock on the door. Norah opens it and stands in the doorway. It's our residence hall advisor.

"Hi! I'm just reminding you guys to be out of the apartment by eleven, OK?"

Norah answers. "We've already told them we'll be here when the Secret Service gets here and we'll leave then, OK?"

The residence hall advisor pleads halfheartedly and then leaves. Norah opens a bag of potato chips and a tub of French onion dip left over from the party. Along the edge of our little dining table, she lays out a neat line of gunk-laden chips for me to eat while she works on the bag. It's something to do while we wait.

It's about ten-thirty. There's a more assertive, more manly knock. Norah opens it. From the hallway, our visitor introduces himself. He's from University Housing. We are requested to leave by eleven. We respectfully decline.

Moments later, it's the Dean of Smoothing Over. We ought to have recognized him by his pleasant and accommodating door-knocking style. Another pro forma plea. We assure him that, although we're not being cooperative, we're not being "uncooperative"; the Secret Service should know we'll all get along fine and nothing bad will happen. He makes vaguely reassuring noises. But, he reminds us, the Secret Service is running the show.

It's eleven. A definite law-enforcement rap. Here we go.

"University police! You are requested to leave this building!"

I ignore my own advice about sudden moves and roll up to the doorway. "We will leave after the Secret Service people have searched." It seems important, somehow, that we're not refusing to leave; we're just explaining when we will leave. It also seems important, somehow, that no one has ever directly threatened us with arrest.

"This building is now under the jurisdiction of the United States Secret Service! Armed guards are posted at all exits!

Snipers are posted on surrounding rooftops! You are within the security perimeter! You may leave at any time."

Norah closes the door and lines up more chips for me on the table. "We can leave at any time."

"Yeah. At this point, I'm not going anywhere until we have a Secret Service escort. All it would take would be for one of those guys with guns to be nervous or confused or hyper or whatever and—"

"Kent State."

"Or Orangeburg." We'd like to laugh and mock this succession of emissaries sent to talk us out, but we're on edge. It's not funny to them, and we won't know if it's funny to us until we see how it turns out.

The room is dark and close with the thick yellow paper blocking both big windows. We've finished the whole bag of chips. I'm thirsty from all the salt but can't drink because drinking would wreck my fluid and peeing schedule. It's eleven-twenty and I wonder why they're taking so long. Do they think we'll give up if they leave us sitting on ice until we've eaten the last chip? Have they decided to respect our legal rights after all, if we insist? Are they bringing in the A-team? Are they hoping we'll come out, so they can shoot us? Have they forgotten we're here?

From the hallway come thumps of multiple law-enforcement feet. Norah waits for the knock and promptly opens the door. "Hello." She's all business.

Badges are shown and a request is made for a search for the purpose of presidential security. I give my little speech. The search can be done with our consent if we are allowed to observe it. We do not consent to anyone being in the apartment when we're not present. They don't exactly agree, but unlike all our other morning visitors, they don't ask us to leave. We invite them in.

It seems like a whole platoon, but maybe it's only three or

four men. Some search while others watch us. After ascertaining that they'll need to cover two big rooms and a bathroom, they get down to it. An agent looks in our refrigerator, pats down our milk jugs, inspects the cavity of our toaster oven, checks out the Blenheims in the cabinet, frisks our ramen noodles. It's a strange feeling. Miss Tidy keeps things neat, but still I have to suppress an urge to apologize for our expired products. They go into the bedroom, open our closets, and expose my collection of little dresses and Norah's black hole of fashion dissonance.

An agent has his hands in my underwear drawer and he's feeling around. At first I'm so glad, glad beyond words, that it's all dime-store panty hose and washed-out cotton briefs—nothing weird to embarrass me. But then—I'm embarrassed anyway. Everything's so horribly dull. No one has ever given me any crap from Frederick's of Hollywood, not even as a joke. How does it look that I don't own a bra?

It's over quickly, but I don't like it. It's just like I told the Dean of Smoothing Over in our first meeting: it's MEN I don't know going through my THINGS! In a moment of surprising self-discovery, I find there's some truth behind my Magnolia Blossom Factor. It's not that I'm coy or shy or have something to hide; a gaggle of personal assistants handle my intimate things routinely. But these men aren't here at my invitation to do my bidding. They're agents of my enemy. Even though I share my private space with a lot of people, it's still private. Or it was. I still don't know what happened to Norah behind the Iron Curtain, but something like it is happening to me now. It's something that shouldn't happen in America.

The agents move toward the door and Norah and I fall in. When and how did she get her shoulder bag under her arm? Has she maintained this flat poker face through the whole event? An agent reaches for the light switch; it has been moved preposterously low to suit me. In the momentary hiatus, two agents cast their eyes, *Dragnet* style, toward the living room wall. Karl Marx looks right back at them. My man. Karl doesn't blink.

The agents, now in the role of protectors, encircle Norah and me as we proceed down the back ramp, across the baking asphalt, through the security perimeter. We're moving at the slow, stately marching pace of my old power chair. Norah stops. "Oh dear." The look on her face could stop a freight train. "I left the signs in the apartment."

"Never mind," I say. "We can't go back."

✦

We charge over to the Student Union and buy more sign-making supplies. At the cafeteria, we get lunch and set about re-creating the signs as best we can. I head up to the law school for that job interview I should have declined. On the way, I get caught in a typical autumn Columbia cloudburst. When everyone else is running to get out of the rain, my nice simple motors chug along at their usual crawl. At least they're working. By the time I shake hands with the recruiting attorney for the prestigious Charleston firm, I'm soaked to the skin. My happy gauze hippie dress is limp and lifeless and far too clingy. My pigtails are dripping. I might have a touch of wet-dog smell. At least this time I'll be spared wondering why I don't get the job.

✦

I meet Norah outside the Horseshoe and we steel ourselves to go through security at the gate. I go in front and Norah rests a hand on one of my push handles. "Go on through," the officer says with a pleasant wave. "You two have a special place, all the way in front. Have a good day!" He doesn't peek into my big bag of books or Norah's big bag of protest signs. Once again, it seems, I'm just a disabled person, inherently harmless, with my nice helper girl. No threat. It's a scene that has been acted throughout the centuries, at least since that big festival day when newly blind Samson, escorted by a nice helper boy, was directed to his special place, all the way in front, in the Temple at Gaza.

We make our way to a spot in what is normally our front yard. For the first time, we get a good look at our window signs. Set off by the soft landscaping that naturally occurs over decades in the South, on a building made of beige stucco with white trim, the black letters on yellow paper really pop.

Most of the crowd in the crip section aren't too happy with our fabulous windows, though. As long as I may live to ponder the mystery, I will never understand how a severely disabled person can be a Republican, but there are some here. Mostly, my disabled comrades aren't very political, but they are polite and eager to please, brought up with Southern notions of hospitality. They keep saying it's an honor to have the president on campus and the signs are inhospitable. I don't think I owe hospitality to people I haven't invited and to whom I haven't been properly introduced. And honor? I'm not sure why Ronnie's here. To please a major campaign contributor? Seal some deal with Strom? Be photographed in a beautiful place? Whatever the reason, I doubt honor has much to do with it.

I'm not sure, now, how to get this crowd to carry protest signs. This group could apply such pressure as to make even my best buddies waffle. The only way to find out is to try. "Norah, you want to unpack the signs?"

As soon as the first sign comes out, an agent pops out of nowhere and is on the walkie-talkie spouting incomprehensible G-man argot. He has under observation two Caucasian female whatevers in whatever sector. . . . It seems we are again dangerous, or at least in need of having our First Amendment rights chilled. Each of us gets an agent to subject us to close observation.

"Oh no," Norah says. A couple of guys in work clothes are covering our windows with brown paper. They're concealing our beautiful, expressive First Amendment windows in plain brown wrappers suitable for shameful things. I want to go over there and question those men until they tell me who gave them their instructions and call a meeting right now, and I mean a meeting with the person running the show, not with the Dean of Smoothing Over. But I don't. I'm worn out from all this craziness. I've got my own personal spy to deal with. I want to get these signs in place.

The show's about to start. There's no time to dillydally around the margins. I need to do like Samson, attack the point of most resistance, grab the post whose giving in will make the rest collapse. I approach the most Republican crip. "You don't want a protest sign? OK. But you know why they put us here in front. Not so we can see, but so we can be seen. You know how things work. Think how pretty they'll look in this pretty setting, with this pretty crowd of polite students. And in the front row, courageous and inspiring us! Young and well-groomed and handicapped! You know if we sit here with no protest signs, we'll wind up in the next fund-raising film for the Republican National Committee."

He accepts NO NUKES. My mission's accomplished.

✦

That evening, our banishment is over. In the front room, Norah has her boom box going and is dancing with Karl Marx. Under the big luminous face of Alexander the Great, I'm lolling on my bed, talking to Beth on the phone. From my account of the day's proceedings, she gets the impression that I kicked butt.

"Well," I say, "we didn't exactly pull the Temple down on their heads, but we did something. We got some protest signs out, and the people saw the windows, even if the dignitaries didn't. The Secret Service didn't have the nerve to pull them down when they were in our apartment this morning."

"What about the speech?"

"What about it?"

"You didn't tell me about Ronnie's speech."

"Oh. SOS. Same old shit."

"A tissue of lies?"

"A wall-to-wall shag carpet of lies. I forget how bad he is. You know, I haven't listened to him speak since the big El Salvador speech last winter."

"Really?"

"Yeah. I watched it with Marie and she was sitting there so polite and interested and everyone declared it was such an effective speech, and my blood was boiling, and not a nice healthy blood-boil like you get from Blenheim Number three. I had to swear off."

"I can't believe it. I remember you couldn't get enough of Nixon."

"Beth, I was sixteen! My adolescent passion had to go somewhere. I mean, he had those beady eyes, that sweaty upper lip, that smell of desperation. I knew he'd get his comeuppance in the end."

"So that's the difference. Ronnie is doomed to succeed."

"Exactly. And now I'm twenty-six, grown up. It's no longer such pure joy to be righteous among fools. Now I know Ronnie's easy lying affability is directly linked to all this stuff happening all over the world."

"True."

"I don't know if there's really any point, but I'm glad we gave them opposition. You know, there was another group. Some kids had organized themselves to do really raucous, boisterous chanting and they took their cues from lines in Ronnie's speech. They knew what he was going to say and had their responses ready. They were tough. They got beat up, thrown out, and kept coming back."

"Who threw them out?"

"Students with opposing views, I presume."

"Or Mr. Phelps and his friends."

"Maybe. What's funny is that everyone's criticizing those kids for disruptive tactics. Nobody's noticed how disruptive Ronnie has been."

◆

A few days later, Norah and I get a letter from the Dean of Smoothing Over, thanking us for our cooperation and commending us for a constructive spirit of compromise. He also promises to restore the wooden ramp that had been removed from our front door, presumably to improve the photo op. My Olivetti has stopped working so I handwrite a polite but prickly reply.

Professor Criminal and Constitution is outraged when he hears that they covered our windows with brown paper. He says it more than once: "I am outraged!" It's a clear violation of the First Amendment: governmental suppression of speech based on content. He asks me to bring in the signs and then raises some pointed questions at the faculty senate. The administration claims that the yellow paper signs might have provided cover for a sniper.

I tell the professor how the Secret Service made absolutely sure no snipers were secreted in my underwear drawer, and we agree it's somewhat surprising to learn that brown paper can stop bullets. Still, I'm not interested in suing anyone. I have too much on my plate without being a plaintiff.

"Well," he says, "sometimes the best you can do is make them stand up and take ridiculous positions."

It's a useful lesson, actually one of the best I get in law school. Like many of the good lessons I've learned, it doesn't leave me fully satisfied.

3

Honk If You Hate Telethons

By this time, August 1991, I'm an assistant city attorney with a monthly retainer that affords adventures in dilapidated housing and also covers most of my law office overhead. I want the city to be happy, so I'll touch base with the city attorney. "Is a city permit needed to pass out handbills and picket on city sidewalks?"

"Harriet, I'll be damned if I know." That's what he always says just before he answers my questions. "We do have a permitting process through the police department. Maybe it's unconstitutional, who knows, but it makes the police happy, and we want the police to be happy. Call them up, and if they don't want to let you do whatever it is that you want to do, just call me back and I'll get it straight."

I phone the police administrative number and get transferred around until finally I'm talking to the officer in charge of parades. "This isn't about a parade," I say, "but the city attorney said I should check with y'all. I happen to be an assistant city attorney myself, you know."

"What are you planning to do?"

"Have a small group on the sidewalks carrying signs and distributing handbills."

"A protest?"

"Yes."

"That comes under parades. What's it about?"

In law school, Professor Criminal and Constitution taught us that this question is irrelevant under the First Amendment. The city may not consider content. It can regulate only the time, place, and manner of public expression. I therefore proceed to tell the officer the specifics about time, place, and manner. I assure him no fighting words will be used.

None of this is what he wants to discuss. "What I want to know is: What's your cause? What's your issue? What are you protesting?"

Oh well, we do want the police to be happy. "I'm protesting the Muscular Dystrophy Association telethon."

"You're promoting the telethon?"

"No, I'm protesting it."

"Why?"

"Does the reason matter?"

"I'd think so. I'm sure you must have a reason or you wouldn't be protesting."

He has a point. "I don't like the way the telethon depicts people with disabilities, including muscle diseases like I have. It's all about stirring up pity, when we don't want pity. And Jerry Lewis ought to be fired. He actually called people in wheelchairs 'half persons.' When this year's telethon is on the air, I want to be out there. You know, I'm not Jerry's Kid! Never was."

"So this is the Jerry Lewis telethon?" the officer asks.

"Yes."

"You know, I never thought he was funny."

"Yeah? Well, funny or not, he's a bigot, and a real charity wouldn't give him a platform. So do I need a police permit?"

"To tell you the truth, Attorney Johnson, a permit probably isn't required, but it would give your cause more credibility."

"What?"

"It's like the city's good housekeeping seal of approval. This anti–Jerry Lewis protest is definitely something we can endorse, so if you'll come down here with a picture ID and sign the necessary forms, we'll be happy to set you up. We can do it while you wait."

This isn't the same First Amendment I learned about in law school classes, not the same First Amendment I encountered when Ronnie came to Columbia. But why am I surprised? Charleston is and always has been a law unto itself.

✦

Whether it's due to the parade officer's taste in comedy or my issue, I'm happy to have the city's good housekeeping seal of approval. I'm hungry for external validation at this stage.

It will take several years to establish the annual telethon protest as a charming Charleston tradition. At this point, protesting is not very respectable—and not at all lawyerly. Charleston culture is based on the notion that power flows from person to person, by means of favors granted and returned, through rituals of civility. Protesting marks you as one of the outsiders, the rabble, the friendless—one of those who can't redress all grievances with a couple of phone calls to the right people. If you're building a solo law practice, as I am, you might reasonably worry about the impact of an outsider-mark on your client base.

Beyond that, protesting is contrary to the teachings of Charleston's civil religion, politeness. Our mothers teach us it's not polite to criticize. Protesting falls clearly within that general rule and criticizing charity is a particularly heinous infraction. If you're a beneficiary, it smacks of mean ingratitude. If not, it's sour grapes. It's so much politer—so much easier—to smile indulgently and say, "They mean well." It's easy because, in fact, they usually do mean well.

I've had a lifetime of saying "They mean well" of telethons and the people who love them. In my childhood, telethons were ubiquitous. Easter Seals sponsored the separate-and-unequal crip school I attended. United Cerebral Palsy bought equipment for some of my friends. March of Dimes declared it would "Stamp Out Birth Defects!"—a slogan that made us defectives nervous. They all wallowed in pity, depicted disability—"crippling" they called it—as the worst fate imaginable. They all assumed the only answers were prevention and cure. In most ways, one thon was like the next. But in one way, MDA stood out from the pack. Its pitch had an added punch of urgency: find a cure before they die!

My mother thought telethons were tacky. She said no when we were asked to appear. She tried to distance me from them, but my own eyes told me that the MDA thon was about people like me and like my classmates Ronnie and James. The poster children looked just like us; we were all literally of the same flesh. Also, coincidentally or not, we were all skilled verbal manipulators. Together in the crip ghetto, my friends and I watched the annual parade of our little doppelgängers being publicly sentenced to death and saw one another through with gallows humor and broad parody. Later, having moved on to the mainstream world, I wanted to go to law school, qualify for scholarships, get a job and a car loan, start a business. But dying children aren't allowed to do such things; they can't be trusted to fulfill their obligations. I therefore squirmed alone and kept my distance.

As time goes on, that distance comes to feel natural. MDA's competitor-thons wither and die. I get busy with other things, including making the world safe for disability. I work with thousands of others to win passage of the Americans with Disabilities Act in July 1990. My ticket to the signing ceremony is framed in my office to symbolize the dawn of a new day. When I think about the MDA telethon at all, I imagine it will soon slide into history.

But still, I squirm. In August 1990, a year before I take out that permit, I see the posters go up in downtown businesses I pass as I roll to work. Once again. Once again, the poster children are a blast from the past; they bring back memories of Ronnie and James and of myself as a child. Once again, the message denies the worth and value of such lives as they are. And— once again—my impulse is to duck and hide.

But with the federal seal of approval newly set on the ADA and the clock ticking toward its effective dates, I am emboldened. Self-powered in my chair, self-employed in my office, at large and unsupervised, I am free to spend the morning and the rest of my life as I please. My route to work takes me past the fancy hotel that hosts the local telethon feed. I roll in and zoom across ice-smooth marble floors to the concierge who sits at a desk at my eye level.

"I see y'all are hosting the telethon again," I blather pleasantly, "and I just got to thinking that y'all might be interested in thinking about a different side of disability." My pitch is so soft the concierge isn't sure what I'm pitching. Neither am I. She calls a manager. I blather until they offer me the use of a nice big room, set up as I may request, for a couple of hours during the Friday before Labor Day. They don't know what I'll do with it. Neither do I.

It's so easy. Maybe they can't refuse a request from a dilapidated crip, especially when she's turned on the charm. Or maybe—as I prefer to think—I'm now one of those well-connected insiders whom business types are eager to please.

As I roll the three blocks from the hotel to my office, the plan gels. I'll call a press conference to highlight the ADA. I'll gather people representing various disability groups to talk about what the ADA means and urge business to comply. There will be no direct criticism of the telethon; after all, it's already historically irrelevant. But, indirectly, in the polite and subtle way of Charleston, we'll be countering MDA's Call to Pity.

I phone people who worked with me for the ADA. They're impressed that I have a free room and a seal of approval from this fancy hotel. The press conference is a great idea; sure, they'll come out.

They come out. They bring friends. Surrounded by Charleston's decorous disability community, a community I have rallied, listening to one person after another proclaim that the problem isn't disability but discrimination and prejudices and myths and fears, I feel strong, strong enough to show my face in public even as the telethon is gearing up. Local TV comes out in force; we make them put the sign language interpreter in the shot and they get the story right. It's a triumph of free publicity for the community.

Two days later, that Sunday morning, I get the bombshell from my mother's hands. "I hate to show you this, but I think you need to read it." It's the *Parade* magazine. Jerry Lewis is on the cover, imagining, "If I had muscular dystrophy."

It begins: "What if the twist of fate we hear so much about really happened? What if . . . when the gifts and the pains were being handed out, I was in the wrong line . . . ? Oh yes, there's the expression: 'There but for the grace of God go I' is used in a variety of contexts, but rarely do people take a solid look from the outside in and see themselves as other than they are. So I decided, after 41 years of battling this curse that attacks children of all ages, . . . I would put myself in that chair . . . that steel imprisonment that long has been deemed the dystrophic child's plight."

I am stunned. Sitting here in my steel imprisonment, having been in the wrong line for gifts and pains it seems, I can't believe it, and it gets worse. Lewis says if you go to a restaurant in a wheelchair, "90 percent of the pasta winds up on your lap!" He waxes miserable about the "indignities" of getting help with bathing and dressing. He says, "Being in a wheelchair makes you feel like everyone is whispering about you." He contrasts wheelchair basketball players with "normal, healthy, vital, and energetic people."

He piles them on, the incidents, the outrageous insults, the stereotypes. Then comes the moral of the story: "I just have to learn to try to be good at being a half a person . . . and get on with my life. I may be a full human being in my heart and soul, yet I am still half a person, and I know I'll do well if I keep my priorities in order. You really cannot expect the outside world to assist you in more ways than they already do, and I'm most grateful for the help I receive. But I always have the feeling in the pit of my stomach that I want to scream out 'Help!' Or, 'See what has happened to me!' Or, 'Is anyone watching?' But those screams are usually muffled by the inner voice that tells me what to do and when, and tells me softly and strongly: 'Be still. . . . Hush. . . . Drive quietly. . . . Try to make as few waves as possible.'"

It's a kick in the stomach. Haven't several civil rights and liberation movements—including the one that won the ADA that we were celebrating two days ago—proven the benefits of making waves? Didn't Hitler's Germany prove the danger of denying full personhood based on genetic characteristics? I'm astounded that anyone, even the likes of Jerry Lewis, could put his name on such a thing. I'm astounded that any magazine, let alone a "noncontroversial" commercial outlet like *Parade,* could run it.

Don't they hear the bigotry?

No, they don't. When bigotry is the dominant view, it sounds like self-evident truth.

For the first time in many years, I turn on the thon and it's still the dark days before the disability rights movement, when crips exist only to remind others to count their blessings. They're still sentencing children to death on live TV, in the presence of the children and their families. Now that I'm old enough to be a parent, this seems a form of child abuse. No matter that they mean well. No matter that it seems to be bringing in tens of millions of dollars. That only makes it worse. If the tote board is to be believed, pity still sells. I can't pretend the telethon has lost its power.

"You should write a rebuttal," my mother says. She's right, but it's a horrible thought, to write a public declaration that I am a whole person. Oh well. I write an op-ed for the *Post and Courier,* the paper that delivered that horrible article to houses all over the Lowcountry. The op-ed is published. People tell me they're touched and moved, but I need to do more.

The posters go up again in 1991. Jerry Lewis remains the unrepentant voice for an unrepentant money machine. It's time to stop hiding, time to tackle the thon head-on—time to do what Lewis's imaginary cripple won't do: make some waves. This year the confrontation won't be subtle, decorous, indoors, with the cooperation of the telethon hotel. This year it will be done the outsider's way: in the streets.

Thus fired up, I decide to pull a police permit. That's how I wind up with the city's good housekeeping seal of approval.

◆

My phone list begins with the people who came out to the 1990 press conference. "No" takes many forms. In Charleston, the most common is the polite question:

I agree with you about the *Parade* article, but don't you think a protest just calls more attention to it?

Do you think Charleston's the kind of place where a protest will be well received?

But don't they do some good with the money? What about the children who need help?

Shouldn't we let it die?

And, of course—Sounds, er, interesting, but I have plans with family. Good luck, though! I'll call you to find out how it went. Let's get together sometime soon. . . .

The director of the AIDS support organization does seem to get it, can't believe anyone would say such things, can't believe anyone would publish them, can't believe MDA didn't sack Lewis, thinks all decent people should be up in arms, knows stigma kills. But he has a previous commitment, a commitment that does seem real and irrevocable. Asking him to send someone else, or to talk it up for me, would be too much. It's too hard a sell, I'm finding.

So I'll reach out to various progressive groups I've supported over the years, to people who don't mind picketing. No takers. After so many rejections from what seemed the natural base, I start pitching at random, to anyone I happen to run into, to anyone with a minute to hear me out.

On the street, I run into Nick. He's never too busy for a street-corner conversation. I've known him and his interesting family ever since he went through grade school with my youngest brother, Ross; he's lately done college in our neighborhood and has lived for weeks and sometimes months with my brothers on the third floor of our house. With interests that include theater, communications, high culture, and low culture, he might spark to the issue. Yes. He might see the protest as street theater. He might think Jerry Lewis isn't funny. But I know this boy well, and there's a more obvious approach: "Hey, Nick!

Come and protest with me Monday morning and I'll feed you when we're done."

"Wha' food you feed?" Nick comes from Edisto Island where it behooves a white boy to speak Gullah if he wants to be beloved.

"Greek food," I answer.

"Greek food, naah. To the Ole Towne?"

"You know."

"Wukay then, I be there. Say when?"

My first recruit. Do I know other young men who will work for food? My brothers aren't interested in my foolishness, but there's Brad. He called me one day last month, out of the blue, wanting a recommendation to law school. I told him I didn't know him. Well, he's in a wheelchair and he's a friend of Dave, my quad buddy from law school, and he asked Dave for a recommendation but Dave said he'd be better off with a recommendation from me. I wished him well, but firmly declined. Now I'm desperate enough to dangle at least a glimmer of a possibility before him. I look for his number among the message slips that are piled on my desk like autumn leaves.

"Hello. Brad? This is Harriet Johnson. If you still want a reference, I've thought of a way I might be able to get to know you well enough to write something." I explain about the protest. To cover the strained silence, I babble about the *Parade* article, about how I'm tired of these people forcing me to lay low, like I have something to be ashamed of, really insulting all of us half persons, confined as we are to our steel prisons. I know he really wants that reference; Dave has given him this absurd idea that he won't get into law school without it. But still he's on the fence.

I offer free lunch.

OK. He'll be there.

My father has been with me the whole time. Dad is probably

the least military professor emeritus The Citadel has ever had. Since his retirement, he's jumped at any chance to protest militarism, racism, sexism, any kind of bigotry; after so many years of buttoned-up conformity, he's like a kid let out of school and would probably pay me to join the protest. But fair is fair. I promise him a free lunch along with the boys.

My team recruited, I need matériel. I write a flyer and fax the text to my sister Beth at her office, where she has a fancy computer with different fonts and print sizes. She does a layout and faxes it back. Before the slick thermocopy paper gets muddy, I have two hundred copies made. Yellow. I also have one hundred "What's wrong with telethons?" brochures I ordered from *Disability Rag* magazine. My legal assistant faxes my press release to local media. I keep markers and construction paper on hand, but I'm out of poster paper so I get someone to take me to the drugstore. There I discover vinyl peel-off letters with which I can make the signs myself:

RIGHTS, NOT PITY

WHY MUST WE BEG? SUPPORT UNIVERSAL HEALTH CARE.

EVERY PERSON IS A WHOLE PERSON

HONK IF YOU HATE TELETHONS

MDA AND JERRY: THIS "KID" IS FED UP

We're set. Almost. There's one more person to deal with: the local telethon host. He is a local news anchor and his mama is one of my mama's very best friends. I don't want him to feel ambushed. I phone and tell him personally. His reaction reminds me that this is a pretty strange thing I'm doing.

It's Sunday night. The telethon is starting. There's some tired tacky showbiz razzmatazz and then Jerry appears in his tuxedo. From him I learn that I'm not the only disabled person who has complained in the past year. He suggests that his disabled critics don't know much about neuromuscular diseases. "My kids can't go into the workplace; they can't do anything!" He goes on, "Please, I'm begging for survival. I want my kids alive. I don't ask you to pity them. I'm asking you to keep them alive."

The lies continue.

✦

The first lesson I learn that Labor Day is that you shouldn't announce the same start-up time to your supporters and the press. I've told everyone ten A.M. At nine-fifty, I'm with my father, the flyers, and the signs on the street outside the telethon hotel, the same hotel that gave me a free room last year. At nine fifty-five the *Post and Courier* arrives.

"Is it just you and your father?"

The vague sense of dread in my stomach becomes a real knot. "Well, apparently so, for the moment, though I do have promises from two young men."

I stop myself. No matter how pitiful you look, you'll look more pitiful telling about the people who said they'd come but aren't here "yet." Better to forge ahead and stick to the message. The reporter and photographer seem hurried, no doubt eager to get the day's big story, at the beach where children are digging in the sand, ladies are laying out fried chicken, girls are lounging in bikinis, dudes are hanging ten—The Last Day of Summer from all angles.

Dad gets the duct tape out of my bag and decorates me with signs. On my right side, it's THIS "KID" IS FED UP. On the left, WHY MUST WE BEG? He has to juggle the rest of the signs as we commence our two-person parade. Walking with us, the photographer and reporter double our ranks. You take solidarity where you can find it. I give the reporter the why-we're-here, making reference to last year's *Parade* magazine cover story.

"Did you see yesterday's story?" the reporter asks.

It was another cover pitch for the MDA telethon. "It isn't so blatant, so obviously offensive, but it is stereotypical," I say. "It's on the courage and overcoming theme. It suggests that we need a special spark of character to get through our miserable days. That reflects and feeds the public perception that suffering is our usual lot."

Dad and I pose for pictures. The paper leaves. As if on cue Nick shows up. He's looking a bit bedraggled as a young guy ought to look on a holiday morning. Dad issues him HONK IF YOU HATE TELETHONS.

We walk around the hotel, directing the signs toward the one-way car traffic. The wide sidewalks are in good condition for Charleston, amply peopled with tourists, mostly white, and locals, mostly black. Dad is the leaflet commando. It's all I can do to "parade"—my bouncy little E&J Marathon, acquired soon after law school, likes to zip and dart and is impatient with this slow walking-person pace.

We round the last corner. Up a driveway, at the car entrance to the hotel, I see a young man in a wheelchair. It's Brad, obviously, trying to be invisible. I can guess why. If you're alone in a public place and you happen to be in a wheelchair, nondisabled people tend to assume something's seriously amiss—you're stranded, your nurse has run off, you're dazed and disoriented, you need to get back to the nursing home. You fend off well-meaning offers of help until you want to disappear.

"Brad? I—"

"Harriet. I thought we'd meet here."

"Sorry. We walked from the other direction. I forgot this entrance was here." I offer him his choice of signs and Dad drops a lapload of flyers on him. Putting on his game face, he gives the flyer a quick study. He asks about the scope of our city permit, careful about staying within legal bounds as befits an aspiring lawyer. On with the parade.

People are now responding to Nick's HONK sign. He's gotten into it, working the sign, getting those honks by acting the role of handsome young man; he's made himself resemble Paul Newman in one of those early Tennessee Williams roles. Brad immediately shows himself as a personable establishment crip—the kind of well-groomed up-and-coming young man who looks you straight in the eye and assures you he'll get the job done, whatever the job may be. To curious tourists, he's approachable and, once approached, he explains our issue clearly and persuasively, using bullet points from the flyer:

"We don't want pity. Pity gets in our way when we are looking for jobs and a place in the community."

"We're glad people want to help. The best way to help is to support our civil rights, like the Americans with Disabilities Act."

In the face of opposition, he stays cool; when he finds an opening, he grabs it, leads them along. Every word seems straight from the heart. No one would suspect he's motivated by free food or any other form of secondary gain. He'll make a fine lawyer. I'll recommend him without hesitation.

Local TV asks why are we here. I give the same simple sound byte with only slight variations. We're showing that there are two sides of the telethon; the money does some good, but the price is too high. The telethon suggests we're all doomed and that isn't true. I have one of those diseases. I'm thirty-four and enjoy my life the way it is. Brad listens, and, like a good trial lawyer, picks up some new themes. We're becoming a team. Dad is getting the handbills out. Brad's explaining them. Nick's working the car traffic. I am the comandante. We have found a rhythm and it's become a pleasant way to spend the Last Morning of Summer, warmed by sunlight, tickled by ocean breezes, engaging with all kinds of people on some of the most interactive streets in the United States.

A big, leathery man is pressing a $20 bill on me. "Here you go, darling." It's spooky: LBJ's voice. He's ornamented in turquoise and silver—from cowboy hat to pointy boot-toes.

"We're not soliciting," I say.

He squeezes the bill into the palm of my driving hand. "Take it darlin,' for the telethon, for the cure, and God bless."

"No, thank you, we're not collecting today. We're passing out these handbills. I'd appreciate your taking one and giving it a read."

With lumbering reluctance, he pockets his twenty and takes a flyer. My father mutters, "That money would have helped with lunch."

The Texan gazes at the handbill as he meanders lackadaisically due north. Then he comes to a sudden cinematic stop. His jaw drops. His neck goes tight, and he's shooting with his eyeballs, top to bottom, till he's hit every word on the yellow page. He turns on his boot heels toward me and my small band of compañeros.

"You're against Jerry Lewis!"

"Er, well, sir, we think——-"

"That Jerry Lewis!" There's blood in his eye. "He—he takes all the money! Takes it! He lives like a king! In France!"

That's not our message and I'm not privy to the account books, but I'm disinclined to get in a fight with him. I have promised the city police that decorum will be maintained.

✦

It's a success all around. Lunch, with tax and tip, is only about $10 per head; the food is rich with lots of garlic and oregano and the boys don't leave hungry. Brad is overjoyed to know he'll get that recommendation and law school admission is therefore in the bag. That evening, we get decent TV coverage, even from Mama's friend's son at the telethon station.

The next day's *Post and Courier* contains the exciting news that there have also been protests in Chicago, Denver, Los Angeles, and Las Vegas. The local account teaches me another lesson: don't expect a reporter to get sense from a steno pad that's spent a day at the beach. While we paraded together, the reporter seemed to understand everything I said. In his article, he gets the goods on why-we're-here. But, ostensibly quoting me, he adds that people with muscular dystrophy have a special spark of courage and determination—a stereotypical view I was criticizing, not espousing. I send a long op-ed. This paper runs it with my picture, complete with WHY MUST WE BEG? in a box with a counterpoint from MDA's CEO that is so patently stupid, so mean and disrespectful, that it goes a long way toward justifying my disreputable actions.

A short time later, my copy of *MDA News* arrives. The letters column contains quite a bit of comment from telethon loyalists. In response to one reader's request, MDA prints addresses of protest organizers Laura Hershey in Denver and Mike Ervin and his sister Cris Matthews in Chicago. I figure they'll get hate mail, so I send them love-and-solidarity letters and enclose my flyer. They welcome me into the tiny ranks of the national telethon opposition. In South Carolina, I'm considered a radical. Among them, I represent the conservative wing. After all, my protest had the city's good housekeeping seal of approval.

News of the protests continues to percolate and there's interest from national media. In January, I get a call from a producer of an NBC talk show. They want me in New York in two days.

✦

Geneva, who still works for me at home, doesn't travel. I'm wracking my brain. Who among my vast acquaintance would take off, leave Charleston on the spur of the moment, abandon all responsibilities to take me to New York—in January? I roll into the outer office, and there she is, the sharp face in front of the ponytail, the college kid my office co-op lately hired to be our runner.

"Mandy. I need someone to take me to New York day after tomorrow."

"NEATO TORPEDO!" There's something of the infant in Mandy: bouncing, exploring, always in motion, never at rest—until she gets tired and falls suddenly comatose, sometimes under the desk of a lawyer who's stepped out for a minute. Now it's like I've given her the best news of her entire life. She's crowing.

"Hang on a minute." There's no one in the waiting room but us, so I'll go ahead with the gory details. "I need to be bodily lifted—in and out of airplanes. It's heavy labor."

"Cool!"

"You'd need to stick with me at all times. Follow exact instructions."

"Sure!"

"Bedpan duties."

"Awesome!"

"It'll be a quick run up there, maybe a good dinner, a TV talk show in the morning, and then back."

"Excellent!"

"Good deal," I say. "I'll tell NBC to make reservations. Oh. Mandy, what's your last name?"

✦

It's an early flight and Mandy has the exuberance of a toddler let out of day care. She is entirely and immediately compliant with all my instructions. Beyond that, she has a strange instinct for strange body mechanics; even without being told she somehow knows which body parts are unnaturally stiff, which unnaturally floppy. When she carries me through plane after plane, no one could suspect it's her first day at this kind of work.

I haven't had time to work out power chair logistics, so I travel in a portable chair. At JFK, Mandy lifts me into a taxicab. As we ride into Manhattan, she stares out the window, grooving on the roads, the traffic, the buildings, the racket, the movement, the overwhelming chaos.

She rolls me into the sudden sterility of the hotel. From our irregular lurching pace I know she's skipping or otherwise silly-walking behind me. The gawks we're getting aren't the usual pity-gawks. People are clearly amused by whatever she's doing, charmed by whatever she is.

At the desk, I produce the confirmation number NBC gave me. "It's a double accessible room."

"Sorry, ma'am, but all our handicapped rooms have one king. We can bring in a rollaway."

"When you do that, it eats up the turning space and it's no longer accessible. Let me see a 'regular' double room. It might work." I'm frustrated. This happens all the time. To get the required turning space, they don't enlarge the room; they remove a bed. Not exactly equal accommodations. I wish I could remember whether the ADA takes effect for public accommodations this week or next.

There's considerable back-and-forth, consultations behind closed doors. The desk clerk returns. "We're trying to make this work, but we're fully booked."

Mandy thumps a complicated bongo riff on the pleasingly hollow countertop. "Hey, man! I can sleep with you!" She presses down with both hands, hops up, and with alternating feet gives the front panel three quick kicks in time with three words: "Not A Problem!"

Under the circumstances, insisting on my rights, if indeed I have any rights, would seem a bit rude. Without kicking, I tell the desk clerk it's Not A Problem. I'll sleep with Mandy. After all, I've seen her sleep in the office, and she doesn't appear to be a bed hog or sheet thief.

A bellman takes us to our room. For showing us the light switches, the thermostat, and TV remote control, he is rewarded with Mandy's unbounded enthusiasm. "Anything you need, just call," he says.

"Right on, Leo!" Mandy says, reading his name tag like an old pal. From a little stash of cash I have stowed in her hip pocket, she vigorously pulls out an appropriate tip. On top of that, she gives him a big thumbs-up as he closes the door.

She tosses me on the bed and flops down beside me but upside down. I'm exhausted from being toted and from travel stress. I'm ready to crash, but the sock full of wiggling toes just left of my head tells me Mandy's not crashing right now and I can't sleep with a buzzing glowing person in my space. Hoping to talk her down, I ask her questions. I've heard she's a formidable force on the soccer field and get her to tell me some pointless details about her play and practice schedule. College major? Art. When she was younger, her family took her to some, like, really major museums but she doesn't remember much. With more questions, I make her recall seeing, at the British Museum, those gates from ancient Assyria, huge stone arches, flanked by monstrous animals. I tell her that when I saw them, I thought, these are scary—these are why Jonah was afraid to go when God told him to go to Nineveh and prophesy.

"What?"

It seems Mandy doesn't know the story of Jonah, so I launch

into the narrative. I know she's paying attention when her foot stops wiggling; her toes flex when the story gets tense. I get to the part about Jonah getting swallowed up in the belly of a great fish, and she says, "Whooooaa!"

Soon after that, after Jonah has been spat out on the bank of the Tigris River but before he fulfills his mission to reveal his truth on the streets and sidewalks of downtown Nineveh, she crashes. So do I.

✦

Nick is now in New York to study acting and directing and whatnot at NYU. Through his parents, I've told him I'm coming and he invites me to feed him dinner. He shows up at the hotel, talking Northern talk now. Our plan is to go to a place where my mother and I ate, as it happens with Nick and my brother Eric, about four years ago. The Brazilian Coffee House Restaurant has a killer feijoida. The problem is we can't find them in the phone book. Maybe I have the name a little bit wrong. Mama remembers the address is 45 Forty-sixth Street, or maybe 56 Fifty-seventh Street—numbers in sequence like that, somewhere toward the middle between one and a hundred, in a Brazilian neighborhood. We'll get in a cab and look for it.

Nick volunteers to lift me. He's done it before. When he and my brothers were in high school, I sometimes went out with them in some kid's car so they could fake people out. First, they let people see a bunch of healthy teenagers pulling up in the disability parking. Look at 'em scowl! Then they unload the wheelchair. Oh, they didn't realize. So contrite. Then one of the big healthy boys sits in the chair and thumbs his nose. Fury! Shock! Utter disbelief! Finally—the surprise ending—me, flopping from the arms of a big healthy boy, undeniably, unmistakably the real thing, and the whole gang hoot their gotchas to the world at large! I figured it was harmless entertainment for young people—maybe a kind of street theater.

Now it's a New York cab.

"Where to?" It's the first time I've ever met a New York cabbie with a New York accent. I hate being a Southerner who doesn't know where she's going, but what can I do?

"Well, the thing is this," I say, as Southerners do. "We want to go to the Brazilian Coffee House Restaurant." I explain about the numbers being in sequence, somewhere toward the middle of one and a hundred, in a Brazilian neighborhood, all that. He gives me a slow smile that is at once condescending and predatory.

"Tell you what. I take you to Foity-foive Foity-sixth and if that dun't woik, we can troy something else."

"Excellent!" Mandy says.

"Fo' true." Something about the situation has caused Nick to slide back into Gullah.

The driver has discerned that I'm the grown-up and waits for my response. "That'll be perfectly fine. Whatever makes sense to you."

We're lurching through the streets and then the cab swerves with frustration. "Wait a minute, dey got that blocked. We'll troy Fifty-six Fifty sevent' foist. That OK?"

"Sure!" Mandy beams.

"Aw right, naah," Nick says.

"I trust in your judgment," I say.

Off we go in a different direction, and then there's another obstacle, and a reversal, and another false start and another. At each change, we all three in our own ways give our consent to the reroute. For Mandy it's always awesome or cool or neato. For Nick it's wukey or sho-nuff. For me, it's—whatever I say in my ridiculous Southern lady lawyer idiom. The driver looks sideways at his ticking meter.

I tell him, "Sir, we're here only for the night. We were too tired to go sightseeing this afternoon, and NBC is paying the fare, so it's OK if you drive us around a little. Just try to find the restaurant in whatever way suits, and we're fine."

He seems incredulous but takes us winding around consecutively numbered addresses. We're having fun. He points out a few sights of interest along the way, including Foity-second Street. We can live with his scorn.

"Luknya!" Nick exclaims.

The driver guesses Luknya means he should stop. It's the building. I remember that awning. But it's an Italian restaurant now. "What do you think?" I ask. It's still a Brazilian neighborhood, and there is a Brazilian restaurant across the street. We decide to check out their feijoida. Probably it's good if they outlasted the amazing Brazilian Coffee House Restaurant.

I tell the driver, "You can put us out here, if you would be so kind."

He figures the fare. It's not so bad, but he seems a bit defensive, like maybe he should have known where the Brazilian Coffee House Restaurant used to be, and taken us right there.

"Tell you what," he says. "You people are so goddam agreeable, I think I'll waive my usual non-English-speaking surcharge." He pronounces it soychauge and we thank him.

We go inside. Mandy has told me she's a vegetarian but she can eat black beans prepared in meat if the meat is removed, so I order up the feijoida. Almost immediately the black beans and all the accoutrements are laid before us. Nick and I inhale the intoxicating fumes, atremble with anticipation. Protruding from the black beans there's a pig's tail and ear. Nick spears the ear and waves it with his fork. "Variety meats!"

Mandy's gone green. Urgently I beckon to the waiter who is standing behind her. "This girl is a vegetarian. Can you make her some vegetarian black beans?"

He winks with the same predatory condescension we got

from the cab driver. "Yes, ma'am, of course, we can prepare special vegetarian black beans, just for her. Give me two minutes."

I imagine them back in the kitchen, scooping Mandy's beans from an enormous never-empty bubbling bean cauldron, picking away sausage and variety meats with amused contempt. In a trice, Mandy has a shallow bowl of black beans, garnished California-style with a dollop of sour cream and a pile of crisp variety greens.

Nick and I are left to deal with the Brazilian national dish, the most soulful of all soul food. Before us are mountains of beans, rice, collard greens, sliced oranges, manioc flour, and meats defying description, all cooked to a fare-thee-well, simmered for days, perhaps for decades. Then, we know, there must be coffee. And flan of course. . . . A daunting prospect. But that's all right, naah. We have plenty of time. Time to chew and swallow and talk crazy talk in Gullah-boy and Southern-lady and whatever Mandy talks about every possible topic. Or almost. We never get around to the telethon or tomorrow's talk show. Why spoil a fine meal?

✦

Morning. Before I remember where I am, Mandy has jumped into jeans and T-shirt and sneakers, ready for action. I start drawling my exact instructions. She's obviously unaccustomed to the complexity of grown-up-lady winter clothing but nothing fazes her for long.

We've been told that from here we go to NBC's studio at Rockefeller Center and from there to the airport. President Bush is in town and the city is in gridlock. Ahead of schedule, we're checked out. With our bags, we sit near the door and wait for the van. Also waiting is a young man, suited and tied, self-propelled in a manual chair. I wonder if he and I are doing the same gig; I'm kicking myself that I didn't ask who else would be on the panel. I'm sure this guy isn't one of the telethon crit-ics I know about. We're all more decrepit; there's not a self-propelled manual chair user in the bunch.

Mandy bounces up. "Yo! Leo!" She's spotted our bellman on the other side of the crowded lobby. A personal assistant is sup-posed to be unobtrusive, but Mandy must be Mandy and I can't fuss in the face of Leo's smile. Mandy taps and wiggles and we wait.

The van arrives and, yes, it is for both me and the other per-son on wheels. We introduce ourselves. His name is Scott. He's from Texas or somewhere, in advertising or something.

We ride the lift into the van and Mandy locks both Scott and me in four-point restraint as though she's done it a thousand times before. Eventually we nose out of the hotel driveway, into the gridlock, and there we sit. "President Bush is in town," Scott says, "speaking to foreign leaders, I heard."

"Yeah, that's right," I say. "I think there are still a few for-eign leaders he hasn't thrown up on yet." Scott's guffaw seems genuine, which makes me think he's not a bad guy. But I also think he is most likely my opponent in the TV debate and won-der why is he putting his crippled self on the line for the thon— if, indeed, he is for the thon?

We are one vehicle among who knows how many, trapped in the presidential gridlock. Scott suggests we get out and roll— seems it's only a couple of blocks—but the driver clearly wants to keep us and there are the bags to contend with. So we engage in chatter that is pointless and pleasant, only slightly stilted, suitable for strangers who have been brought together for ritual combat on network TV. By look and gesture Mandy is telling the driver, her newest friend, that this is a really, like, weird, conversation. Maybe she's never met an establishment crip be-fore, but I've encountered quite a few. Scott reminds me of some of the young crips I knew at the University of South Carolina. He's sort of like Brad.

At length we make it to our destination, and after incalculable time tied down in the van, it's a frantic dash to the studio, where I'm introduced to Dr. Leon Charash of New York, MDA's medical director. He reaches down and I greet him with my two-handed political handshake. Scott and Leon appear to be old acquaintances and it's clear I've guessed right about which side he's debating.

The fourth panelist rolls in. It's Mike Ervin, one of the Chicago protesters with whom I've corresponded. Mike and I nod in greeting instead of shaking hands; given our combined bodily immobility, any kind of physical contact would be way too complicated to attempt in front of a crowd.

In my heart, though, I give Mike a warm embrace. It's love at first sight—at my first sight of his shoes. They are small, soft, cotton, made in China. His have laces, mine ankle straps, but they're functionally equivalent and they tell me his feet are like mine, too soft for regular shoes, apt to lose regular shoes during transfers, with limp but sensate toes that sometimes get scrunched and need adjusting through the cloth. His clothes are likewise like mine, soft and unconstructed so nothing bunches or hangs funny or binds the small movements that are possible. The similarity of our clothes implies similarity in how our flesh feels in them. I believe I know how he feels in his body.

It hits me hard that not since my childhood in cripdom, a place where my body type was not unusual, have I shared that kind of knowing with anyone. I shared it with Ronnie and James, but they died in their late teens; for many years now I've lived in the mainstream world where the crips you encounter are of a different kind and I've been of a different substance and form from all the people surrounding me, like the last local survivor of a rare species. Now, I've met another. As I've already learned, Mike is a rare bird indeed: smart, funny, on the warpath, no establishment crip, and sure as hell no darling dying child.

But there's no time to marvel. It's almost showtime and we must get prepped. There is concern about the effect of bright lights on my high round forehead, but I decline makeup. I'm rolled on a stage in front of a studio audience, alongside Mike, Scott, and Dr. Leon, positioned and repositioned, lit and relit, miked and remiked. The technical people ask me where I'm from and then they say, oh Charleston was so beautiful in *The Prince of Tides*, and I say, oh that was Beaufort pretending to be Charleston because we were torn up by Hurricane Hugo at the time, and they say oh well it was beautiful scenery, and I say oh yes it was and much of it looks just like Charleston. All the while I wonder exactly when Mandy will fall into one of her comas. So far she's doing fine, more than fine, working side by side with the crew, crawling around the cables, playing with a roll of tape, loving all the lights and cameras and action.

An advance guy tells the audience what to do when the applause sign flashes and how to behave when the green light is on. "Some of our guests are in wheelchairs," he says unnecessarily, "but they're just like other guests. Even though they're in wheelchairs, it's OK to challenge them. You don't have to agree with people just because they might be in wheelchairs."

"Or just because they might be doctors," I say, loud enough to be heard to the back row. I suspect Dr. Leon is not amused.

At length the green light flashes and the cool blond on-air personality strides out to the well-prepped applause. The discussion is introduced by a short video with clips of protests and a surprising seal of approval from Evan Kemp, Bush's head of the Equal Employment Opportunity Commission, who says from his power chair in his power office that pity is a barrier to employment of people with disabilities. Then the first question, for Mike: How can he oppose the telethon when he suffers from one of the diseases the telethon targets? "First of all, I don't suffer," he says. Bingo. The ableist language, the assumption that having a disability inherently means suffering, is so pervasive I didn't even notice it. Mike is absolutely right to object, right at the top of the show.

For the next forty minutes or so, we do the ritual as the rules prescribe in a time before shouting and interrupting have become fashionable. We exchange well-rounded sound bytes, glib answers to crisp questions. We're not scripted, but each of us has a role to play. Leon is the true believer, Scott the committed token. Mike is nemesis—uncompromising, bordering on snarly. By default, I am the nice cop, the petite Southern lady with soft consonants and a fuzzy sweater dress. I guess if Jonah got the call to speak today, it might be in a forum like this, after a time swallowed up in gridlock.

A man in the audience says MDA's support meant everything to him when his wife was dying of a neuromuscular disease; he's visibly, viscerally upset at what seems like a personal attack on kind caregivers. I wish I could talk to him privately, as one human being to another, but we must talk publicly, in representative capacities. I say I'm very glad to hear MDA was helpful to him. On the monitor I see the camera pull in tight. The close-up signals sincerity in TV language and it annoys me because I am in fact sincere and don't need it signaled. But that image, Monitor Harriet with her thoughtful pale skin and intelligent brown eyes and one earnest braid commencing behind her left ear, can't be avoided, up close and personal, slowly moving in. Before the closeness becomes unbearable, she dutifully delivers the next good-cop punch: our challenge to MDA is to do good without doing harm.

Another bereaved person challenges Mike. Mike would feel differently if he had lost a loved one to neuromuscular disease.

No, Mike answers, not true. He has lost friends. One died on the couch in his apartment. I want to hear the whole story; I want Mike to explain how he can think our dignity is more important than the possibility of curing diseases that can kill people. I want to tell about Ronnie and James and through the telling begin to figure out why I feel the same way. But this is a TV debate, not a real conversation. We can't slow down and explore the raw reality that has brought us where we are. Our job is to shoot zingers back and forth.

So the volleys fly in this strange mixed-doubles game, from Harriet, to Scott, to Mike, to Leon, to Mike, to Leon, to Scott.

The applause sign flashes. Green light turns to red. It's over. The formula talk ends before the real conversation has begun, before I've probed what fears have drawn an intelligent up-and-coming establishment crip like Scott to the wrong side of this debate, before I've told Mike how much I love his shoes, before I've said what I want to say about living in a world that insists that people like us are suffering and that lives like James's and Ronnie's and Mike's friend who died on the couch were less because they were short.

With the ease that is the birthright of the ambulatory in-towner, Dr. Leon has thrown himself back into his customary habitat before Mike, Scott, and I are freed from our cables. With Mandy and Mike's attendant—who happens to be the male equivalent of Mandy—Mike, Scott, and I roll out to await transportation. Because of the continuing traffic problems, we've been warned to expect a protracted wait. Good. We're keyed up. We'll have time to talk.

Now there is also time to take in Rockefeller Center's famous lobby, which was a blur of confusion as we raced in. All around, the monumental wall paintings by Diego Rivera proclaim equality, with human bodies in place of protest signs and stories in place of slogans. In the crowded public space beneath the murals, three people in wheelchairs, small figures, far from monumental, sit and wait for the next thing to happen.

As we wait, alive and improbably together here and now, we put our time to good use. We talk. Now our slogans and signs are replaced by our stories and flesh-and-blood experience. It's a kind of talk that doesn't settle any questions, doesn't alter any fixed opinions, doesn't aim to change the world. Yet, inevitably, subtly, it affects us.

For me, the conversation represents reconnection with the crip world. The crip world of my childhood was a place where I felt at home and valued; leaving it was a wrench. This is a new place, all grown up, with grown-up hopes and fears and struggles and responsibilities and rights, a place of belonging for the person I am now. We have differences: Mike is the feisty rebel; Scott the slick inside guy; I am finding that the good-cop shtick comes naturally to me. At the same time, we share the strange experience of living in and around the nondisabled world and resisting the stereotypes that would confine us and that sometimes threaten our lives.

This discussion is too real, too rich, too much our own, to offer for public consumption. It's not ready for the streets of our hometowns or the studio in New York or the gates of Nineveh. The public audience is not ready for this conversation. We are.

4

What the Hell, Why Not?

Susan, a lawyer in my office and the greatest genius I know when it comes to meddling, sticks her head in my doorway. "So I know you've heard the scuttlebutt about the Charleston-City seats in the County Council race."

I know that not one but two candidates have been removed from the ballot with less than a month to go before the election. I can't remember what happened with the first guy—an attack of apathy, maybe; I know the second guy didn't live in the city, a requirement for the Charleston-City seat on County Council. But what I know isn't scuttlebutt. It's been in the *Post and Courier*. "What do you know?"

"Runyon's filing for one of the seats."

"Naturally." He's usually up for that sort of thing.

"The other one's up for grabs."

"Can they reopen filing this late?"

"Apparently so."

It's an odd race. As originally configured, there were two Republicans and two Democrats. Countywide voters select any two of the four. There was talk that we'd be better off with only one Democratic candidate, who would be first choice for all Democrats and the default second choice for all Republicans who don't like one or the other of their nominees. Now it's back open. "Do they want a second Democrat?" I ask.

"Anne Frances says she made a commitment to get a full slate." Anne Frances, a lawyer in Susan's vast social circle, is the county Democratic chair. "I was thinking you should file. I'll donate your filing fee. I can also drive you around. Be your campaign manager. I have some free time."

"What does Anne Frances think?"

"She'll be fine."

If Susan says someone will be fine, they'll be fine, but it might be best not to inquire how it comes to pass.

"Why do you think I should do this?"

"Because the people love you."

"Why else?"

"It'll be fun. If you get elected, it's a convenient office. They meet around the corner. You can roll from here or unload the van in the King & Queen parking garage. Much better than traipsing up to the state legislature in Columbia." Susan knows that logistical concerns have great weight on my scale of values.

"I can't possibly win."

"Winning isn't terribly likely, but it'll be interesting." She pantomimes shifting my gears, turning my steering wheel. "Think of the places we can take the van!" I can almost feel her turning corners too hard, popping curbs. Day in and day out, she's earned a reputation as a calming presence in divorce court, a soother of jangled nerves, but she's a surprisingly aggressive driver. We always have a blast in the van.

I check my mental calendar. It's pretty light for the next four weeks. What the hell, maybe I will—if Anne Frances can't find another candidate.

This week Runyon's seat is open for filing; next week the

second slot opens. I wait a couple of days and then phone Anne Frances.

"Are you still looking for a council candidate?" I ask.

"Oh! Yes! I am." There's a breath burst with each syllable; it sounds like she's leaning back in her swivel chair with the back of her hand pressed against her fevered brow.

"Have you heard Susan's latest scheme? She wants me to file." I say it in a way that would give Anne Frances permission to guffaw, if she were the guffawing type. She doesn't even chuckle; I suspect she's blanching. Her blanch is pretty dramatic considering that her skin is so fair to begin with, and set off by dark hair and ruby red lipstick—but of course I can't get the full effect on the telephone.

"Is this just another of Susan's schemes or is it to be taken seriously?" she asks.

"Isn't a Susan scheme always to be taken seriously? This one sounds pretty nutty, but she's set on it, and I usually do what she says. She's never led me astray." Anne Frances's silence seems pained, but maybe I'm projecting. I've put her on the horns of a dilemma. Maybe. I go on. "Anne Frances, if you don't want me to run, please say so. I'll tell Susan to give this one up. I don't want to hurt the ticket. If anyone else wants to do it, that's absolutely fine. There's no time to put on a primary!"

"Oh my God. A primary! We just can't have a primary!"

"I was joking."

"Oh my God. The thought absolutely never occurred to me. Can you believe it? Never! What if two people file? It would be—my God—just too awful for words!"

"Anne Frances, it won't happen. The election's in four weeks. You'll be lucky to get one credible candidate." Even one noncredible candidate, I think. "Don't worry."

But I've lost her to the agony of dreading the short-fuse primary from hell that isn't going to happen. I end the conversation by telling her I'll file for the second slot if no one else wants it, unless she thinks I shouldn't. Meanwhile, I'll talk it around.

✦

This is in October 1994. You know, of course, that this will be Newt Gingrich's year, the year the Republicans take out that Contract on America and Democrats go up in flames. We won't discover this historical fact until the votes are counted. At this point, most Charleston County Democratic leaders think we might reverse the tide that seems to be making more and more voters push the Republican button. We're being hammered by new Republican voters in the resort communities, young professionals in the suburbs, and Snowbelt retirees all over. But the conventional wisdom says these voters are economically conservative and socially liberal, just like Bill Clinton, and if we can make our party and get candidates just like Bill Clinton, we can get them pushing our button.

So says the conventional wisdom—the white, male, prosperous, middle-of-the-road, just-like-Bill-Clinton conventional wisdom. My wisdom follows a different template. Two years ago, I was county cochair of Tom Harkin for President. During 1988 and 1984, I was at the state convention for Jesse Jackson. I think what's getting our candidates hammered, year after year, is the vast bloc that decides every election—the people who stay home and don't vote. The disconnected. The ignored. The answer is not to get all slicked up and play to the fickle middle but to stir up that inchoate majority. The lesson to be learned from Ronald Reagan, I keep on saying, is that Americans aren't as moderate as they're cracked up to be. They'll go for clarity, even if it's extreme. And if fake sincerity plays so well, maybe they'd like the real thing even better. Who knows? It might take some getting used to and might not work the first time, but it's an experiment worth trying.

✦

Anne Frances calls me back, calls Susan, calls around, and discovers that I really might file if no one else does. I know she'd like a Bill Clinton type, ideally a baggage-free Bill Clinton type, and I don't qualify. I'm obviously not the type, and I do have some baggage—not Clintonesque baggage packed with sex and real estate, but baggage containing things like picket signs and support for socialism. My agenda isn't what's considered sellable in Charleston County.

I truly don't want to cause the other candidates any angst. I've been involved with local politics for eighteen years, in responsible positions for five years. Despite certain differences, I'm proud to be one of the Faithful. When my party loyalty has wavered, all I have to do is think about South Carolina Republicans.

I go to one of our first-time candidates—a professional man with a natural high-gloss finish. He's invested a lot of time and money running for Council in another district. I ask, would I hurt his chances in any way? Oh no. But, he says, campaigning is grueling. Maybe I should wait until another year, some time when I'd have months to prepare and raise money and maybe even win.

As the week goes on, I run into more than one personable thirty-something white male lawyer who tells me Anne Frances has asked him to run for County Council. "But I'd have to be out of my mind!" one says. "There's no way a Democrat can get in this late and win."

"Yeah, you're right," I agree. So, the county party chair is still hoping for a credible candidate. She may have to settle for a nut.

I phone the city attorney for advice. He's not available, so I ask for his wife and law partner, the deputy city attorney. "Harriet, you'd make a great candidate," she says, "and a terrific councilmember if elected. You've done such great work for the city. The county would be incredibly lucky to have your brains and your hard work." Whenever I get such praise I start steeling myself for the however or but. "But," she says, "it's not a good year. Have you seen the national polls? Looks like we're going to get creamed. The county's been getting tougher and tougher for Democrats. Eventually the tide will turn, but this would a terrible year to jump in."

That's it. No way will I do this without the city's blessing. "Well, you're probably right. I know the general thinking is that the party should go with moderate, middle-of-the-road candidates, and I might be too odd. I mean, the whole thing could degenerate into a referendum on the telethon protest."

There is a pause. "Hey now. I forgot all about that. You know, you could win this thing. You are well known throughout the community. Visible. You have a real following. And your issue crosses party lines. All kinds of people dislike Jerry Lewis!"

She says she wants to talk to her husband and to the mayor.

Within the hour, there's a call from Anne Frances. She sounds like she's calling from the other side of a catastrophe. "Harriet. The mayor wants you to run."

This must be painful for her. Our brilliant, beloved, undefeatable Democratic mayor cannot be denied. I ought to give her a quick answer and put her out of her misery, but it's a moment to savor. "The mayor wants me to run? Really? Why on earth?"

"He says you'd be a strong candidate and a great councilmember, that you've done great work for the city."

"Does he think I'll appeal to swing voters?"

"He wants you to file. Will you please do it? Filing opens at my office at noon on Tuesday. Can you come over right then?"

I agree. I tell Susan we're off and running and I need $480 for the filing fee.

✦

Anne Frances's office is across Meeting Street, halfway between my office and the building where County Council meets. Susan and I head out at the appointed time to walk over there. There's a traffic light at the corner where Anne Frances's building sits, but no curb cut. We walk down one more block. There's no light. Susan steps into heavy two-way traffic that seems perilously close, and I follow like a baby duck. I'm glad she's here. I am not confident of my ability to judge speed and distance, probably because I never went anywhere alone until I got my first power chair at age twenty-one—in the sixteen years since, street-crossing faculties haven't become automatic. I know drivers are looking out for conventional pedestrians but sometimes wheelchairs don't register.

Then it's back up the block to the front of the modern office building where Anne Frances works. Susan opens the door. The vestibule has two steps. I've been here before; I came in by van through the back parking lot. We try to go around, but no matter how we do it, there is no accessible path from the sidewalk into that parking lot. If you're in a wheelchair, you can't get there from here. I could get in my van and drive in from street level, but my van's in my driveway at home. If the county were in charge of these sidewalks, this might be a good campaign issue. But it's the city's jurisdiction, and as a city attorney, I'm a bit constrained. I'm assigned to dilapidated housing, not curb cuts.

Susan says she'll go inside. I'll wait in front. It won't be the first time I've transacted business on a city sidewalk; my last passport was issued in front of the historic post office.

It's a pleasant, warm day; this lull is something I ought to savor. Once I sign those papers, I'll be busy. I pull up against the building and enjoy the air. Passersby ask me if I'm stranded, as they always do. In a situation like this, I am stranded, sort of, but there's nothing for them to do. I say I'm fine.

The door opens and Susan comes out. I expect Anne Frances next. I'm looking forward to solemnly shaking the county party chair's hand, seeing her Snow White face. But instead Susan dumps papers in the bag on the back of my chair. "I signed everything for you. It's a done deal."

"Thanks. What's next?"

"Eat lunch. Then there's a meet-the-candidates forum."

✦

I've been to many candidates' forums as audience member, facilitator, and Democratic questioner. Presenting myself as a candidate ought to feel much different, but to my surprise it doesn't. Immediately, I find it's easy to be plain and natural if you're totally unprepared and everyone knows you have no idea what you're talking about. I wasn't planning to run. I haven't been paying attention to the issues. I have a vague idea that the plan to close the Charleston Naval Base—potentially an economic calamity—might become an opportunity to redefine what kind of economy we have, but otherwise I assure potential voters that I'm serious and conscientious and a good listener and quick study. If elected, I'll figure out the issues. People are very, very nice. Some connect me with the telethon, but I'm not sure they remember which side I'm on.

At the forum, some people ask me for campaign literature. I don't have any. So back at the office, I type up a one-page bio and campaign statement. Susan reminds me to include my address and instructions on how to make out checks. That reminds me that I need a campaign account, so I phone my banker. Susan roughs out a to-do list. Her husband can take my photo and produce a campaign brochure. She'll work on TV and radio.

"What?" I say.

"It's a countywide race. You need to be on TV and radio."

"I'm not spending my own money, OK?"

This week we'll hit a few events and lay the groundwork. Our big announcement—to kick off the campaign in earnest—will come after filing closes next week, only two weeks before the election.

I fax a press release announcing that I've filed. The next day, the *Post and Courier* runs a nice edit of my press release, including a head shot they have graciously cropped from a file photo taken at the first telethon protest. I look like a respectable, if earnest, pale, and thin young woman. At Democratic events, the Faithful congratulate me on getting some press and clamor for campaign materials. I get laughs by offering my plain one-page handout as the temporary campaign brochure. A day or two later, Susan reformats my text into bullet points with larger type on front and back. "The temporary campaign brochure, second edition," she says. We'll revise it every day or two. The Faithful can collect 'em all.

Systematically, Susan is haggling over quotes for media time and production, printing, and signs.

"I don't want to do signs," I say. "I never heard of anyone who was persuaded to vote because they liked a sign."

"You've got to have signs. For the people who put up signs."

She's right, I guess. Each party has its cadre of sign warriors who erect signs by day, steal the other side's signs by night, and in the morning fulminate with righteous wrath when they discover that their own signs have been stolen by evil, lawless opposing cadres. Our sign warriors want to know: How many? How big? Where?

OK, we'll do a few. If we get some money.

✦

There's a little glitch to send any party chair's blood pressure off the charts. Another candidate has come to Anne Frances's office and is filing. She begs me to talk him out of it; she's sending him to see me. I don't know him, have never heard of him, have no idea how this is to be done. Discouraging candidates isn't my forte, and I surely don't have any rationales likely to convince him that I am better than he is. I presume Anne Frances has told him the mayor wants me, which is my only objective selling point. My basic campaign spiel about being unprepared and ignorant won't work here. Maybe it's what provoked him into filing.

With mannerly desperation, I invite him to tell me about himself, but he says very little, so I yammer about the process, that we're only allowed one name, since we already have Runyon, and we need to decide now, so someone can take on the Republicans. One of us needs to withdraw.

Why not me? He doesn't ask, but I wish I could tell him.

He says he'll think it over.

I send word around that I can withdraw if that's best, but now the party wants me on the ticket. Meanwhile, I continue going to various events, mostly rallying the Faithful, who are mostly African American, but also Irish, Greek, and Jewish, with the occasional WASP for comic relief. Everywhere I go, I pass out the temporary campaign brochure, third edition, with a growing sense that this is an absurd and interesting and pointless and engaging enterprise. I am hoping I get to stay in the race.

Then Anne Frances tells us the other filer has decided to withdraw. Since I gave him no good reason, his decision is received as a grand and magnanimous gesture. The unknown two-day candidate becomes a party hero.

✦

"Such a deal!" Susan's been talking to the people with cable TV. "They haven't been getting any political advertising and they're keen on breaking into that area. I've negotiated a proposal for donated production of a thirty-second spot and they'll run it at five dollars a hit. With no minimum."

"You're kidding."

"So we need to put together a script. I'm thinking there isn't time to rehabilitate your image."

"Probably not."

"So we're going to run on your negatives. It'll start with a cheap photo montage. LAWYER. DEMOCRAT. ADVOCATE. Advocate meaning telethon protester. Put together your news clips and I'll shoot the 'lawyer' and 'Democrat' pictures. While I'm at it, I'll get a new head-and-shoulders shot for the newspaper. The Mexican dress you wore for the telethon protest isn't quite right. But the dangly earrings are good—definitely."

I ask about the plan to have her husband take my campaign photo. "He'll do the real one. Mine will be the temporary photo."

"OK. Fine. It all sounds great."

"Another thing: the cable people will even let us pick which shows to be on."

"Wow."

"To start with, I figure we ought to saturate *Civil War Diaries* on the History Channel from now 'til the election. Everyone watches that."

"Definitely. It's a good show," I say.

"That's where we pick up our swing voters. Now, let me tell you what I've found out about black gospel radio."

◆

Susan gets me on black gospel radio because she likes the guys at the station. They're jokey and jivey and very Christian. I like their studio. It's all eight-track, 1970s technology. No fancy electronics here; the engineer turns dials and flicks mechanical switches. On one of their cartridges that's been reused and relabeled countless times, I lay down my spot:

> I'm Harriet McBryde Johnson. I'm running for Charleston County Council.
>
> You might know me as the wheelchair lawyer who pickets the telethon. People ask me why I do that. The answer is, human dignity is not for sale.
>
> Why am I running for County Council? Because government, too, should treat every citizen with dignity and respect.
>
> When the base closes, what kind of community will we be? If you want a voice in what happens, vote for me, Harriet McBryde Johnson, and the Democratic ticket.
>
> I'll do my best for you.

" 'I'll do my best for you,' " one of the radio men repeats. "Is that your slogan?"

It sounds pretty weak, I think. "I don't think so. I don't think we have a slogan yet. Maybe we'll run a contest. Got any ideas?"

"A contest!" one says.

"Create-a-slogan!" another answers, and so in the ancient tradition of call-and-response razzing they keep it going about ideas, about the contest—create-a-slogan!—and what a couple of jokey ladies Susan and I are. On departing, I give them the latest edition of the temporary campaign brochure. I don't ask for a copy of my tape. I'd have no way to play it, and eight-tracks are in short supply. Every cartridge is needed in the Lord's service.

◆

Filing closes and two weeks before Election Day, I am duly certified as the party's replacement nominee. The announcement
event has already been planned and core family and friends
alerted. People have been working the phone lists for the
County Democratic Women's Club, over which I presided during the Hurricane Hugo years, and of the City Democratic
Party, of which I've been beloved hardworking secretary for the
past five years.

By force of habit, I want to go early to make sure everything
is set up, but Susan won't let me. I'm not the organizer, she says,
I'm the candidate, and the candidate must make an entrance.
It's time to start when we get out of the office and head by foot
and chair down Meeting Street, to the intersection of Meeting
and Broad streets, Charleston's famous Four Corners of Law.

Across either street are monumental buildings representing
the federal government, the state (including County Council
Chambers), and religion (or, "the law of God"). The nearest corner is City Hall, the corner that counts, the deputy city attorney
once told me. Others might disagree, but for me city government has been disproportionately what counts, and I don't
mean city government generally but this particular city government. Charleston city politics mirror much that defines
Charleston and Charleston people—rich variety, the perpetual
dance of connection with disconnection, the battles of then with
now, an embrace that strengthens as it smothers. The only thing
Charleston has that is missing from Charleston city politics is
classic good looks, that surface beauty that draws the tourists
here. Our politics can be ceremonial and stately, but no one
would call them pretty—even when the azaleas are in bloom.

Now that I'm running for countywide office, aiming toward
a new Corner of Law, I'm expected to worry about the entire
hundred-mile-long sliver of land along and in the ocean, seg-
mented by water and marsh, connected by bridges and cause-

ways. The rules I'm running under require that the candidates for this seat live in Charleston-City, but the voting is at large, over the whole county. To get my votes, I'll need to cover a number of towns and suburbs, old fishing villages, new resort communities—even North Charleston. But first, there are courtesies to exchange here at City Hall, the power hub of the city that is the center of the universe.

City Hall's stucco front, a color between lilac and gray that isn't mauve, seems calculated to make the sky look even bluer than it is. The building's most impressive feature is a grand curved double staircase made of white marble. We go under the staircase, through a door, down a ramp to the basement. There, as I expect, is Maureen, the switchboard operator, rejoicing at my sudden candidacy. I lead Susan to the elevator. Good old Otis. I tell her to push 2. I'm a regular in this building.

I roll into City Council chambers, a grand ceremonial room dominated by grand ceremonial portraits of old and historic officialdom, all meant to impose and intimidate. In this room, too, I am a regular; I've had lots of fun here. Susan moves a chair so I can park behind one of the council members' desks, which have always reminded me of a Charles Dickens schoolroom. Like most nondisabled furniture, the desk is useless for me; the bottom is too low to park under and the top surface is too high to be useful. But parking here is how I signal that I'm seated, that things will begin soon but not immediately. Susan thinks TV will be here if we wait a few minutes.

Below the portraits, a crowd of friendly living people fill the seats around the room. The Democratic Women came through. I smile and nod and poke the air with my fingers; my hand won't flatten nor my arm reach out for a proper political wave. I'm told the mayor is on standby and will come out whenever we say. He is our chief and therefore entitled to make an entrance grander and later than mine.

We're calling this thing a press conference to avoid having to serve the Faithful food and drink, and based on long experience I tell Susan the press won't come out; they reasonably prefer to charge money for political advertising. But Susan has called in a chip with someone at one of the local TV stations. They've promised. She says we'll make the evening news. Yeah. I can hear it: "On the lighter side . . ."

I listen to the chitchat around me. Susan is telling someone with characteristic aplomb, "Our strategy is, a vote's a vote. We'll take 'em all. Of course she's smart and honest and would do a great job. But if people vote for her because they don't like Jerry Lewis or they like her dangly earrings or whatever, that's fine. We'll get her picture out there and people will say she's inspirational. We won't say that, but we'll take inspirational votes. Hey, this close to the election, we'll even take pity votes. She can set 'em straight once she's in office." I'm not at all distressed when she gives up on the TV news crew and sends for the mayor.

Mayor Joe Riley walks into Council Chambers like he owns the place, which, in a way, he has, for the past nineteen years. There's no denying his enormous impact on how the city looks and functions. Although at times he's shoved change down choking throats, his persona is hardly domineering. He's small and slim; although his hair is graying, he's still perceived as boyish. This crowd includes people who've known him since boyhood in the rough-and-tumble of Charleston's Catholic schools; to everyone here, he's part pal, part hero. He has opposition, of course. For some, Riley-hating is a consuming life passion. Generally, the way people feel about him is bound up with the way they feel about the city. At some visceral level, this individual political functionary, this city, these people, are all one collective. And for most of us the collective inspires a love like family-feeling. There are conflicts, deep divisions, sharp differences, but ultimately, anything can be forgiven.

As he goes, Mayor Joe shakes hands and kisses some of the women. He's not a great schmoozer; with a significant hearing loss, he can't follow conversation in a noisy room. I roll away from the desk to signal that I'm standing. He shakes my hand and touches my back as Southern politicians do. I touch his arm as Southern politicians in wheelchairs do, then follow him into the well of the room and park beside him, keeping some distance between us in hopes that his ornate Victorian rostrum won't make me look small. I am looking forward to hearing the mayor speak. It's always a kick to hear his light reedy voice and his bodacious Charleston accent; on this occasion, I will get to hear that voice and accent speaking in praise of me.

He takes notes out of his pocket. The buzzing room goes silent. "Friends," he begins. "What we have here is a blessing in disguise."

He pronounces it the Charleston way—Blassing—and I know instantly it's yet another moment of my life that I'll never live down. He goes on to an unequivocal, enthusiastic endorsement of my unexpected candidacy. The praise is lavish enough for a funeral. Then I deliver my own remarks, an excellent compendium of generalities. Whenever I get at all sonorous, the crowd echoes my words back to me. It's like church. Call and response and the whole room my amen corner. In this high-paneled room, the applause thunders. It's like a real campaign event! Susan ends the proceedings with a down-to-earth pitch for contributions. The mayor shakes more hands. People line up to touch my back and give Susan checks.

We get back to the office and count the money. As a press conference, it's a successful fund-raiser. Because we didn't rent a room or feed a crowd, it's pure profit. There's a big check from my brother Eric, a psychiatrist, and good ones from several lawyers, and many ten- and twenty-dollar contributions that touch me. Now we can pay for the cable TV and black gospel radio and the signs.

✦

Even after I've shaved my morning routine down to the minimum, it's a struggle for Geneva to get me presentable for the coordinated campaign meeting at seven-thirty A.M. Susan picks me up in my van and we zoom across the Ashley River to the temporary campaign headquarters. That's not something we made up. It's something the county party does each election cycle—gets use of some unoccupied store or warehouse owned by one of the Faithful and sets up a depot for volunteers and literature distribution. It's run on the cheap with borrowed equipment and only a couple of phone lines. The serious phone banks are done nights and weekends in friendly offices, sometimes including mine.

Anne Frances is holding court, managing to appear both perfectly controlled and dreadfully harried. An assortment of candidates and campaign representatives share intelligence about fish fries, barbecues, and parades. We make speeches to one another and carp about life's injustices and hum about conspiracies against us. I announce my create-a-slogan contest. The only real business is Anne Frances's announcement that each campaign is assessed $500 for the coordinated get-out-the-vote effort. There's balking, but not from me. I have no illusions that my loyal supporters will be able to cover the county on Election Day.

Also present are a number of sign warriors. They are distraught that my signs have not yet arrived. We offer the temporary brochure, fourth edition.

"We need road signs!" they say.

"And what about the Face?" someone asks.

"The Face!" comes the seconding chorus.

"Harriet Johnson Face!"

I forgot. In our African American community, the Face is big. If you go to a funeral, you will be given a program with the decedent's Face on the cover. Ditto for the bride and groom at a wedding. An event isn't an event without a Face for distribution. A campaign with no Face? Unthinkable.

We go back to the office and Susan fiddles with her computer—fancier than mine—until she's produced an 8½-by-11-inch flyer, suitable for posting in windows beside the business license, with a place for the Face. The temporary campaign photo, showing my wheelchair, long braid, and dangly earrings, fits fine. Off to Kinko's. In bright yellow, it's something to satisfy the supporters until the real signs come in.

◆

From the time I started pondering a campaign, I've been looking forward to going to church with Susan. It's a ritual in the South. During election season, white Democratic candidates go to black churches. They're received warmly, honored like ambassadors from a foreign galaxy with every possible courtesy—and then muttered about. "We never see them but in late October, early November. . . ." "They come around when they want votes. . . ."

I'm eager to play my part, see if I can do something different with it. Of course, I'm unavoidably white, unavoidably looking for votes. But in local politics disability seems to qualify me as something like a person of color, a minority for sure, one of the oppressed. Here, cripdom was racially integrated ahead of the nondisabled world; the Crippled Children's School bus went into everyone's neighborhood. Another odd factor is my out-of-the-closet irreligion. I go to church twice a year, most years—

late night only. On Christmas Eve, it's midnight mass at the Catholic cathedral where the mayor worships and my mother sings in the choir. A week later, I ring in the New Year at an African Methodist Episcopal watch night service. I go to both for the pageantry, the mood swings, the experience of being in a big noisy party without cigarettes or alcohol. I am made welcome but no one pretends I am part of the fellowship. For me, church campaigning might be more natural than for the typical white glad-handing candidate, snowed by all that courtesy, oblivious to the muttering that will come. What if I openly acknowledge the congregation's muttering rights? Might be interesting.

Susan has other plans. "You're not doing black church. They must get tired of all these white candidates showing up at election time."

I give her a little argument. As stupid and ineffective as it is, church campaigning is expected; skipping it might be perceived as a snub. I like the singing and clapping and stomping and shouting. The preaching is so good. Maybe the text will be from the thirty-seventh of Ezekiel.

Susan is firm. "I know you love a dry bones/get-out-the-vote sermon, but you're spending Sunday morning with white Presbyterians."

Up to now, Susan's manipulation has always seemed to spring from the purest motives, securing the common good and promoting the general welfare. Now I have the disquieting thought that she might be a sadist, cleverly disguised as an earth-mother lawyer with a rare sense of fun. White Presbyterians.

It gets worse. I should have realized that Susan won't be my churchgoing companion. She has her own regular Sunday gig at Charleston's most liberal Protestant church, where she is assistant pastor—the kind of assistant pastor who knows her way around the place, from the furnace room to the belfry. She promises to deliver the votes from her church. To deliver me to the Presbyterians, she's arranged for Mandy to drive my van.

Mandy, our office runner, is by now living in the basement apartment in Susan's house. Anyone living in Susan's basement—no, anyone living on Susan's street—is subject to being drafted into Susan's schemes, so Mandy has no more choice in the matter than I do. She shows up at my door in tidy skirt and blouse, stiff as a third-grader at a new school. At the moment, it's hard to see in her the dynamo who took me to New York about three years ago. She drags herself into the van and drags the van across two long bridges to another part of the world.

At the Presbyterian church, I'm greeted by the friends who have invited me, no doubt at Susan's suggestion. I'm sure they'd be glad to introduce me around, but there's no established protocol. This church doesn't expect campaigning; it certainly isn't clamoring for my Face. Too bad. Susan's husband finally took the permanent campaign photo and produced a lovely permanent campaign brochure we had printed on paper approximately the same color as City Hall. Mandy and my friends line up in a pew. I park in the aisle. The dignified service brings back memories of childhood visits to my mother's church of origin. They sing and pray with foreordained words. They attend to a sermon that is brief and well composed. They seek out their god with their minds, through books. No doubt the place is window-to-window swing voters, but the thought of my reaching them here is preposterous.

When the service has ended, my friends introduce me to their minister. I give him the two-handed political handshake, then head out with Mandy, relieved that she made it through the service without crashing under a pew. The lift on my van has an intermittent electrical short and now it's out. Mandy searches my bag for the steel ratchet I've been carrying and hooks it to the motor wheel.

"So! Harriet!" Mandy says as she turns the ratchet and cranks me up, "What do you think THAT was all about?"

"I have no idea."

"I think maybe Susan's, like, scamming to get us in church. Maybe that's why she's running you. You know? The whole thing is just to get the two of us in church."

"But why? She surely couldn't think we'll catch the spirit there."

"Naah," Mandy says. "She's not that kind of Christian, trying to save souls. It's maybe just the idea of getting the two of us in church. You know how she is."

I ponder this as Mandy winds the ratchet and I inch upward. "Mandy, sometimes the motor comes back to life. Give it a try."

I don't think to tell her to remove the ratchet and now the motor is engaged and this massive bar of metal is spinning right over my head in air space where the motor is now pulling me.

"Shiiiiiiiit!" I holler.

Mandy kills the motor. The ratchet flies off, barely misses both of our heads, and crashes into the asphalt. We are near collapse, from fright and then from laughter. Startled Presbyterians come to investigate the commotion. We're unable to explain what's just happened but let them know we're OK.

We get in the car and Mandy closes it up. "Shiiiit!" she repeats in my particular accent. "Man! Oh! Man!" she says in her own, "I bet you got lots of Presbyterian votes with that! Man!"

◆

"There's a problem with the signs," Susan says. "They got the order wrong. But it's OK. We've got signs."

We wanted signs like the ones put out by Runyon, the candidate who got into the race the week before I filed. They're made of flimsy cardboard, biodegrading right before our eyes, perfect for the last-minute replacement candidate. Instead, we got heavy plastic that looks like it will outlast the human race and whatever's next. Deep indigo letters on white.

I phone Wayne, one of the sign warriors who seems to specialize in putting them up, not stealing them. "The signs are here. How many can you use?"

"How many you got?"

"Fifty."

"Whew. Fifty. For a county a hundred miles long. That's a lot to cover. Please," he says, "don't tell anyone else they're in, because with only fifty, you can't let people be putting them in their yards. Let me come by and show you my sign plan before you do anything else. I've been thinking about it."

I know I'll get in trouble with the other sign warriors—and that's trouble I don't need—but I agree.

As fast as he can drive, Wayne shows up at my office with an armload of big maps from the county planning and zoning office. We find an empty conference room and move chairs away from the table. He unrolls the maps and makes the pitch. He wants all the signs. He's identified the most-traveled intersections, the most-bottlenecked streets, the places where voters in large numbers will get the greatest impact. The plan is based on serious data. I'm impressed.

"But here's the best part." He's trying not to explode with excitement. "I got a good buddy will lend me a cherry picker. I can get 'em up so high, ain't no way Republicans can steal 'em. Which is good because if they got stolen, ain't no way you could get more up between now and the election. We only got fifty to cover the whole county. It's tough, but at least these will last. You got good heavy plastic. Not like Runyon's."

I give Wayne the signs. I hope the other sign warriors will forgive me.

✦

I tell Susan and my default office lunch partner, Tim, the story of my morning in church. There is a consensus of the campaign committee, comprised of Susan and whoever else happens to be around, that we'll rely on cable TV and Wayne's signs—which are suddenly omnipresent and spectacularly visible from lofty heights—to deliver the swing voters. In the home stretch of this sprint of a campaign, I'll focus my energies on the Democratic base. Each day, Susan picks me up and we divide our time between the law office and the campaign trail.

Of course, I can't ignore the *Post and Courier*. On its masthead, it proclaims itself as "The South's Oldest Daily Newspaper." As Charleston's Only Daily Newspaper, it has influence. Its endorsement is good for some swing voters; as a poll manager, I've seen many voters take the *Post and Courier* slate into the voting machines.

Along with the other three candidates for those two Charleston-City seats, I am summoned to a structured interview. There are five questions about the issues, one about ourselves.

I'm not dazzled by my Republican opposition—but when have I ever been dazzled by Republicans? One seems to think the race is for school board; the other is stuck on platitudes about running government like business. Runyon, who has been so ubiquitous in local law and politics that you almost can't see him, is very good. He's been around and pays attention. He has plausible ideas about how to sort out some of the county's intractable problems. It occurs to me that he might do good on County Council and he'd have a better chance if I hadn't come into the race to split those default second-choice votes. I wish I were better prepared, but there hasn't been time to read the paper or talk to people in a serious way. So, instead,

I make some effort to be charming. I get the panel of reporters laughing at my jokes. I tell them about the create-a-slogan competition. If I'm lucky, they'll go for style over substance and give me one of the two endorsements.

Back at the office, Jack, a guy I've known since law school, is hopped up about launching my Internet campaign. He's loaded and configured software so I can log onto a local dial-up bulletin board and respond to questions posted there. He's been promoting this as a groundbreaking event. Just as I'm the first local candidate on cable TV, I'll be the first in cyberspace.

The format suits me. I log on. I read the questions. I ask my friends for the answers. Jack is full of ideas on using technology to make county government more efficient; Susan proposes remote locations and drive-in windows to pay taxes and child support. I adopt their nuts-and-bolts ideas and key them in.

The board is also peppered with the favorite litmus tests of the right wing. Jack tells me the guys—and they're all men—on the bulletin board tend toward survivalism and radical tax opposition. Jack himself is liberal by South Carolina standards, but as a Civil War reenactor and computer buff, he runs with an unusual crowd. I decide I may as well tell the truth. I support gun control, abortion rights, and the right to burn the flag. In my legal opinion, the federal income tax is constitutional; I am not persuaded that a fatal flaw in its enactment obviates the duty to pay.

After a few hours, I log back on. A man who purports to represent a large group he doesn't precisely identify or clearly describe says they are deeply opposed to my opinions and philosophy, but they can tell I haven't been bought and am not for sale. They pledge their support. To a man.

We've bagged some swing voters. I bet my spot on *Civil War Diaries* has softened them up.

The *Chronicle,* the African American weekly, has been printing my news releases verbatim and is donating ad space to run the permanent campaign brochure full-text with Face. There's a glowing endorsement of both me and Runyon. Maybe the *Post and Courier* will follow suit.

Not exactly. A glowing endorsement goes to Runyon. The other goes to the Republican who would run county government like business. At least the *Post and Courier* politely omits the names of the unendorsed. Maybe no one will notice.

◆

The county party is having its traditional preelection fundraiser, a $5 fish fry that will be counted a great success if it doesn't lose a whole lot of money. The buzz says this one might be a success because the beer has been donated. The public address system will cost: my brother Mac, a sound engineer, has the party over a barrel because he has the skill to make candidates audible but not deafening in this National Guard armory. I'm looking forward to making my brief remarks. It will be a warm, responsive crowd, almost as good as black church, and without the muttering.

Susan's secretary has figured out how to print labels. My family is now armed with JOHNSON—COUNTY COUNCIL stickers, which they're sticking on people as they come in. I'm delighted to see Mayor Joe wearing one as he makes his way through the room giving mayoral handshakes and back touches and kisses; his hearing aids must be aroar or more likely turned off.

I'm having trouble hearing and being heard; the conversation of people on legs buzzes several feet above my head. I park beside an empty chair and the Faithful take turns resting their feet and wishing me well. To my great relief, the sign warriors are full of compliments. My signs look great! They cover the county! The best locations! Indestructible! Unstealable! They tell funny stories about getting the Harriet Face (8½ by 11, yellow) posted in the Dollar Store, the Greek restaurant where I host the post-telethon-protest luncheon, and barbershops and beauty shops and Laundromats all over. People want copies of the permanent campaign brochure to pass out in their neighborhoods. I'm astounded by the energy and enthusiasm that have grown around Susan's latest scheme. There's always something in the air this close to Election Day. People get crazy.

A friend who works directly in the election process brings me intelligence on things I never thought to worry about. It took some doing, I'm told, but they got me on the face of every Shouptronic voting machine. They've added my name to the absentee ballots, one by one, with peel-off stickers. The election worker moves close, a little conspiratorial. "Now, you understand, we're not allowed to show bias. When people ask why there's a sticker, we can only give the facts. Like, you know, a candidate had to be added two weeks before the election. She's that smart lady lawyer, *in the wheelchair*. Smart as a whip! We can't say much. I wish I could do more." With due pomposity, I say giving the voters a fair election is all I ask.

There's a slight muting of the crowd noise and I see the world's most senior junior senator, Ernest (Fritz) Hollings, making a grand entrance. All he has to do to enter grandly is walk through the doorway. His height, his ramrod-straight bearing, his booming Charleston baritone, his square jaw, his Dixie grin, and his gleaming silver hair do the rest. My mother presses a JOHNSON—COUNTY COUNCIL sticker on his lapel and I see his wife, Peatsy, asking where I am. She leaves Fritz to his hand-shaking, lady-kissing, and back-touching and makes a beeline to me. She collapses into the empty chair like she's just survived a grueling day of shopping.

"Harriet!" She addresses me like an old sorority sister, then crackles with repressed ladylike fury: "If I could cancel my subscription to the *Post and Courier* I would!" If there were an

Olympic competition for political wives, Peatsy would win all the medals. Of course she noticed the discreetly silent non-endorsement.

The senator eventually makes his way to me and hunkers down. As always when we meet in these big crowded rooms, he gives me the latest Washington news on tort reform, which he pronounces "taut refawm." He's pegged me in his mind as a trial lawyer; it's not precisely on target—I don't do wrecks and job injuries—but I am routinely pegged with vastly less accuracy, often by people who know me much better.

The speeches start. This is a watershed election. Last time we elected a president. This time we'll bring it home. Next time we'll make fools of all the pundits predicting one term! I'm still stinging because, by failing to get Tom Harkin nominated, I allowed Clinton to steal the party's soul, but the crowd's enthusiasm is contagious. Knowing that all these people are talking, phoning, passing out brochures, and putting up Faces, I start to imagine wild things. The ticket includes some outstanding public servants; Anne Frances has recruited some promising, credible newcomers. Maybe they have coattails a last-minute entrant might ride on.

My turn comes and I don't know what I say except that it's a bit serious, maybe when I talk about the process—I'm in love with the process at the moment, a system in which anyone who has a maybe-sadistic earth-mother friend with $480 to spare can offer herself for a position of public trust. Mainly I'm funny. I don't think I'll be making an acceptance speech, really, so it's a good time to acknowledge the people who have helped. I announce that the create-a-slogan contest is still open. "You could be the winner! But you can't win if you don't enter! Time is limited!"

Now I need to eat. It's slow going to chew and swallow when people still want to talk to me, but even cold it's delicious, this standard $5 political meal—salty fried fish, red rice with sausage, green beans glimmering in pork fat, a square of yellow cake—or is it sweet cornbread? By the time I'm done, the crowd has thinned and it's mostly my parents and brothers around me. Brother Mac is breaking down the sound system, pulling up cables.

"I've got your slogan," he says.

"Yeah?"

He delivers it in his excellent radio voice: "Send Johnson to County Council. Give 'em what they deserve!"

◆

On the Friday evening before the election, Susan phones me at home. "I have to go to Ohio. I'm sorry. I have to go."

Her father has had a massive stroke and is on life support. I've never met him, but I know a side of him through Susan. He's a towering figure in her life and in the lives of several communities. "I have to go now. I won't even have time to stop by and vote absentee. I'm sorry. I'm really so sorry."

Susan won't stop apologizing. My first impulse is to tell her it's of no importance whatsoever. I can call on a number of other people to do what she's been doing. Forget about it. Her one vote won't matter. But none of that would be true. On some crazy scale, what she's been doing does rank as important. Her contribution has been uniquely valuable. Her vote is vital. Each vote is.

All I can do is say I'll see it through and wish her and her family well. In that moment, I wish I were a praying person, so I could promise to pray, but I'm not and she knows it.

◆

My father covers the weekend engagements. I'm glad they don't include church. I get a Sunday morning off and in the early afternoon we head out to the stump meeting in a rural, mostly African American community in the north end of the county, the area that took the brunt of Hurricane Hugo five years ago.

The entire Democratic slate showed up at the fish fry in downtown Charleston, but here in a school cafeteria nearly fifty miles away, candidates are sparse. Runyon's here, and I'm pleasantly surprised to see the well-polished newcomer who encouraged me to file some other year. Most of the candidates are black. Applying the current political wisdom, this forum would be written off by all of us as a waste of time. The last-minute push would be in the population centers, with swing voters, maybe on the telephone. The people who come to this forum, all black, mostly elderly, will almost certainly vote, and vote Democratic. They're in the bag. Why bother with them?

It seems to be about respect. Mr. Gussie, the longtime organizer of this event, travels to Charleston one night every month, to represent his community at the county party executive committee. He's far more faithful than most of us Faithful for whom traveling to the meeting means a five-minute car ride or a fifteen-minute walk. Every other year, he brings a full slate of delegates and alternates downtown to the county convention. For years now, I've exchanged pleasantries with Mr. Gussie at those meetings; ever since the roll call at my first county convention in 1976, Jimmy Carter's year, I've cheered for that crowd from the country. But until making this long drive over the Cooper River Bridge, beyond the last suburbs, past marsh and fields and more fields, I never truly appreciated how this community keeps itself connected with my community. It has earned more respect than it gets.

In the country, on both ends of the county, Democrats do things with ceremony and dignity. They speak slowly and as they speak they stand straight, look you in the eye, and nod their heads in a way that comes close to bowing. There's none of the amusing bombast I heard at the fish fry. Here politics isn't a game. It's about treasuring the right to vote and using that treasure well.

When it's time for Mr. Gussie to introduce me, he seems flustered. He might not be 100 percent sure what office I'm running for—after all, when he organized this event my name wasn't on the slate. No problem. I can tell them the story. His introduction is simple: "Miss Harriet," he says, "has been a Democrat as long as I can remember."

I might take issue with that, tell him his gray hairs attest to a memory going back farther than he allows, but I don't.

◆

On Monday, I am ready to declare Mac the winner of the create-a-slogan competition. However, his slogan is so good it deserves a crowded field to beat out. I want more entries. "Get serious," I tell the lawyers and legal secretaries at work. "The election is tomorrow. I need slogan ideas."

Default lunch partner Tim steps up to the plate. "Vote Harriet. What the hell. Why not?"

I'll call it a tie. Mac's slogan will play with the Faithful and with the antitax survivalists on the Internet. Tim's is for the more typical swing voter. But there's no time to get either slogan out. No time for a permanent campaign brochure, second edition.

◆

Election Day. Geneva turns me over and I wake up with a knot in my stomach, as I do on most election days. Normally I work out Election Day jitters by managing the polls. It's a fourteen-hour day, political work at its most basic and a haven from the pointless speculation that fizzes and simmers everywhere else, but candidates can't work the polls. My plan is to do what other candidates do: go vote, glad-hand and get glowered at in the precinct, and spend the rest of the day in ineffectual dithering. I might as well get the whole candidate experience.

If Susan were here, she'd arrange an entourage and maybe a photographer when I go to vote. But it suits me to roll over there on my own. In the bright light of morning, I've fully recovered from the notion that I might ride my co-candidates' coattails to a seat on County Council. Now if I were a praying person, I'd pray that I get at least a thousand votes, so people won't cringe and wince and discuss how surprisingly friendless I am. The last thing I want, as a young professional woman with a neuromuscular disease, is to come off looking pitiful. I also don't want to let Susan down.

I move along the sidewalk beside Colonial Lake, a square pool of water flanked by grand houses and linked by pipe to the ocean, where poor city people sometimes catch fish and crabs to eat. A car pulls up. The window rolls down and it's a young white woman with a baby seat beside her. "Hey!" she says. "Turn around!" I turn and face her. "Yeah! You're that candidate . . . with the dangly earrings! I love them! I voted for you. Good luck!"

I holler my thanks and remember the wise words of my campaign manager, now absent, now grieving. A vote's a vote.

In the precinct, a poll manager asks me to remove the JOHNSON—COUNTY COUNCIL sticker from my battery box. There ensues a small altercation to which I'm not a party. A Democratic poll manager argues that candidates are allowed to wear name tags and there's no rule against placing the name tag on the battery box. The precinct captain decides my sticker can stay.

The Shouptronic machines can kneel to wheelchair height as defined in design specs, but for me it's still too high. For me, there's no secret ballot, never has been; instead the rules allow me to have assistance from a person of my choice. Often I ask a first-time voter or a child; sometimes I torment some major Republican by directing her to push buttons she'd rather not push. This time, I'll make it completely random, whoever's ahead of me in line when I show up. It's an old white man in a windbreaker and cloth cap.

I present my registration card and sign the poll list. With my cloth-capped neighbor, I first do the nonpartisan school board races and referenda. Then I tell him to push the button for the straight Democratic ticket. Below that button, a line of lights come on and it's like a Christmas tree lighting. Beside those lights are the names of some admirable public servants, some credible Bill Clinton Democrats, and a few odd ducks, including me.

"That's it." My ad hoc voting assistant pushes the green VOTE button and the machine rings. We emerge from behind the curtain and I roll out onto the city streets.

◆

At the victory party, the bad news takes shape early. Democrats are getting creamed all over the country, at all levels. The deputy city attorney was right. The bravado at the fish fry was wrong. The only Democrat to win countywide will be a Democratic woman who is running for school board with no party label. The only Democrats to win as Democrats are winning in African American majority single-member districts. Those highly desired white swing voters are swinging overwhelmingly the Republican way.

But the first few precincts reporting give me the 1,000 votes I want. More come in. When they're all counted, I get 26,800, fourth of four in my race, a bit more than half what the top vote-getter gets. One amateur party statistician makes a case that I would have polled 40 percent in a two-person race against either of the Republicans; I don't get it, but the consensus is that I've made a brilliant showing. People thank me for running. I'm told I was the subject of get-out-the-vote sermons at two black churches; I'm squirmy to think about the inspirational terms that might have been applied to me when I wasn't there to object, but also very moved.

In the bitter recrimination meetings that inevitably follow crushing defeat, I suggest my vote may offer a measure of our party's bedrock base. Maybe my campaign picked up a couple hundred swing voters through cable TV, the Internet, my pitiful/inspirational/dangly-earringed Face, and word of mouth from friends to friends. But I was in it for only three weeks, raised and spent only $3,600, and did no phone banking or direct mail. I guess at least 26,600 people voted for me simply because my light was underneath the Democratic button.

There's an old saying, of course, that some people will vote for a yellow dog so long as it's a Democrat. I think Susan's scheme was about giving the yellow dog a human face. I count this role an honor. I tell the Faithful we should be encouraged to find that there are so many yellow-dog Democrats in Charleston County, even in a very very bad year. These are people to build upon. Maybe we can mobilize them to undercut the base of what was, once again, the biggest vote-getter: None of the Above, the choice of the nonvoting majority.

But the conventional wisdom draws other lessons. It says I'd have closed the gap with a little more money. A few more signs. Broadcast as well as cable. White gospel radio as well as black. That endorsement from the damn *Post and Courier.*

The *Chronicle,* which often takes a jaundiced view of the party's nominees, is kind to both me and Runyon. We fought the good fight. We have proven ourselves. According to the *Chronicle,* we should have won. We needed two more weeks. That's all.

5

Unconventional Acts

Four years ago, I was with Harkin for President, hell-bent on stopping Clinton, daring to hope for a nominee who might care as much as I do about disability rights. Two years ago, my County Council campaign served up an alternative to the Clinton model, the model that seems to be sucking the life out of politics. Now, in May 1996, I find myself on the floor of the South Carolina Democratic Convention as a Clinton delegate. What can I do? We're all for Clinton now. The party is united. The old feuds are in remission. So, why bother to spend the long day in Columbia? I guess because I'm part of this thing. Last year, inspired by a meeting led by Jesse Jackson, I moved up from secretary of the City Democratic Party to become Mayor Joe's party chair. I've been coming to conventions for so long that if I were to skip one, people might worry.

I know almost everyone in the Charleston County delegation. Mr. Gussie and I exchange slow rural head nods. In the aisle, suburban sign warriors recount battles and skirmishes they've fought along the roads. On the podium, Senator

Hollings is abooming. It's a fine performance of a shtick he's perfected with decades of practice.

This time I'm running for national convention delegate. Why not? It's a little project to help fill the day, and, as a conspicuously disabled person, I can do my bit to make the convention look like America. My campaign flyer stands out from the competition. It's the skuzziest, a cheap Xerox of my 1994 campaign Face, on paper with so much recycled content that it smells like pluff mud. A couple of friends are getting them out. On this flat floor—we're at the University of South Carolina basketball stadium—I could move from one county delegation to the next to chat up the voters, but I'm saving my energy for the caucus.

Hollings says something stupid and I snarl, "What a bunch of crap!" Peatsy Hollings, that perfect political wife, turns back from the seat in front of me and gives me a meaningful look that just might be sympathetic. At length the ceremonial speeches end, we elect party officers, and it's time to select delegates.

I'm contending in a surprisingly crowded field. The first vote is organized by congressional district. Mine, a white-majority district, snakes over segments of several eastern counties. Unfortunately, most of my Charleston County Democratic friends live in the black-majority district that ends two blocks from my house. I lose out. Never mind, there are other opportunities.

The afternoon wears on and I lose ballot after ballot. Losing gets my blood up. By suppertime, I'm keen to go to Chicago. Hungry and tired, we're told to elect two more women to balance the delegation. By now about three-quarters of the crowd has gone home. Among the statewide Democratic rump, the people who stay to the bitter end, I see a good many friends, lawyers mostly, former Charlestonians, Harkin supporters, people I know through school or disability advocacy.

They elect me on the last vote. From the list of also-rans a slate of alternates is quickly chosen. I have won a place on the floor in Chicago.

◆

A week later, all delegates and alternates are summoned to Columbia. From the delegation chair, Mayor Bob Coble of Columbia, we get the news: this delegate business will cost serious money. We're assigned to the "flagship" convention hotel where Clinton and Gore will stay with their delegations. This is quite a perk, a boon because the Democratic national chair for operations is Don Fowler from South Carolina, but the bargained-for convention rate is over $200 per night. Thanks to Don, we will have front-row seating at the United Center, the vast arena where the Chicago Bulls play.

I write a list of accommodations I'll need. Accessible transport from the airport and around Chicago. A floor pass for my personal assistant. An accessible area to sit in my chair, with my state delegation. Assurance that all events will be accessible. The state leadership promises to get answers from the Democratic National Committee.

From late May until August, there is a stream of phone calls and faxes on logistical details. I get a call from the state party: "Harriet, I've got good news. All events are accessible. The airport shuttle leaves every fifteen minutes and all vans are lift-equipped. You will have a designated spot with our delegation. If you need help on the floor, the DNC will assign a volunteer."

"What? I need my own assistant. My sister Beth has already volunteered." I'm flustered. I don't want to admit that I'm a bit afraid. Without help, I might not be able to move through the crowds. I might be trapped.

Realizing I might need reinforcement, I send an e-mail to Mike Ervin, my brother-in-arms against the telethon. He's in Chicago; local crips always know the scoop. He tells me to call his sister, Cris Matthews, who's been working with the local organizing committee.

I call Cris. "Hmmm," she says, "Mike says you're a lot like me. Is that true?"

"I imagine. I'm a lot like Mike."

We're talking about our disabilities. Cris gets down to the nitty-gritty. "So you need serious help in the bathroom?"

"Yeah, when I go. But I don't go often and it's easy enough to schedule. The real problem," I confide, "is that I don't know what it'll be like in those crowds. I might need someone to bust through them for me. Someone who will be ready the instant I say go."

Cris understands.

I ask her about the amazing accessible airport shuttle. "I don't think so," she says, "although they have taken lots of accessible city buses and reassigned them to the Democrats." She doesn't sound too pleased.

Directly and through intermediaries, the DNC assures me there will be no access problems. They keep telling me about this totally accessible shuttle. I fax them my flight information just in case. The only problem seems to be Beth's floor pass. Cris is working on that.

A progress report from Cris: "It doesn't look good. I explained about the bathroom, that you have to be lifted, that you need privacy, all that. I told them you might need to be positioned in your chair or need help getting through the crowds. They still say you can use one of their volunteers. I thought I was getting to them when I pointed out you're a lawyer and you'd sue if their volunteer dropped you—but they still say no." I thank her for trying.

Within the hour, a call from the Democrats: "We've approved a floor pass for your sister, subject to Secret Service clearance." I give Beth the news. She's ready for action.

✦

It's August 24, at O'Hare Airport. As Beth and I arrive at the shuttle stop, a van is about to leave. It has no lift. We approach a young woman with a DNC badge and a walkie-talkie.

"These vans are not handicap accessible," she says. "There will be special transport for you."

When? She doesn't know. What's their number? She doesn't know. Who does know? She doesn't know. Ask the person on the other end of the walkie-talkie, I suggest.

"We're Delegate Transportation," she says. "You need Disability Services."

"As it happens, I am a delegate in need of transportation. And I was told the shuttles were accessible."

"Who told you that?"

"Disability Services. Everyone."

"Not me." The walkie-talkie woman turns her back and busies herself with important things.

I see a woman in a manual wheelchair with the look of someone who's been waiting for a long time.

"How long have you been here?"

"An hour."

"What's the deal?"

"I don't know."

I can't believe it, but I'm not surprised. It's a contradictory state I seem to live in these days; six years post ADA, I've come to expect access, on one level, but I know the old world of you-can't-get-in still lives. You never know what you'll get. The existence of rights—rights on paper—implies a duty to assert them. I roll out to the curb where carousing delegates are filling those inaccessible vans, one after the other.

"Good afternoon," I tell them. "You are boarding a discriminatory shuttle service. Did you know this shuttle discriminates?"

African Americans look shocked; European Americans look uncomfortable.

"This van is for walking people only. No wheelchair people can ride."

Suddenly walkie-talkies are all over the place. They rush past me to the other conventioneers. "A special van is coming for her."

I see all the faces—white and black—register relief.

"They say a van is coming," I say, "but this woman's already been waiting an hour. Your van is here. Ours is not here. You're going. We're waiting. That's second-class service. Separate and unequal."

A woman steps into the van and looks back with a very sweet smile. "I hope your special van will be here *real soon*." She almost pats my head.

Another group flocks to another van and I start another harangue. I get the same reaction: shock, discomfort, reassurance, condescension.

The walkie-talkies offer to reimburse taxis. No, my power chair won't fit. But the other woman on wheels agrees. I feel like hectoring her about solidarity—my hectoring neurotransmitters are pumping and I want her to help me get a sit-in going. But then, in her place I might take a cab myself.

At least my hectoring has motivated the walkie-talkies to get me out of the way. Finding me a lift-equipped vehicle has become high priority.

Finally, the special transport arrives. It's a sixty-passenger bus, bright yellow with big black letters: Cook County Public Schools. A Cook County school bus driver, guffawing about all the hullabaloo, delivers us in solitary splendor to that pricey flagship hotel.

◆

Preconvention events are under way. Tonight, the South Carolina delegation has a train trip to a party in historic Pullman, outside of Chicago. Ever since I got the invitation, I've been trying to get someone to tell me if it'll work in a power chair. Mayor Bob, who is proving a very accommodating delegation chair, has been looking into it. Beth and I go out in the morning and check back with Mayor Bob when we return. He still doesn't know. He seems really concerned, though. Of course he understands I don't want to get on a train without knowing that I'll be able to get off on the other end.

In the early afternoon, we've arranged to go to a concert/rally sponsored by *The Nation* magazine and various progressive organizations. Cris and her husband, David, plan to come, too. The event has me chafing about being a delegate for a president whose policies too often reflect his swing-voter-dominated politics. Just last March, he signed legislation that ended welfare as an entitlement and took SSI away from thousands of disabled children and noncitizens. Early in his term, he dumped Lani Guinier, the perfect nominee to head the Department of Justice's Civil Rights Division, as soon as a couple of powerful Republican senators told a few lies about her. What was I thinking about when I offered to come here and renominate him? Is there no limit to how far I'll go to keep from being bored?

In the end, I take heart, as I have at other times, from the words of Jesse Jackson. He's from South Carolina; he must remember how it is in small places, places where the connections are close, where opting out would be irresponsible, and where there's nowhere else to go. He preaches a defiant persistence: "Stay and fight another day." The Clinton forces may have captured all the votes, including mine, but I resolve to make my party loyalty their worst nightmare.

Beth prowls around the accessible spaces and has no trouble finding and bringing over the woman who's "like me." Meeting

Cris, I feel the same kinship I felt when I met Mike in New York, thrilled to find this new sister, a woman with presence and power and the twistiest spine I've ever seen. Cris and David propose that we all go out to dinner. I'd like to go to Pullman, but what if it doesn't work out? I'd be livid. Cris and David have a van and know their way around. The choice is clear.

After a good meal, we wander around a touristic riverfront development and wind up on a tour boat. It's accessible and no one stops us or asks for money, so we roll on. We don't realize until we've set out that the boat's been chartered by Democrats. Some guys give us signs and instruct us to wave them and cheer loud. Hillary Clinton is arriving in a tall ship—and we are in her escort flotilla.

It's awfully silly but dutifully we wave and cheer. In spite of ourselves, we get excited when we spot the first lady—look! the blonde in the pretty pastel suit right under all those big microphones! The carousing charter group is on the top deck. Left to ourselves on the main deck, Cris and I enjoy crip talk—so lacking in my daily life, clearly abundant in hers—while Beth and David tease us with the compare-and-contrast game. Cris is twistier; Harriet thinner. Same verbal style; different accents. Similar political philosophies, but Cris is into animal rights and Harriet isn't.

Astonished, as always, by the long twilight of Northern latitudes, Beth and I stroll back to our room. We have four telephone messages, all from Mayor Bob.

"Still working on the Pullman trip. I'll call you back."

"It will be accessible, but we're not sure exactly how."

"Harriet! Thanks to Don Fowler, we have a lift-equipped bus! It'll take us straight from the hotel to the party. Be in the lobby at six."

"We're leaving. Where are you?"

Oops. Mayor Bob went out of his way to help. No telling where Don Fowler got that bus. I hope they'll forgive me.

◆

The next morning's meeting of the Disability Caucus makes me feel good about being here. We're the Disability Nation, with all kinds of disabilities, regional accents, and personal styles. There are in-your-face activists, policy wonks, and officials in suits. Black and white and Asian and other. Men and women. Everything but Republicans.

The meeting starts late. It turns out the meeting place has been changed and no one told the Sign interpreter. When the discussion starts, it opens with—what else?—logistics.

We're told this will be the most accessible convention ever. Because of advocacy by disabled delegates last time, there will be no segregated wheelchair seating. We will have places with our states. The bus shuttles to the United Center are three-quarters lift-equipped, and the convention will have both Sign and real-time captioning gavel-to-gavel.

After my experience at the airport, I'm skeptical, but most of the people who are talking have disabilities. That gives them credibility. The discussion quickly moves to politics.

Becky Ogle talks about how we can make a difference in November, and how November will make a difference to us. She's smart and feisty and wears a pointy-toed Texas cowboy boot on her one foot. Then there's Tom Harkin—my man!—talking with real expertise and authentic emotion about the ADA. I roll up to shake his hand after the session and he seems to remember being on stage at a Baptist church with me and Jesse Jackson in 1992. Cabinet officers brief us on disability policy. No one talks down to us. We are important members of the coalition. Judith Heumann, the great disability rights pioneer who had to sue the state of New York to get a teaching certificate, speaks to us as head of Special Education and Rehabilitation Services. I'll write her name at the top of my reasons to back Clinton. No Bill, no Judy. I'm almost reconciled.

✦

The buses to the United Center leave right in front of our hotel. So that's what they mean by "flagship." They do have lifts. I roll into the first bus in line and an efficient Chicago Transit driver rams my big wheel into the clamp. I'm jammed in with a hodgepodge of cheerful Democrats, off for shared adventure.

South Carolina is seated just to the left of the podium. My spot is right beside the aisle. We arrive so early that there's no TV except C-SPAN. The floor is crowded but not packed.

In the evening, network TV arrives; the floor gets more crowded, more intense. Occasionally a camera or boomed microphone swings perilously close to my head; each time Beth jumps up to deflect disaster. With the major speakers come thicker crowds down front, blocking the aisles. Fellow delegates help Beth keep them moving so we can all have breathing room and an occasional glimpse of the podium.

The DNC has assigned a staff person to our aisle, a man with a walkie-talkie. I try to get him interested in crowd control, but it's clear that his job is to pass out signs and cue our "spontaneous demonstrations." He is there to make sure we look good on TV.

They've been building up to tonight's major prime-time speaker, and now they're introducing him: Christopher Reeve. When the introduction ends, the hall lights are dimmed. Onto the stage he rolls and then sits, gleaming under a dramatic spotlight. The crowd is on its feet, wild with welcome, with excitement, with awe. Yes. They are awed by the mere sight of this man sitting, smiling, looking around. He hasn't said a word and they're going crazy. It's real. There's no prompting by the DNC.

I find myself in the middle of sixty thousand drop-jawed souls, witness to a late-twentieth-century pentecost. Physically, Reeve is way above the sixty thousand, isolated by that spotlight. Symbolically, he's the object of devotion, not a member of the fellowship.

He's speaking now. I try to listen, but things have become surreal. I look up at Reeve.

I look up and I see . . . a ventriloquist's dummy.

How could I think such a thing? I'm horrified. If these worshipers could read my thoughts, they'd tear me up and throw me to the dogs. I try to banish the idea but it won't go.

I tell myself Reeve's playing out the peculiar drama of his life the best way he knows how. He's being used, but what can he do? This is a new role for him. He has no script.

But, there he is, Charlie McCarthy.

Where is this image coming from? No quad I've ever known has struck me this way. I'm pretty quadlike myself, with my floppy arms and legs. Maybe it's the lighting that isolates Reeve, the staging that objectifies him. Or maybe it's the contrast between his physical persona and the physical vigor we've been conditioned to expect on the podium of a national political convention.

No. It's the face. That smile running from ear to ear. Those eyes rolling around in their sockets. The face is commonly considered animated, but I see something wooden.

I'm warmed by the sudden sunburst of TV lights; a camera crew is setting up. They want crip reaction to the Reeve speech.

"Beth, can you block me?"

She stands between me and the camera. The crew establishes a new sight line and she leans right into it. They call someone on their cell phones.

Reeve's measured syllables are perfectly timed with his mechanical puffs of air. The pauses make what he's saying seem important. Even in the dim lights I can see the faces in the crowd, transfixed by the sight of him, fascinated by the sound of him. The gleaming presence. The ventilator whoosh. The limp body propped up in dress-up clothes. The talking head that once was Superman.

My camera crew decides Beth's not going away. They load up their gear and head elsewhere.

Moments later, on the giant TV screen in the rafters, there's a woman in a wheelchair with both arms crossed over her chest, scowling. Quick cut to a nondisabled white woman, tears streaming across a smiling face, backlit to highlight her moment of inspiration. The lights pick out a variety of delegates. White, black, old, young, male, female. Everything but crips.

It's melodrama. The kind of telethon melodrama I just can't bear. How could they bring it here, to a national political convention? This is my party. How could they do it?

The speech ends and the lights come on. Emotion has run through the vast space, in one of those communal experiences that touches each individual and transforms the group as a whole. But as Reeve and the crowd have enjoyed their communion, I have been placed outside the circle. The force that has been let loose in the hall redefines me as it defines Reeve, as a disability object, presumably tragic but brave, someone to gawk at, someone to make them grateful that they are not like us.

I tell myself I'm overreacting, and I want to believe I am, but I'm almost shaking when I join the line at the elevators. A misty-eyed stranger kneels down beside me and clutches the hand I'm trying to drive my chair with.

"Wasn't that just *wonderful?*"

"No," I blurt out, "it wasn't at all wonderful. I thought it was pretty bad."

"Well, I thought it was wonderful." She springs up and pivots away with an angry shoe-clop on the hard floor. How dare I refuse to be inspired?

On the bus ride back, everyone rhapsodizes about how inspired they are. Gone is the usual where-are-you-from chitchat. I stare at the black floor mat and withdraw from the group that has set me apart.

We get to our room, way past ready to collapse into our beds, but there's a blinking light on our phone.

A message from Mike Ervin: "Hi. Some people from Chicago are meeting tomorrow for a press conference to deal with the Christopher Reeve—er—problem."

Beth writes down the details. We'll be there.

◆

The next morning, I arrive at the Disability Caucus meeting to find the gang from Chicago outside the door passing out flyers. I'm overjoyed. Mike introduces me to his comrades, including a number of activists I know through the disability press. A flyer by Mike and his wife, Anna Stonum, deals pointedly with the Christopher Reeve—er—problem.

Chicago TV news shows up. They shoot video of the group and then zoom in on my red delegate badge, proof of my authenticity as a genuine Democrat from the Deep South. Up here, I guess, I'm exotic. They set up lights. Mike and I agree to talk.

There's so much noise I can barely hear what Mike's saying. Is he really calling Reeve a whiner? No, not exactly, but close. I think Mike might be going a bit too far, but a wave of gratitude washes over me. He's a champion, fighting back—his fight is not against Reeve, but against the greater foe, the force that put Reeve on that platform.

Now I'm up, the nice cop.

I've done a fair amount of TV, but not in the Midwest. Here, to be understood, I need to tighten my consonants, drop some of the diphthongs; yet, I need to sound like a delegate from South Carolina. I flex my face.

"Christopher Reeve is going through a tremendous transformation. It's impossible for most people to imagine, but it happens to thousands of people every year. It doesn't make him a disability spokesman. He's still learning. He wants to be cured, but for us it's more important to live our lives, the way we are. He doesn't speak for us."

In thirty seconds it's over. Now I can let my mouth return to mush.

I recruit a couple of people from the Disability Caucus and we put an edited version of Mike and Anna's flyer on the convention floor. We can't find a cheap copy deal in the middle of Chicago so we print only two hundred copies. But they get around. A disabled delegate gets his tall skinny attendant to slip through the throngs and drop a few in each state. As the speeches drone on, they are passed from hand to hand, and read.

✦

In the afternoon, at the United Center, Beth and I make sure we're in our seats before Justin Dart speaks. Dart is an authentic disability rights leader; in his trademark Texas cowboy hat, he traveled the country to galvanize support for the ADA and then to inspire people with disabilities to get active in politics. He is also a lifelong Republican who held high office under Reagan and Bush. His defection from Bob Dole—a disabled veteran with a good voting record on many of our issues—seems like big news to me.

But not to the DNC. They've scheduled Dart for early afternoon. America's prime-time image of disability will remain Christopher Reeve.

It's exciting to see one of our own roll out on that huge

podium. But there are no DNC cheerleaders to organize a "spontaneous demonstration."

"JUSTIN!" I yell at the top of my lungs. "JUSTIN!" It's the only yellable thing I can come up with. I don't have much cheerleading experience.

Too gallant to let a lady yell alone, some rowdy gentlemen from South Carolina roar along. Then the rest of the delegation takes it up. They're also yelling in Ohio, across the aisle, and behind us in Washington. From our various places around the hall, we citizens of the Disability Nation use our combined voices to make sure that our leader gets a proper welcome.

Dart's talk—concise, cogent, almost oracular—is over before the crowd's enthusiasm has worn off. He rolls off the stage like the hero that he is.

A Charleston delegate who's sending daily news reports home leans over with his notepad. "Who is he?"

Thus it comes to pass that the *Post and Courier* covers Justin Dart.

✦

Tonight, August 28, Vice President Gore is to speak. When we come into the hall, our DNC cheerleader meets us with a warning.

"It's going to get hairy. They've issued about five thousand extra floor passes. They want the aisles packed for TV when Gore speaks."

I can't believe it. The hall was already packed to the point of misery. I've been hemmed in between the raised seats and a constant river of people pressing against me as they try to navigate the aisles. Now, five thousand more?

As the hall fills, the stream of walking people and swinging cameras stops. Blocked. I am trapped behind a solid wall of butts. Right in front of my face. Big ones, little ones. Men and women. The butts of America. I look up at the ceiling. I try not to panic.

Then a big body slams right into me. The space over my head must look like a hole in the bottleneck; the guy just walked right into me. A moment later, it happens again. A big object, maybe a TV camera, swings over my head. All the camera crews, the pages, the floor managers, the aides, the correspondents—all those who think they have urgent business at the platform—head right at me, realizing I'm here only when they hit me.

I yell at our DNC staffer. He's got his hands full of signs and his ears full of walkie-talkie instructions on our next spontaneous demonstration. I keep yelling and a helpful fellow delegate taps his shoulder and points to me.

"Y'all need to get this aisle moving," I shriek.

"I told you it would be hairy."

"It's dangerous. Call security. They need to get the aisle moving."

"I can't," he says. "They want it packed."

He goes away. He has signs to pass out.

Beth is standing up to try to let people know I'm here. But she's small and they don't see her either, until they're too close to stop. They trip on my unexpected chair. She blocks them with her body, but still they slam through. Most of the blows fall on my chair, not my flesh, but the constant assaults are too much. I'm not built for this. I'm too small, too frail, I think. I'll get killed.

"Let's leave," I yell.

I don't stop to think how we'll get through. I'm only vaguely aware that my steel components can inflict pain; if I hit them, they'll find a way to get out of my way. Desperation propels me forward.

I don't know how, but I make it through the aisle into the

more open space right below the platform, where it's too close to see. Our DNC cheerleader catches my eyes through the crowd. "Thank you," he mouths, making little clapping signs with his hands.

Thank you?

I'm leaving for my personal safety, and they think I've done them a favor! They want me out.

In that second, my desperation turns to rage. I'm a Democrat. I'm a delegate from South Carolina. I belong on the floor. Those five thousand people with new floor passes don't. They can't run me off.

I zoom through the service corridors and pass through an open door and yell at the first white man I see. Yes, it's racist and sexist but I'm too steamed to care. "We need some security on the floor. It's dangerous. Someone needs to get the aisle moving."

Calmly he pulls up a chair and leans over until he's at my eye level. "OK," he says, "tell me about the problem."

The bastard's been to sensitivity training. I can tell by the way he's acting. I tell him about the problem. He uses active listening techniques and offers validation. But then he says no. They want the aisles packed. The bottleneck looks good on TV.

I won't be placated. "I'm a delegate. I've got a right to be on that floor. I'm going back out there, and I want some security."

"If you go back out there, we can't guarantee anything. We can't protect you."

With his soothing ways, he's entered my physical perimeter. This doesn't calm me down, but does empower me to waggle a skinny finger in his face. I am a woman possessed.

"Look. If you people can't protect me, I'll have to just—call Minister Farrakhan—and get some Fruit of Islam on this floor."

I can't believe what I'm hearing from my own mouth. I mean, I'm no pal of Minister Farrakhan. I don't have his phone number. It's absurd, but it strikes a raw nerve. The man has jumped up and is on the cell phone.

As I've been haranguing, Beth has been wandering around the office. On the floor she has found a piece of paper with a big Access symbol on it. In the corner, an old sign with a plain white back. On a table, scissors, glue, and markers. She's working on a sign. RUDE DEMOCRATS BLOCKING MY VIEW.

"Why not 'banging into me'?" I ask her.

"People wouldn't get it," she says. "They'll get this."

The man sees what we have in mind. He's yammering about party unity, the need to project a good image . . .

I roll out into the corridor. Over the loudspeaker, Gore is telling about his sister's death. It's a small human story, scripted and packaged, so we'll know the scripted and packaged candidate has a soul.

I let the words roll past and wait for cues that the speech is about to end. When Gore goes off, there will be movement on the aisle and I will try to zip back to my place. Beth is holding the sign; accompanying the drone of Gore's speech is a buzz of people telling me I shouldn't go out there, and if I do I shouldn't take the sign.

"It's up to y'all," I say. "I don't ask for a clear view, just security. If you provide safety, no problem."

The walkie-talkie guys that line the corridor are on the move: Secret Service. I hadn't even noticed them. They speak to the sensitivity man. "We need to clear this area so the vice president can come through."

I speak to the Secret Service, politely. "I'm not leaving. I've been run off the floor, and I'll be damned if I'll be run out of this hall, too."

The sensitivity guy thinks I don't understand. "This is where the vice president will be coming through."

"Fine. Good. I'd like to speak to him. He should know why I didn't stay to hear his speech."

Beth and I have badges showing that we've been cleared by the Secret Service. We're certified nonthreats. But letting the vice president come our way is not an option. After a hurried walkie-talkie call, the whole unit is redeployed. Gore is rerouted to the corridor on the other side of the arena.

We go back on the floor. Within moments, I'm getting slammed again. Beth stands up on her seat and hoists the sign high in the air. It shows up on the TV feed. Instantly, there is security on the aisle. The standers are required to move on; camera crews have a clear path and room to swing their gear. Relief rolls over me like a wave.

✦

It's the last day of the convention. I wake up trying to decide whether to go back on the floor for the nomination and the president's speech, or surrender my credentials.

The South Carolina delegation meets first thing in the morning. Everyone is there because that's where the daily credentials are issued. As the meeting is ending, I ask Mayor Bob for the microphone. "I wanted to explain about last night, about that sign, RUDE DEMOCRATS BLOCKING MY VIEW. I want y'all to know it wasn't really about rudeness. I can tolerate rudeness. It was about safety. The DNC deliberately created a crush on the aisle, and it was dangerous. I asked them for help, but they refused. They thought I should leave instead. But I had a right to be there. I am representing Democrats from South Carolina. With about two hundred other delegates with disabilities, I'm also representing a constituency of about fifty million. The DNC wouldn't listen to me, so I figured I'd use the power I had—to make them look bad on TV. Well, it was amazing. The sign went up and right away the problem was solved. There comes a time when you have to stand your ground."

The delegation cheers. The cynic in me says it's a reflex; they'll cheer at anything after this four-day pep rally. But the applause does me good. I know what I'm going to do.

"I'm going back on the floor tonight. I could be more comfortable, staying in, watching the president's speech on TV, but I am going back. I want to ask for your help. Back me up with the DNC. Also, I ask you not to be part of the problem. Remember that a wheelchair is not a piece of furniture to lean on. Give me some space. And, please! Keep your butt out of my face!"

The South Carolina press is there. They crowd around me and ask for details.

"Will you take your sign tonight?"

"Sure."

"Will you hold it up?"

"Only if I'm crushed again. It's up to the DNC."

The stories they write will go in papers all over my state. Every one of them will quote me as saying, "Keep your butt out of my face."

We'd like to go to one of many interesting caucuses or meetings or skip out for tourist adventure, but instead I spend the morning on the phone. I dread going back on the floor. I want security. I call Disability Services. "This mailbox is full and will not accept messages." I dial every number anyone has ever given me. I ask for a barricade and offer to go to the United Center now, to meet with the carpenters and come up with a plan. I'm told there will be no barricade; I can sit in a separate section. I insist: I will stay with South Carolina, and I want safety. I try to explain how the aisle could be reconfigured. They hang up on me.

We get to the United Center early, hoping to be able to talk to people before things get too hectic. Our cheerleader greets me with a big smile. I soon see why. They've put up a barricade.

It's made of vertical metal bars that are taller than I am. On the corners, they've tied balloons marked "Person with a Disability." There's a similar arrangement behind me, in Washington State, where there's another delegate who uses a wheelchair.

The view through the bars is like looking out from prison, but the barrier affords precious airspace between my face and the wall of Democratic backsides. Here in protective custody, I'm safe. It's a mark of how stressful it's been that I am grateful for my cage.

Now I can enjoy the scene. The roll call is a kick. The president's speech is beautifully crafted and perfectly delivered. They don't call him Slick Willie for nothing. I wait for the line about welfare reform, to see if anyone will boo. It comes. He calls on every business person who's ever criticized welfare to give welfare recipients jobs. It's a sentiment we can all cheer, even those of us who are still furious about the law. In spite of myself, I admire such finesse.

The speech contains hundreds of punchy sound bytes, but it's not choppy. The taglines are structured in blocks, related by theme, by sound, by structure, by mood. At the end of each block, there's a huge applause line. Just before each applause line, I hear Clinton hold back, bringing the energy down. Then it goes back up and the energy is released—applause. When the applause ends, another block begins, leading up to another crescendo. It's a very Southern form of oratory.

I hear that low key and I know another block is reaching its end. The whole hall, probably without knowing why, is waiting for the applause line. It comes. A quote from Christopher Reeve.

The applause comes, but it's polite, tepid. There's a little muttering. I can't see, but I imagine Clinton biting his lower lip. He moves on quickly. Why did the big line go flat? Two days ago they were maniacs for Christopher Reeve. Something's changed.

Did we disabled delegates have an impact? Were we all scowling in our respective states? Did our flyer saying Reeve didn't speak for us bring some reality back onto the floor? I don't know.

The Comeback Kid comes back. The speech ends to thundering frenzy. It's time for the balloon drop, a convention fixture ever since it was introduced by Nixon's boys in 1968. I look up at the ceiling where the balloons wait in enormous nets. How enormous, I haven't noticed until now.

The nets open and the balloons rain down. They hit the bleachers, the raised seating on the floor, thousands of people standing up, and flow down, down. I realize I'm the lowest point—the drainage hole—for the whole arena. I see the balloon swirl coming at me. I might be screaming, but it's so noisy I can't tell.

Beth hits the floor to snap a single shot of my predicament. Then she's up, with three other people, pulling balloons off me as fast as they can. Still, within seconds, the balloons are way above my head. I tell myself there's plenty of air. It's fine. It's fine. It's fine. But it's a strange sensation, to be engulfed, swallowed up, and absolutely unable to escape.

When the deluge finally stops, they dig me out. I sit stunned. Beth is laughing at me and I don't care. She takes a picture and I don't care.

I sit and wait for the balloons to clear, the way we wait for the streets of Charleston to clear after it's rained during high tide. Beth is still highly amused. "I've been looking at those balloons all week," she says. "I wasn't sure it would really be this bad, though!" Now I'm only knee-deep in balloons. Now I can see the floor again. Now I imagine I may be able to navigate the aisles. Where do all those balloons go?

The floor empties of people. The press and wall of butts and the whole state of Ohio have cleared out. I look through my metal bars and see the Clintons, the Gores, and all the dignitaries up there grinning.

They don't look a bit frazzled.

◆

The convention's over. It's my free day in Chicago, the Friday before Labor Day. Mike and Cris are having their telethon protest; on Monday, I'll do my own back home. My secretary has already obtained the police permit and sent out invitations— today she'll do reminder calls and make note of the RSVPs for the postprotest luncheon.

Beth and I meet the protesters at Grant Park. It's the place where antiwar protesters were beaten up by the Chicago police in 1968.

"Mike, do we have a police permit?"

The question makes Mike laugh. I try to remember the criminal law I learned for the multistate section of the bar exam. I think it's criminal trespass if you are asked to leave and refuse. At least in South Carolina.

"Listen, Mike. I don't do civil disobedience, especially not in Chicago. I'm a chickenshit with a law license, OK? If anyone asks us to leave, the Ladies from Carolina are leaving. There will be a hole in the line."

Mike tells the group to roll down the curb cut into Michigan Avenue, single file. I like the plan. We won't block traffic. Blocking traffic is a crime in any jurisdiction, I'm sure.

As I roll out, I hear Cris. "Hey, why don't we just block traffic?"

We fan out. I'm in the middle of a line of power chairs that bisects the street. Horns are honking. We're moving, but not at speeds customary for motor vehicles in Chicago.

A couple of cops arrive. They count us. They talk on the radio. Reinforcements come. Another count, more radioing. Higher-ups, in mufti. Another count. With considerable unease, I wait for the order to cease and desist. It never comes. Instead, they set up barricades and direct traffic around us.

Thus protected by the kinder, gentler Chicago police of 1996, I feel the road roll under me and take in this marvelous cityscape. The tall sleek buildings, the wide street, the open air are so different from the narrow old streets where I live and work. I'm strolling in the middle of Michigan Avenue with my buddies and I feel set free.

There's a fair amount of noise, but no singing, no chanting. I yell out what I think is an appropriate chant: "HEY HEY! HO HO! JERRY LEWIS HAS GOT TO GO!" The others take it up, in their midwestern accents. But when they say the second line, it's changed: "TELETHONS have got to go."

They're right. The issue is bigger than Jerry Lewis, just as democracy is bigger than Bill or Al or Christopher Reeve or Justin Dart or Mayor Bob. Or me.

After a week of getting pushed around and shoved aside and struggling to be a member of the group, I find myself a part of things at last. I'm one point in a line. It's a lovely, strong, straight line, a line on the move. It's a line of people who have seized the streets and made them our own.

6

Trial and Error

By power chair, I zoom from my house toward the Four Corners of Law. I'm headed to the federal law corner for the first day of a jury trial in the United States District Court. I've been associated as cocounsel for the plaintiff by my friend Margaret, a tough divorce lawyer now branching into employment litigation.

I've been practicing law for nearly twelve years now, but I've had very few jury trials. Usually we conduct discovery, go to a judge with a few motions, and the case is resolved one way or the other. This one is going to trial, and Margaret has asked me to do the opening statement. I'm nervous, but I've suited up for the occasion. I can't wear those woman-lawyer suits seen on TV, but my raw silk turquoise dress drapes nicely around the curves of my back. I'm wearing my best black shoes. They're velvet and cost $6 at the local hippie store. And, of course, serious jewelry. A simple gold bracelet, pearl earrings, sapphire ring. It's my kind of power dressing. Everyone will know I'm a force to be reckoned with.

There's a lot riding on the opening. It's commonly said that most jurors are convinced—or not—during the lawyers' opening statements. I've heard hints that I'm the wrong person for this job. It's a case under the Americans with Disabilities Act. Our client was fired, she says, because she told her boss she'd need back surgery. The problem is that, beside me, she doesn't look like a "person with a disability." In fact, she looks great in a suit. The company lawyer will surely tell the jury there's no way this plaintiff can file an ADA lawsuit when there's nothing wrong with her. How do I convince them otherwise?

I stop obsessing and enjoy the ride. It's familiar territory. I know every bump in the slate sidewalks, every gap in the old bricks. I know when to slam full speed ahead, when to slow down, when to dodge. As I get closer, I merge with a stream of lawyers and clients striding on legs from downtown offices to court. I flawlessly navigate the challenging terrain without clipping anyone. I'm good. I belong in this world. Nobody can mess with me.

I stop for a line of cars. Beside me an elderly black lady waits at the bus stop and looks me over. I'm used to being gawked at, but this is different. She's looking at my clothes, my jewelry, my "look," and her smile is openly appreciative.

I nod at her the way we nod at one another in Charleston.

"You look so beautiful," she says.

I give her the classic aw-shucks smile.

"You look just like a Doll Baby!"

A Doll Baby? Not a tough, terrifying litigator?

My smile freezes and I say, "Thank you, ma'am." She means well. And I know there is a certain Doll Baby Factor at work. My body is undeniably small and ragdoll-floppy. Against the vivid turquoise dress, the extreme whiteness of my face and hands must look like—well, porcelain.

The traffic clears and I cross the street. I roll another block past the old post office to the Hollings Judicial Center. I'm waved through security and roll down a hall and up the elevator to the courtroom. I'm trying to get focused.

I'm still jumpy when the judge calls for plaintiff's opening but I find the spot where I can meet the eyes of all twelve jurors. I introduce myself, the plaintiff, and Margaret, and explain it's Margaret's case. She will be questioning the witnesses; I'm here to help with the legal arguments, honored to be invited to address the jury.

These expected formalities restore my sense that this is my place. Echoed on marble and mahogany, my voice comes back strong, clear, and just genteel enough. I'm ready to confront the issues. I talk about invisible disabilities and think I see a tiny nod from the juror who reported chronic health problems on the jury questionnaire. I say the ADA protects people who can do things, but other people unreasonably think they can't. Discrimination can mean treating people as different when they're not; it also means ignoring differences that need accommodation. I review the evidence. Formality gives way to folksiness. One by one, the faces show understanding.

As I thank them for their attention, I'm conscious of twelve faces looking at nothing but me. Clearly, they're responding not only to my words but also to my visible persona—to the tiny woman in a wheelchair, wearing gorgeous fabrics and precious metals and stones. A different kind of lawyer. I dare to hope that Margaret's guessed right and my look won't kill the case.

I turn back to the plaintiff's table and I know those dozen pairs of eyes are watching the arc I make, like a skater, as my tires etch the plush carpeting. For a moment, I wish appearances didn't matter. I wish I could simply master the law and the evidence and do my job.

But then I look back at the jury. They're still with me, and I'm glad.

The Doll Baby has spoken.

✦

It's like every other jury trial: we're here because facts are in dispute. There's no dispute that our client got fired shortly before her third back surgery in about four years. The question is why. Before we get to that central issue, the law sets up others. Is she a "person with a disability" under the ADA, that is, does she have an impairment substantially limiting a major life activity, real, or on record, or as perceived by the employer? Is she "qualified," or able to perform the job with or without reasonable accommodation to her disability? Did she request an accommodation? Was her needed accommodation "reasonable," that is, not an "undue hardship" to her employer? Only if we prove yes to each issue do we get to the real dispute: Was she fired because of her disability or for a "legitimate, nondiscriminatory reason"?

If the jury members don't see our client as a credible, hardworking person, we're sunk. If they do like and believe her, we have a chance, but only a chance. We have the burden of proving discrimination.

Margaret is building a circumstantial evidence case, the kind of case that gets a bad rap in law dramas but is usually the only case you can make in the real world. Nowadays, in 1997, people rarely admit to discrimination, at least not in front of witnesses likely to talk.

Our case opens. Margaret calls our client to the stand and lays her tidy notes on the podium. Beautifully tailored and impeccably groomed, Margaret looks distinguished, from the strong stance to the striking white hair that makes me think of the great Southern icon, Robert E. Lee. It so happens that, like many members of the Charleston bar, Margaret idolizes Robert E. Lee. But the Lee she reveres is not the loyal son of Virginia who took up arms reluctantly, nor the vanquished gentleman of Appomattox: he is the maniac who ordered tens of thousands to certain death at Gettysburg. With a Chicago-Irish accent and a direct attack that would have made Lee quake in terror, Margaret is without doubt one of the most adversarial people I've ever known. When she presents a circumstantial case, she leaves no stone unturned, nor any bug found thereunder unsquashed.

Under Margaret's questioning, our client chronicles a long, responsible white-collar work history. Then, she tells about a slowly escalating series of medical problems: back pain, surgery, physical therapy, again and again, with lingering difficulties she tries to work around. Anticipating the criticisms to come from the company witnesses, she presents a picture of hardworking competence in challenging circumstances. She's no heroic overcomer, but an ordinary working woman who needs her paycheck and does everything she can to accommodate herself to the job, until finally she has to ask that the job bend to accommodate her. She doesn't pretend to be perfect. She is humble, but not defensive. She recounts in detail the private conversations with the managers, which we all know they will deny.

If she's lying, I think, she has an awful lot of nerve. But if she's honest, she has even more. It must be hard to sit in that box and tell your story knowing you'll be called a liar. It takes a kind of bravery to submit to judgment and ask twelve people you've never met to take you at your word.

Margaret flips through her notes. "One moment, please." She walks back to our table. "Did I get everything?" she asks.

"Of course you did," I say.

For the next several days, it is my job to listen with more than my own ears. With the ears of the judge, I try to make sure we get into evidence the facts legally required to establish each element of our case, without which he will be obliged to dismiss the case at the close of our proof. With the ears of the jury—twelve different sets of ears, the ears of strangers whose thoughts are unknown to me—I need to ensure that we're engaging, clear, and persuasive. And, finally, I listen with the ears of the members of the Court of Appeals, or, more accurately, with their eyes. They work in a plain text world. If they wind up with this case on appeal, they won't see these witnesses' faces or hear their voices but based solely on words will have to decide whether the jury's decision—whatever decision—must be sustained or reversed. I try to envision the transcript this trial might become and make sure every nod becomes a clear yes and that objections are stated on the record. Because the Appeals Court cannot consider errors not objected to, one of the jobs of a trial lawyer is perversely called preserving error.

Alan, the company lawyer, rises to cross-examine. Margaret and I have known Alan for over ten years, beginning when we worked in three different offices in what Charleston considers a modern high-rise. Later, I joined Margaret's office co-op and we moved to a converted carriage factory a few blocks away; soon Alan's firm moved right across the hall. Now Margaret has moved her shingle to Broad Street, the South's most intimidating legal address, leaving me to move into her former office, a large pleasant room with tall windows, sometimes still referred to as the Viper Pit in Margaret's honor. Alan is still across the hall, a familiar presence during my comings and goings.

But this is the first time I've seen his jury-trial persona. While Margaret stands firm, Alan roams all over the place, apparently bent on impressing the jury with his height and limb length. It makes sense. Margaret's job is to make the story clear. His job is to muddy it. Without being harsh or ungentlemanly—male aggressiveness against a lone female doesn't please Southern juries—he pokes holes in our client's chronology, displays a certain attitude, and drops hints about what's to come when the jury eventually hears from the owners and managers of the company, three brothers who happen to be Citadel men.

I'm paying attention to a contentious line of questioning. When I got into the case, Margaret and Alan were having a brouhaha because our client got some disability benefits after she lost her job, while she was recuperating from surgery. Alan wanted the judge to dismiss our case on the theory that our client, as a matter of law, couldn't claim under the ADA to be "qualified," that is, able to do her job, when she got money for being "disabled," that is, unable to work. I helped Margaret with a brief that asked the judge to exclude all evidence about the benefits; the ADA doesn't divide the world between "disabled" and "nondisabled" but targets disability discrimination whenever it occurs. What some other body of law has to say about an individual's general employability has nothing to do with her ability to perform one particular job. The ADA ought to cover people who would otherwise be on the disability rolls, we argue, given that one of its express purposes is to reduce the social cost of dependence.

The judge has ruled that Alan may cross-examine our client about what she wrote on the disability forms but may not reveal their purpose; it's up to the judge, not the jury, to decide whether any damages should be reduced on account of benefits received. Although splitting the baby may have worked for Solomon, here the result is not happy. Ordered to hack the statements from their context, Alan engages in some of that stilted, bizarre dialogue that maddens everyone but lawyers— and tends to madden me, too.

Now I think Alan might be exploiting the constraints, suggesting to the jury that he'd prefer to tell the full story, but he's being prevented because the plaintiff has something to hide. He asks a question that I think goes too far.

"May I approach the bench!" It's not a question when I say it, but a bit of an outburst, and out I burst from the counsel table, zooming in high gear across the courtroom. Too late I realize that the judge's desk—a black marble structure suitable to entomb a Renaissance pope—looms about three feet above my head. Approaching is physically impossible; no way can I whisper my argument out of the jury's hearing. With no idea what else to do, I slow down. To a creep. I am about to halt all together and mutter, "Never mind, it's OK," when the judge stands up, bounds down, and sits on the steps in front of his dais. Because it's rude to be taller than a judge, Alan pulls up a chair and sits. Our colloquy is like a summertime chat in front of a neighbor's stoop.

When the judge stands up, I say, "Thank you, Your Honor," loud enough for the jury to hear. It's a cheap little trick, something lawyers do to make the jury think they've won the point. Of course, Alan does it, too, so the jury is left with no way of knowing which of us won the point but with the accurate impression that we're both full of shit. The judge having clarified his prior ruling, the confusion resumes. I'll let Margaret do our bench-approaching from now on.

◆

After our client has been subjected to cross-examination, redirect, recross, and reredirect, our case moves on. While Margaret questions another witness, her paralegal tells me the neurosurgeon has arrived in compliance with our subpoena. To avoid paying neurosurgical rates for him to hang around and get increasingly annoyed, we plan to get him on the stand at the next opening. I go out in the hall. "Thank you for coming," I say as though the subpoena isn't mandatory. He is visibly surprised by my appearance—Margaret isn't in the habit of warning people how I look—and doesn't quite take it in when I introduce myself. When it fully registers that I am one of the lawyers, he lets me know his time would be better spent repairing spines, and not mucking about with this dispute.

"I have reviewed the chart," he says, "and you won't like what I have to say. She is not disabled. The surgery was successful. She could go right back to her old job with just a little consideration in a few areas."

I tell him I do like what he's saying. This isn't a personal injury case where we want money for what she can't do; we're not pumping up a lurid tale of pain and suffering and loss. This is a job discrimination case and we need to prove that she is able to do the job. We want simple answers to straightforward questions: What is the impairment? How does it limit life activities? Can she perform her job? We agree that our client should have gone to work after her surgery; the ADA's purpose is to make employers do what's reasonable to enable a person to work. It isn't right to fire people for medical problems that have been corrected. If they can work, they should be allowed to work.

On the stand, he gives us what we want. But Margaret likes to prove everything twice. The other physician is available only through a deposition transcript. From the tall lawyer's podium, Margaret reads her questions. From a small table we've placed in front of the witness stand, I read the answers with what I hope is an appropriate hint of doctorly authority. We then work through a long lineup of witnesses and documents dealing with our client's job performance and the events leading up to the termination. I listen, making sure the ducks are arow.

The original plan was for me to examine some of the witnesses. Margaret wants the jury to know that I am not here merely for window dressing, and I could use more jury trial experience; most of my work is in Social Security appeals, behind closed doors with one judge to convince and no opposing counsel. But soon it becomes clear that getting me up to speed would be a major inefficiency. Margaret has interviewed and deposed every witness and has talked to many others who won't be testifying. She knows what's in those boxes of documents. All the details are buzzing in her brain's active RAM. I'm not as good with details. My strength is that I know about the ADA and am one of the fastest producers of effective written legal gobbledygook in the state; I'm better deployed on the papers and on legal arguments to the judge.

As things have evolved, I'm no longer worried about the window-dressing problem. Before she starts with a witness, Margaret reviews her notes with me. Before she concludes, she checks with me again and sometimes asks another question or two on my advice. She is as close to being deferential as a person like Margaret can be. The jury may think I'm calling the shots.

The days are exhausting. Sitting still and quiet behind a table always wears me out. I don't know why. Maybe it's the physical strain of stillness, my body missing the gentle jostling of power-chair movement and the bit of wiggling I can do. Or maybe it's the psychological effects of inertia, the emotional strain of being under observation but not in interaction. Listening is hard work for one who talks easily. From one side, all day, day after day, I'm pelted with Margaret's Chicago staccato, hammering questions. From the other, it's Alan's Lowcountry adagio, rolling along.

Fortunately, there's a Charleston federal court tradition of generous lunch breaks. In the old days, everyone would go home to the main meal of the day and a nap. Now it's a quick bite and work to fill the time. The judge and his clerks attack the piles of paperwork they can't deal with while court's in session. The lawyers agonize and dither and get ready for the afternoon show. After the first day, I tell Margaret I'll be having lunch on my own. I'm being horribly rude, ditching her and the client when the trial has them keyed up—but she doesn't give me any argument. I don't have to confess that I'm on edge. I might go ballistic if I don't clear my head, do some wiggling, see what's been happening at the office, eat a relaxed lunch with Tim and Susan and give them the blow by blow. I tell Margaret

I'll come back to the court room fifteen minutes early and we can talk then.

Even with the breaks, I'm drained. I don't know how Margaret and Alan go so long, nonstop, fueled on courtroom adrenalin. As the trial drags on, I sometimes get so punch-weary, I think I've morphed into one of those silly movies like *My Cousin Vinnie* and can't help giggling, at least with my eyes. Fortunately, our judge is practiced at not noticing, as I had reason to appreciate on a recent Election Day when he came into my precinct to vote and found me and another poll manager in flagrante delicto, rifling through the ballot box. (It was completely innocent, I assure you.) Now, he's running the trial with tact and courtesy to both sides. If he gives either side any slack, it's ours. He might be afraid of catching Margaret's famous ire. Or he might be Alan's cousin.

◆

We rest our case, and Alan rises first to move to dismiss and then to take his Citadel men, one, two, three, through their paces. A witness who benefits from the company's regular patronage says our client did a poor job. Other witnesses needle at various details. On cross-examination, Margaret needles back. It's all about when they discovered these alleged performance problems, when they decided to fire our client, when she told them about the surgery, if she told them about the surgery. There's no dramatic Aha! or Gotcha! moment. The facts are in dispute. That's why we need a jury to tell us which version is more likely to be true.

When our rebuttal case ends, the judge dismisses the jury for the evening. Closing statements will be first up tomorrow. This evening we work on jury instructions.

Before the trial started, both sides submitted requests to

charge, proposed instructions for the judge to give the jury before they deliberate, and objections to the other side's requests. I was the primary writer for our side. Individually numbered and titled, each charge is a statement of one point of law that is relevant to the case. The judge has considered our requests and has printed out a comprehensive charge he proposes to issue. I've reviewed it and I think it's reasonable, not skewed to either side, likely to stand up on appeal, and as clear and coherent as legal writing can be expected to be. I'm inclined to see if Alan will agree; maybe we can dispense with the evening argument. But Margaret would disapprove of such nonadversarial behavior and everyone might realize I'm kind of low-energy. So, sure, maybe the charge could be improved a bit, and, well, we might need to preserve error. I compare our requests to charge with the judge's draft, item by item, and record my points on one sheet of paper.

It's supper time when we get back in court. With the jury gone home, the atmosphere is more relaxed. "Let me hear from the plaintiff first," the judge says.

I stay in place at the counsel table, with my page of notes. "Your Honor, we request that you charge plaintiff's number seven."

I expect the judge to say "Denied," whereupon I expect to say "Thank you" and move on, bip-bap, so I can go home and eat and get off this tailbone that's been sitting in this chair for too many hours.

Instead Alan rises and ambles to the podium. He plants one foot on the box. "Your Honor, I'm reminded of that old story . . ."

I try not to giggle. The judge ought to cut Alan off by denying me, but he allows a full-blown argument and asks me to respond. By this time, Margaret has dug out the relevant sheaf of papers and turned to plaintiff's number 7 so I can see what I'm talking about. Alan's right. There's only the tiniest difference between our proposal and the judge's draft. Dutifully I argue the point, but without much starch. Finally, at last: Denied.

Next. "We request plaintiff's number eleven."

This time the judge helpfully reads our proposed language from his copy. Again Alan argues in full, and now he's walking around, hemming and hawing. So we go, back and forth. Usually denied, occasionally granted, none of it making much difference. I'm getting annoyed with Alan. He's been getting under my skin through the whole trial, acting tall! I decide it's time to put a stop to it.

"Your Honor," I say, "the hour is late and I suspect we're all a bit tired. I wonder if counsel for the defense might be allowed to argue seated at the counsel table."

"No, Ms. Johnson, I believe counsel for the defense should remain standing, but he will stay behind the counsel table and not range over the courtroom."

Alan retreats and things move quicker. I am reeling off numbers and getting summarily denied, with no discussion, the way it should be done.

I'm nearing the home stretch. "Your Honor, we ask for plaintiff's thirty."

"You want me to charge plaintiff's thirty?"

"Yes, Your Honor."

"Why should I do that?"

"Excuse me?"

"I'm asking why should I charge number thirty?"

I have no idea. I don't know what it says. When Alan got corralled and the pace picked up, Margaret stopped flipping pages and now she's having a hard time finding thirty. I stall. "We ask for number thirty because it is an accurate statement of a principle of law that applies in the current case."

"Where did you get it?" the judge asks.

We still haven't found it. "The source is noted at the bottom of the charge."

The judge reads the proposed charge aloud. "I don't see a citation on this one."

"You don't?"

"No, there's no citation. You usually have a reference to the code, a regulation, or a court opinion, but not on this one. Do you know where you got it?"

Margaret, poised stiff and still, is hissing in my ear. Say something! Tell him a source!

"Your Honor, if I didn't put the citation on it, honestly—"

Margaret is in viper mode, ready to strike, I fear. Don't tell him you don't know! Don't tell him you don't know.

"—honestly, at this point, I don't know."

"Thank you for your candor, Ms. Johnson. Could it have come from your fertile imagination?"

"Maybe," I answer. It's all over. It's bad enough to be having this conversation with a judge in open court, but Margaret's hissing is what's killing me. All I can do is talk over it. "Well, Your Honor, whether I found it in an authoritative source or made it up, I believe it is an accurate statement of the law that applies to this case."

The judge rereads it silently. "I believe so, too. I'll charge it."

◆

Closing arguments come right on the heels of the first "All rise!" of the morning. The podium has been pushed away to give the lawyers strutting room in front of the jury box.

After so many days in court, my forensic wardrobe is exhausted. Today it's an olive green embroidered cotton shift over a yellow silk shirt, with a yellow jade dragon pendant. It's slightly bohemian but I think a Doll Baby with an unconventional body like mine can get away with it. Margaret's and Alan's power wardrobes seem as boundless as their stamina, crisp-pressed and ready to go.

Margaret steps out. "Ladies and gentlemen of the jury," she says with her midwestern clip, "this is where the rubber meets the road."

I'm not sure what she means. Neither is the jury; they've bolted up with surprise. This must be a Chicago expression now being spoken for the very first time in South Carolina. She quickly explains that we are getting down to the real business of the case, when twelve men and women have the duty to decide what most probably happened. In line with the instructions we know the judge will give, Margaret lays it all out, detail by detail, and disposes of the defense's counterarguments as she goes. There are blowups of key documents. Timelines. Quotations. She's driving it all the way—tires hugging pavement, inexorably, no turns, no detours, no stops, mile after mile. It's ten times the detail I would have used, but the jury isn't bored. She communicates absolute conviction. The clerk gives a signal: one minute. She brakes, starts to lose control, but veers for that last-minute swerve into the damages case. I realize we haven't put a lot of energy into convincing the jury to order a big check. We've been focused on proving that the defendants broke the law.

Alan's summation is much more like one I'd have done. It paints his themes in broad brush, gives a few factual examples, but doesn't try to be comprehensive. His job is to sow uncertainty. As the judge will instruct, the plaintiff has the burden of proof; therefore, he wins if he can derail just one of the many essential elements of our case. He makes hay about those mysterious forms in which the plaintiff said she was "disabled"; she admitted she was unable to work and shouldn't be believed now when she says she was able to do her job. He scoffs. It doesn't work on me, or on Margaret, or on our client, but this dismissive air might work on the jury, might make Margaret's vehemence look ridiculous. Will the jury think we've done right to make this into a federal case?

Our side has reserved three minutes for rebuttal, and they go to me. I have the first and the last word though otherwise I've been nearly silent, so far as the jury is concerned, throughout the whole trial. I'd like to use our time to beef up the damages case, but Alan didn't mention it and the rules require me to rebut, not supplement. I don't think the jury needs more back-and-forth on the minutiae. I need to deal expeditiously with something Alan has raised and set a tone for the jury to begin their deliberations. My handover must be consistent with my role as an advocate who has mostly been seen but not heard.

I tell them I've been sitting and listening, just as they have. It's clear there's a dispute about the facts. The trial has settled nothing. In several areas, either version is possible. It depends on who you believe or what you infer about the unknown from the known. We don't have certainty, so we have twelve people to consider the evidence, discuss it, and reach a conclusion. My co-counsel has explained in exhaustive detail why we think the company most probably violated the law. The jury has heard why we think our version is more likely than the company's. No need to repeat all that.

But I do want to say something about one thing. The company makes a big deal of the fact that the plaintiff filled out a printed form describing her as "disabled." The law we're suing under nowhere uses the word *disabled*. It's the Americans with Disabilities Act. It's about protecting Americans—people—from disability discrimination. Not just nondisabled people. Not just disabled people. Many people—regular working people—have *disabilities* but don't become *disabled* so long as their disabilities are accommodated. Words are used in a lot of different ways. I filled out a form that called me "disabled" so I could park in the disability parking. On my office door I have a sticker that says, I'M DISABLED, BUT NOT DEAD YET. When I put that sticker up, and called myself disabled, was I saying I'm unable to work? Of course not. Was I giving up my rights to fair treatment under the ADA? I hope not.

I talk fast because the time is running out and, any second now, Alan ought to rise up, act tall, and object. I thank the jury for their service and whir back behind the counsel table, alongside Margaret and our client, the working woman to whom we've given a day—no, a week—in court.

✦

The jury returns a verdict for our side with a modest damages award that we declare entirely fair. But the wrangling shows no signs of ending. The specific amount of damages is puzzling. So is the fact that the jury found a violation of the ADA but not of the Family and Medical Leave Act, with its more specific mandate for people who need time off work. There's ammunition for Alan to suggest, in a motion for a new trial, that the verdict is inconsistent, a compromise rather than consensus, and should be set aside. I want it to be ended and so does our client, but I can't help wondering if a new trial—in which we might beef up our damages case and spend more than one minute arguing it to the jury—might add another zero to the check. Alan should be careful what he requests; he might get it. On our side, there is one of those contorted motions to preserve error. We don't think the verdict was a compromise or inconsistent, but, if it is, we join in requesting a new trial.

Then Margaret and I petition that the defendant company be ordered to pay our fees and expenses. Our claim is several times the amount of the damages award. It's all itemized in detail. Margaret claims the hourly rate she normally gets for litigation in family court, for every minute preparing and trying the case. My hours are far fewer but I ask for $250 per hour as a nationally recognized expert in the ADA. In an affidavit, I swear I'm worth it; three of my friends provide corroboration. The judge well knows I have little jury trial experience, but he also knows I don't waste my time. I don't have the energy.

When the motions are filed, the judge's clerk asks all the lawyers to come for a conference. When we arrive, we are ushered into chambers and told the judge will be with us shortly. He never shows up. It's an obvious ploy to make us try to settle the case. It works. We reach agreement in concept, and I cheerfully leave it to Margaret and Alan to slug out the details. I know Margaret will fight for my fees even harder than she'll fight for her own; with her adversarial habits working for me, I can be magnanimous.

At one point in the posttrial wrangling, Margaret tells me we have a lien on some heavy construction equipment, including a tall crane. I fantasize that Margaret might foreclose on the crane and get it awarded to me. I could use it to hoist myself into inaccessible political cocktail receptions and lend it to Democratic sign warriors and be a hero at election time. But in the end, the secured debt is discharged. Although I'm happy to get paid, sometimes I still think about the crane that might have been mine if things had gone otherwise.

Of course, if things had gone still otherwise, there would have been no crane, no payment, no return of any kind on the investment of our time and of Margaret's money, and, what is most important, no vindication for one ordinary person who believes the law was broken and is ready to bear witness, even knowing her word will be contradicted by others. Today, increasingly, when the facts are in dispute, the answer is not to submit them to a jury but to accept the corporate defendant's side. Not long after our verdict, the Supreme Court begins its steady pummeling of the ADA. Now a plaintiff like our client—the kind who looks good in a suit—is apt to be tossed out of court as not "disabled" enough to deserve ADA protection.

My jury argument that the ADA is for anyone who happens to fall victim to disability discrimination is not one I can make today. As a lawyer in court, I am required to argue within the law as it is, as defined by evolving precedents. But as an activist and a citizen, I have the freedom and the duty to agitate to make the law what it should be. When the ADA was passed in 1990, the disability rights movement won a decades-long fight for comprehensive civil rights protection. Now, we need to return to Congress and fight to win back what the courts have pared away.

7

Believing in Dreams

There's no avoiding the math. In July, I turn forty. How will I handle it? I've been worrying about that ever since I got past the shock of turning thirty. This time I prepare to defuse the event with a two-phase plan.

Phase one is completed. For my thirty-eighth birthday, I demanded and got a surprise party. Because no one makes a big deal about thirty-eight, my friends assumed I was forty then and now they think I'm playing Jack Benny when I say I'm thirty-nine. It looks like I'll be spared the black balloons and the tombstone cake.

Phase two is intended to cover the possibility that, on my birthday, the essential futility of all things might hit me as a bad thing. As life rolls over into a new decade, I need something to look forward to. I put out word that I'm in search of an interesting fall vacation. Laura Hershey, the leader of the telethon opposition in Denver and now a boon e-mail companion, says she's going to a disability rights conference in Havana in October and I should go, too.

It's perfect. My family spent six weeks in Cuba in the summer of 1959, just after—as they say—the Revolution triumphed. I was only two. That summer, it is said, I learned to talk in scrambled Spanish and English; my mother claims I sang "Adelante Cubanos" with a passable accent and excellent pitch. Beth, a strong personality at age four, allegedly taught all the neighborhood kids to say "One, two, three, Go!" in English the day after we got there. In my childhood, I remember my mother recounting all-night radio broadcasts by Fidel Castro; I thought of him as one of her favorite movie stars, along with Oscar Werner and Maximilian Schell. For my dad, I suppose the trip influenced his interests in socialist theater and agrarian reform. Growing up in the Cold War South, I held it a distinction that we spent time in a socialist country, a beautiful land of hope and excitement.

Within two years of our family visit, the United States severed diplomatic relations, sponsored an invasion, and imposed a trade embargo. The island we reached by ferry from Florida became remote. Now, to go there legally, you need a permit from the U.S. Treasury Department. This conference has obtained the necessary permits for both participants and personal care attendants; Beth jumps at the chance to go as my assistant. The trip requires a layover in Mexico and therefore a layover in Atlanta. With so many transfers, odds are my power chair would get broken, and getting it repaired in Cuba might be impossible. Better to take the stripped-down manual chair my legal secretary found at a yard sale for $35. The brakes aren't good but it's very portable—and kind of cute.

As I am working on arrangements, Laura decides she can't go and suggests I take over her assignment to write about the conference for *New Mobility,* a disability magazine. I e-mail the editor. He gives me the assignment—based, he says, on Laura's recommendation and on my "obvious verbal charm." A trifling flirt, I figure, but I'm glad for the assignment. Now I can answer the Treasury Department question about how I intend to disseminate the knowledge I gain in Cuba. I'm in good shape to travel to the other side of forty.

◆

The day I go to Cuba, I'm lifted fifteen times. Lift Fourteen is the most harrowing. A pair of paramedics tote me down steep stairs from the belly of the plane to the tarmac. Havana's Jose Marti Airport has no jetways. It reminds me of Charleston before access laws existed, when if you wanted to go anywhere, you had to be prepared to be carried.

Inside the airport, we are directed to a cubicle marked DIPLOMATS. Normally I'd assume this to be special treatment for special people, but this time it means we're from the U.S.A., an enemy state. The door closes. The inside knob has been removed. Trapped! The militiaman leans out of his high window to compare me with the less-lined face on my soon-to-expire passport. Close enough, apparently; I hear the rubber stamp slam down. The door opens and Beth and I are admitted into the friendly chaos of Cuba.

Punchy from travel-weariness, we find that our Spanish works. Sort of. We're from the United States. We're attending a conference. About the undressed. I mean disabled. I have all my bags. I am waiting for transport. Special transport. With an elevator for the chair, I hope.

In no time, the special transport arrives: a smoky, rusty city bus with some seats removed and a lift that would look right moving crates of beer. There are no tie-downs, so Beth wedges her leg against my wheel and holds tight. I wish I had a seat belt in my chair. By the time we unload at a fancy German-owned tourist hotel, the contrast shocks the system. "It's like something out of the Third World," I say. One way Beth and I amuse ourselves when we travel is by making dumb remarks.

We know that we've returned to a different Cuba. With the collapse of the Soviet Union, most Americans see Cuba's Marxist-Leninist state as an anachronism. Before 1990, 85 percent of Cuba's trade was with the Socialist bloc. Now that is gone, along with billions of dollars of Soviet subsidies. At the same time, the United States has tightened the trade embargo. The island is largely cut off from the global economy. Imports are down 75 percent, the gross domestic product down 34 percent. In what they call "This Special Period," Cubans are experiencing real hardship. But the government has declared its goal of a self-sustaining economy that provides every citizen with necessities. The top priority is food production. The main hope for development is tourism. Here we come.

◆

The next morning, we're not sure what time it is. There's no clock in the room. Probably our watches are right; it's probably the Eastern time zone. But does Cuba have daylight saving time? Some parts of Mexico don't. At home, the time change is this weekend. Assuming Cuba has daylight time, does it change back at the same time? The bank of clocks in the hotel lobby are wildly varied. We head into the restaurant for breakfast and ask the host for the time. "Don't worry," he says, "the buffet is still open."

We follow some disabled people to the conference registration and then we're pulled out and directed somewhere else. We're not sure why. Maybe because others have prepaid and I had to bring a bag of money. My checks and credit cards don't work here, but U.S. dollars are the common currency.

After going through a mysterious series of lines and appearing cluelessly at a number of desks, we are issued name tags and a conference schedule. There isn't the expected satchel full of papers, booklets, and brochures. We take places in an auditorium,

Beth gets out my legal pad, and I plug the translator into my ear. We consult the schedule. If we figure out where we are on the agenda, we can deduce the correct time. Forget it. They're not following the schedule. Probably.

There are various ceremonial welcomes and performances by singers and dancers with disabilities. I learn I am one of more than two hundred people from eighteen countries. There are nine from the United States, some Germans, Canadians, and Spaniards. The rest are from Latin America, mostly Cuba.

Although some panels relate to other countries, the main focus is disability in Cuba. The first session provides a detailed introduction to the conference sponsors, the three official Cuban organizations of people with disabilities. One is comprised of people who are deaf and hard of hearing, one is of blind and visually impaired people, and the third, ACLIFIM, Asociación Cubano de Limitados Físico-motores, is made up of people with "physical-motor" disabilities, what we call crips.

These are Cuba's establishment crips, working within their system, as it is. But it's not the kind of establishment we're used to. Our official committees endlessly host conferences, issue PR, and write reports, all to try to convince government and corporate power to do right. The Cuban organizations are real participants in policy-making: they represent their constituencies and some seventy-five thousand members as trade unions represent theirs. In Cuba, policy evolves from discussions that include the whole constituency; the process is dialectical in the literal sense. Beth and I soon get used to being called *compañera,* comrade.

Clearly in Cuba there's nothing like ADAPT, the grassroots organization that uses direct action and civil disobedience to try to force government to redirect money from institutions and to fund services in our homes. But then, there's nothing like the MDA telethon either. Evolving in the U.S. system of multiple, linked power centers, our organizations use media, government, and business to work for varied and sometimes competing goals. In Cuba, power is centralized—the economy, politics, law, and information are all controlled by the socialist state. The disability organizations mirror this centralization.

Centralized systems resist change, but when change happens it can be fast. For example, we learn that Sign language was forbidden in Cuban schools until the Deaf organization got the government to reverse policy. Once that happened, it took only three years for Cuba to research various "underground" Sign systems and standardize vocabulary and grammar; in one fell swoop Cuban Sign was standard in deaf education. Unfortunately, the minister of education tells us that speech is still among the "skills" needed for university.

✦

Everything is scarce, even for us, although we've been told the tourist sector gets priority. Our hotel runs out of coffee one morning and milk the next. A snack bar, shining with crystal and brass, sells nothing but bread and white cheese, until they run out. At the same time, labor is abundant. Because Cuba guarantees a job for everyone and industry virtually collapsed with the Soviet bloc, the hotel is wildly overstaffed. Two waiters count coffee orders. Excess bartenders lean on the bar and conga in place. When their shifts end, staff hang out in the lobby with the guests. They are not required to be invisible, and certainly not subservient.

There are all kinds of rules we don't understand. At the conference, in the hotel, everywhere—there are procedures, and no one explains them. We never do figure out the time. When we ask Cubans, we get answers like: The bus will be leaving soon. I'll be here for another hour at least. It isn't too late.

The second day of our stay, we're excited to see a lunch buffet set up; it will be nice to order by sight. But a hotel staffer pulls us out of the line. We say it's fine, to us the line is good, the line pleases us much, no problem. They insist we sit at a table and order from a menu.

As we wait in suspense to discover what it is that we have or-dered, three German men are placed at our table. One is young and quadriplegic. The older man may be his father. The big af-fable one must be the personal assistant. The PA speaks pretty good English. "Do you know," he asks, "why we are not permit-ted to stay in the line?"

We can only speculate. Maybe they are trying to help the disabled guests. No, we see other people with disabilities—including some who look like they could use help—going through the line undisturbed. Maybe there's a billing problem, since people from the United States have to pay cash. No, say the Germans, our credit cards work here, and we also got pulled out of the line.

"Maybe they think you're Americans."

"Could be. Vee all look alike, don't vee?"

◆

Conference participants are invited to tour "special" schools. Beth and I sign up for the Solidarity with Panama School, a school for crips.

With a large number of international crips, we pile into those crazy lift-equipped buses and ride past crumbling stucco mansions, now subdivided into apartments. Again, I think of Charleston before a huge infusion of government and corporate capital transformed our downtown into a lovely tourist attrac-tion. On the streets I see people in shades ranging from ivory to dark chocolate. Like Charleston. There is dense vegetation—palm trees, bushes, vines—eating up the built environment, ex-haling rich oxygen. Like Charleston. Only more so.

We get off the bus and roll into the beige lobby of the school. That sense of being back in time gets stronger.

"Looks awfully familiar," I tell Beth. She sees it, too. It's like the "special" school where my friends and I used to hang out in the lobby when visitors came. Gathered in little clusters, these kids are like us, except that I don't see the expected scattering of really hardcore crips. I mean the ones we used to call (with all the tact of childhood) the droolers, the spazzos, the hideous. Where are they? Off in less tourist-worthy facilities? I'm afraid to ask. I remember reports of punitive treatment of people with HIV and note that psychiatric disability has been absent from our conference. Some faces of disability remain unseen in the new Cuba.

The principal gives a lecture. Much of it I don't understand, but I hear there are special schools throughout Cuba. These kids are here because they need special services not available in regular schools. That's what they said about us, too.

We are invited to roam around. Go anywhere. Talk to anyone.

We look for the special equipment. One room is full of drafting tables with high, built-in seats; few of the children I've seen could sit at them. There's no sign that they've been used. They're probably castoffs from some trade school; at my old school, we occasionally got such strange donations. Another room has the standard equipment of low-tech occupational therapy, the same stuff we had in the 1960s. On a paved area outside, kids are zooming around in their chairs. I, too, love rolling on nice smooth blacktop—and it's rare in historic Charleston. Then we see the physical therapy area. Floor mats, parallel bars. Nothing fancy. Any of it could be placed in any school.

Four girls sit at a card table. They act cute, answer questions, pose for pictures. I think of my childhood friends. We, too, used to act cute and engage visiting dignitaries in conversation. But when the visitors left, we had a contest among ourselves: Who'd met the stupidest visitor? Bonus points for a pat on the head!

Now here I am, one of those visitors, a nosy forty-year-old woman from a foreign country. I don't like it, but what can I do? I ask Beth to take pictures for *New Mobility*.

We wander some more. There is a bulletin board about Che Guevara, the revolutionary hero who was assassinated in Bolivia by our CIA. His bones have just come home to Cuba and the country is in a state of high emotion.

I notice that the place smells fine. That means it's clean—the nose doesn't lie in a tropical climate. We pass the library. There are very few books, as in my old school, but maybe in Cuba no worse than in a "regular" school; things are so scarce.

I see a teenage boy sitting alone in the hallway. His disability is not apparent. He is slight and slim, with a lovely face and skin like a cafe cortado. I bite the bullet and ask if he'll talk to me. He shrugs. I start with the basic questions, but then I back up.

I say, "When I was a young girl—"

I stop, looking for the past tense. The boy wants to help. "You went to this school?"

"No, not this school. A similar school, in the United States."

His eyebrows shoot up. Like most people, he's amazed to meet someone from the terrorist country that murdered Che. I continue, without the past tense. "In our school, groups come to visit us, and we hate it! Oh no, we say, another group! Always some group! We must smile, answer stupid questions—"

The boy covers his mouth in an ineffective attempt to hide a grin. He will neither confirm nor deny, but I start to hope I won't be named the Stupidest Visitor when the kids run their contest.

"May I ask you stupid questions?" I ask.

"Certainly," he answers.

With Beth's help—she can conjugate verbs—I learn he's seventeen years old. He's studying academic subjects. He doesn't know what he'll do when he leaves the school. He might like to go to university. He might get a job. He doesn't know. In my school, there were some kids who had wild hopes of a fantastic future. They said they wanted to be president, teachers, lawyers, the next James Brown. We called them impossible dreamers. But the cool kids didn't express hopes. I'm not sure why. Bad luck, maybe?

"Would you like to ask me questions?" I ask.

"No." He laughs behind his hand. It's obviously the first time he's been invited to ask questions. We say good-bye. "Don't you want to take my photograph?" he asks. We do.

The encounter creates a brief and tenuous connection, but the boy and I remain strangers to each other. I'll always wonder how his life is going, but maybe I'm also afraid of knowing. I can only hope that his world will change, as mine has, and that he will realize some of those dreams he doesn't express.

The children gather to sing patriotic songs, joined by a paraplegic American man who has a guitar and a store of Cuban revolutionary anthems so impressive as to surpass Beth's and mine. The children are undeniably cute and sing well, but it's too much like the forced cuteness of my crip-school childhood.

One of the buses is being loaded, so I gesture to Beth to head out there. The lift clatters and clacks and I'm in—staring at the ghost of a San Francisco city map and a sign saying the bus was donated by Pastors for Peace. Beth wedges me in beside the quadriplegic German. There we sit, the bus fully packed, idling. There's no breeze, no air-conditioning. Through open windows we hear the children and the American with the guitar sing on. Inevitably, it's "Guantanamera."

The German personal assistant is looking frustrated. Those Germans like to know what's going on. "Excuse me," he says, "do you happen to know why the bus is not going?"

I answer slowly and deliberately. "I think, in Cuban law it is a crime for a bus to depart during the singing of 'Guantanamera.'"

He explains to the others, in those words that sound like funny made-up German. I think I hear *ein crimen*, maybe something like *Guantanameragesingschaft*.

My joke seems to improve in the translation and I guess it's as reasonable an explanation as any.

✦

Later, we are bussed to another hotel for a pool party. It's a gorgeous night to inhale the thick tropical air, but I'm unnerved. After many years of controlling my own movements in a power chair, I'm jittery at being pushed around, especially in a chair with no brakes along the edge of a swimming pool with no safety barriers and only about five inches of water.

Beth parks me at a table a safe distance from the pool and goes off to get tapas. Some Central Americans sit down, including a man on crutches and braces, probably postpolio. He cranks up the routine flirtation that polite Central American manners demand. He has been watching me, it seems. With my sister, is it? Why don't I get rid of my sister, who is always watching me with the eyes of the secret police? Why don't I get a power chair, that I may escape to adventure? It's too silly. In fact, I am my family's most policelike member and habitually roam the streets entirely unescorted. Never mind. He can think I am constantly chaperoned, tightly tethered, as any respectable unmarried lady should be.

Beth comes back and we watch the crowd. One of the blind men has the worst-behaved guide dog I've ever seen. She wanders, sniffs, probes, explores, as much as an unemployed dog fully at liberty, but never making a sound, never straining the leash, and somehow enlisting every human present to collude in the boss's deception. Without making a sound, a man shoves the dog's nose out of his crotch and a woman whacks it out of a plate of tapas. Meanwhile, the boss follows in the ordered route the dog ordains for him, oblivious to the dog's frolics and detours. Around the man and the wayward dog there are increasing numbers of people in wheelchairs and walking people looking straight over the heads of the people in chairs, moving close, right on the edge of that waterless pool.

An accident waiting to happen, I think, and it pops out of my mouth in Spanish. *Un acidente esperando a pasar,* the Central Americans repeat loudly and it goes all the way around the pool. Apparently it's not a tired old cliché in Spanish, and it must be helped by those multiple meanings of *esperando*—waiting, expecting, hoping.

The tapas are somewhat the worse for wear, but the dance band isn't. There's a glitzy, sexy girl singer and a full complement of full-employment musicians to mix old standards and novelty dance crazes that seem to be common to the Spanish-speaking world. As always with Cubans, everyone dances. Or almost. Beth, a serious dancer, doesn't know the steps and is waiting for a serious dancer to ask her. And sometime in my childhood in the disability ghetto I decided that wheelchair dancing was undignified. I now know I was wrong; we can in our own way play with sight and sound, combine rhythm and form, move in our chairs and with our chairs, and glide and spin in ways walking people can't. But this isn't the night. Not without my power chair. Not with Beth here watching me with the eyes of—a serious dancer.

It gets late, and a large group assembles and is waiting in plain sight of the bus and driver. No one knows when we will leave. I start questioning the ACLIFIM members.

Courteously, they assure me they're not in charge, there's nothing they can do. I press on. Who is in charge? Is he here?

Let's ask him. Let's tell him about the problem. I'm sure he would like to solve it.

Too late, I realize I've gone beyond what's considered polite. My pushiness isn't appreciated.

Cubans eagerly tackle big problems—in a big way. The revolutionary generation stamped out illiteracy, eliminated unemployment, provided universal health care. That spirit endures. Cubans are determined not to go back on a single constitutional guarantee, and to include all people, including people with disabilities. Collectively, Cubans are activists. But individually, they seem passive—waiting patiently, shrugging off small problems that could, so easily, be solved. For people like me and the Germans, it's an upside-down world.

◆

When we get back to our room, we see that our full-employment chambermaid has pleated our bedspreads into fans; she has also been folding our towels into swans and writing us sweet notes in labored English. Beth destroys the artful fan and puts me in bed. For a little bedtime torment, she hands me Pablo Neruda's *Book of Questions*. It's a collection of very short poems in interrogative form. I can't get any sense out of the Spanish. Putting our heads together, we work through one and come up with an English question that's like something from a Berlitz tourist phrase book on LSD. When we flip to the printed translation, it's crazier that we could ever have imagined.

Beth thrives on the adventure of lost bearings, the giddiness of culture shock, the hilarity of being out of control. This is why we travel, she says. For me, it's not an experience to seek out. Whether I'm traveling or at home, I'm in a world that seems taken by surprise by the presence of people like me. This routinely makes life's details so complicated that I always do what I can to smooth them over—including enlisting the aid of people

like Beth who roll with the punches. I would like to know what
time it is, but I suppose it doesn't really matter.

✦

Back in the auditorium, conference speakers tell us the special
period is forcing a reappraisal of disability policy. When Cuba
was a Soviet dependent, it was a kind of poster child for Marxist-
Leninism: its subsidized research facilities were a showplace for
Soviet high tech. Today, Cuba must do more with less. The result is a greater emphasis on community-based services, primary
care, family involvement, and improving access to mainstream
jobs and resources. Not all together a bad thing, I think.

Overwhelmed by facts poured through our plastic ear-
phones, we escape the conference. We've taken up with Anne, a
woman from Washington state. Anne signed on as a personal assistant for a disabled friend; when her friend had to cancel, she
decided to come on as a floating PA. We spend an afternoon in
Old Havana. Curb cuts are nonexistent. Sidewalks and streets
are full of holes and broken pavement. It takes both Beth and
Anne to drag me around, and I'm glad I opted against the
power chair this trip.

We get to the open-air market near the cathedral—where
private entrepreneurs are permitted—ready to spend exactly
$100 each, our limit under the U.S. embargo. The street has
been blocked and my chair won't fit. The sidewalk has a very
high curb; right on the corner a large chunk of cement is gone.
I'm about to tell the others to go in without me, when a man
pops up and helps them haul me up in the air and over the barricade. We thank him and he shrugs. It's no big deal.

Throughout the day people help, without making it a big
deal. It's the old socialist formula, "From each according to ability, to each according to need," played out one to one. It's hard
to pin down, but I get the feeling that being a crip is no big

deal here. People talk to me. On a family trip to Mexico, people were afraid to look at me; they sometimes made the sign of the cross, my mother helpfully explained, to protect themselves against the evil eye. In Paris, cabs wouldn't stop. Even in Charleston, where I am so much at home, people tend to address my able-bodied companions. In Havana, I'm a person.

We go to the Museum of the Revolution. We bypass two steps by cutting across the sloping lawn, and bump up three more. Inside, a sign says there's a fee to use the elevator. As soon as we come in, there's a staff conference.

"You can use the elevator at no charge," they tell us, "but it doesn't go to the fourth floor."

We tour the photos and memorabilia documenting the horrors of the old regime, the guerrilla struggle, and the continuing revolution. There are big crowds at rallies in the summer of 1959. We wish our parents were here to tell us where we might look for ourselves. Beth and I have been to so many museums together that she knows how long I will want to look at each thing. We take in the full exhibit about Che Guevara, which depicts him as a talented, all-around good guy, a sort of revolutionary Eagle Scout; he's not at all the dangerous, romantic commando variously feared and venerated in the United States. We linger at the display about his murder. Coming from the United States, being here at this moment when Cuba is Che-obsessed, it seems a duty.

In the elevator, we point to the button marked 4. "Doesn't work," we're told by the full-employment elevator operator. Our guidebook says the fourth floor houses an anti-U.S. exhibit, with the politically incorrect name of the Hall of the Cretins. Beth, a North Carolina resident, is pretty sure her senator, Jesse Helms, will be there. After we've toured the third floor, Beth proposes to walk up the stairs. Anne is willing to hang out with me. "No," says a guard, "it is time for you to go down now."

We don't argue. They probably think the anti-U.S. exhibit will offend us.

The three of us sit in a park and make some instant friends: two young men who seem to be at leisure in the middle of the afternoon. I keep expecting them to launch into some hustle, but it doesn't come; I guess we're experiencing the famous Cuban love of conversation. One, who has lots of mouth, pretends to think Beth is Meryl Streep. He brags that he is the best worker in his factory, so honored by his comrades that he gets elected every year to go out to the country and help bring in the sugarcane. The other tells us he follows Marxism and the Yoruba religion. He reaches into his shirt and pulls out a brown leather pouch hanging on a string. "I don't know how to say it in English."

"Mojo bag," I tell him.

"Mojo bag," he repeats. I'm happy to have given him a phrase from the Lowcountry branch of the African diaspora.

Our new friends don't carry on about my disability. We talk about Cuba, the United States, racism in the South, what will happen when Castro dies. Maybe the years of egalitarian propaganda have had an impact. Maybe these Cubans have managed to learn what the disability rights movement tries to teach— that it's all one struggle and we are in it together.

◆

Cuba's disability policy is conveniently set forth in its 1995 Plan of Action for People with Disabilities. Despite the paper shortage, there are copies for all of us. I'm excited to get a handout. It's in ordinary bureaucratic prose, far simpler than Neruda's questions, so I can read it for myself with the help of my Wal-mart electronic translator. It's a concise document, describing thirty-six programs in thirteen areas. It ensures that there will be no architectural barriers in new construction. As to existing barriers, there is a systematic process of inspection and prioritization; however, there's no timetable for barrier removal, since the construction industry is in such disarray. It calls for employment in regular jobs. In education, there are provisions to ensure that special schools prepare students for higher education and for productive work. However, mainstreaming is still a matter for study and experimentation. The plan is silent about personal assistance services. How does a quadriplegic Cuban get out of bed in the morning? The whole issue seems to be off the radar, as it is in the United States outside of movement circles.

The plan reveals a system where well-intentioned experts decide what's best for people with disabilities—as they decide for people without disabilities. There's not much about choice or freedom. But then, I ask myself, what does freedom really mean for the average crip in our system? Living hand-to-mouth in the community or languishing in a nursing home, the average crip is guaranteed liberty and due process—but not health care, housing, or a living wage. Knowing how little choice there is at the bottom of the pecking order, I'm impressed by a society where inequality is not accepted as a regrettable fact of life. In Cuba, inequality is intolerable—it's unpatriotic!

The material and social achievements of the Cuban Revolution are undeniable. A government official tells the conference: "The promise of the Revolution was to enable every person to enjoy life and to contribute to social transformation." That promise remains unfulfilled, but our own society has never even promised so much.

✦

Anne has been spending time with Beth and me by day and going out with some blind guys at night, a pretty grueling schedule. At home, she runs a greenhouse and is keen to see the botanical gardens. With a few more hours of meetings under our belts, Beth and I decide to go along.

Visitors are normally taken around on a motor cart, but there's no lift or wheelchair parking place or anything like the kind of seat I might sit in. We say we'd like to walk. It's very hot, they say. We understand. The park is very big, they say. We know; we will see only so much as we can walk through. Can we have a map? No, no paper to make maps. Beth and Anne study the map on the ticket window and plan a route. I have no directional sense and I'll go where I'm pushed.

There is great concern that we will perish walking around the gardens; repeatedly they make us decline the cart I can't sit in. We set out and I'm happy, being rolled around in the tropical heat, only a little concerned about Beth and Anne's exertions as they drag me over paths the jungle is beginning to reclaim. Our introductory map study has told us each area represents some particular part of the world. We rely on Anne's botanical expertise to tell us where we are: Indochina, Northern Brazil. . . . To me it all looks like Cuba.

The place is vast. The unmarked paths seem to be going in circles, but every time we get to a crossroads, an old man rides by on his bike and points back, urging us to retreat to the restaurant. We press onward. Anne points to a tree. "Here's one you should recognize," she says. We don't. "It's a magnolia! You have magnolias in South Carolina!"

Now I can see it, but this isn't a genteel Southern magnolia. This is a monster deviant Land of the Dinosaurs magnolia, unlike anything I've ever imagined.

We are the only brave souls walking through the park. The motor carts come by rarely. The bicycle man, in green work pants, no shirt on his leathery skin, seems to be our escort, instructed to keep a distance but to be sure we find our way back to the restaurant.

We are far from civilization, way out in the African veldt. We think it's time to head back, but now we're not sure how. The bicycle man is nowhere in sight. Beth and Anne make a guess, choose a route, and on we go. I have no idea. Even though I haven't burned a calorie from exertion, I'm getting hungry and awfully tired and thirsty. I hate to think how Beth and Anne feel after dragging their bodies and mine through the heat. Still no bicycle man to point us to the restaurant. Maybe North American fools are given only so many chances to save our silly lives, and then we're on our own.

We clear a stand of trees and in the distance see a small building. A shed or maybe the restaurant. We make a slow progression, hoping it has water, food, people who know the way out.

We make out a sign. The word *soda.*

"They have soda!" I say.

We strain to figure out what kind, not that we care, so long as it's wet.

We make out another word. *Galleta.*

"Chicken soda?" I don't know which of us says it, but for the briefest moment we all believe it and think it sounds acceptable. Anything, anything wet, even if during this special period it must be made from poultry parts. Far more appealing than soda crackers.

✦

I'm a fairly vehement disability rights advocate. "You can't put a price tag on civil rights," I say, whenever someone mentions the cost of barrier removal, personal assistance, or job accommodations. Cuba shakes me a little. If you can't get paper to print phone books, spare parts to keep factories going, bricks, mortar, and paint—how much can you spend on disability rights? Who gets priority? Disabled Cubans or disabled tourists whose money can bring in more goods? Should a computer be used to train scores of university students or enable one child with cerebral palsy to communicate? Scarcity means there are winners and losers.

And scarcity is laid at the door of the United States. "Inadequate services are not due to a lack of political will," an official from the Ministry of Labor and Social Security tells us, "but due to the cruel embargo from the North." Ironically, the embargo—aimed at undercutting public support for the Cuban government for these thirty-five years—has the opposite effect. People pull together when faced with an external enemy.

I wish the United States could be on their side instead. I can't help being impressed by this ramshackle society, tackling the biggest social problems in the most trying circumstances.

"Every morning," says one official, "we wake up believing in our dreams because we have seen them become real."

It's propaganda, I know. But it's impossible not to be moved, in Cuba at this time in history. Cuba was a Spanish colony for four hundred years, a U.S. outpost for sixty years, a Soviet satellite for thirty years. And now, for the first time since 1492, Cuba is in charge of its own destiny—and thumbing its nose at the world's remaining superpower. I head home hoping Cuba will find a way to adapt to a changing world without surrendering the vision that makes it unique.

However it goes, I hope to return. Next time, perhaps it will be as in 1959, before the embargo. Cuba will again be near the American South. We'll drive the van to the tip of Florida, over the Keys, onto a ferry, and across the island. I'll roll out onto my lift and inhale that delicious air that's like home, only more so. I'll find these people, now connected to my world, but still struggling, daring to hope, believing in their dreams and challenging me, even past the age of forty, to believe in mine.

8

Getting Thrown

My little gray 1986 E&J Marathon has been through the mill, poor thing. In August 2001, on the way home from a fine visit with Laura Hershey in Denver, Delta Airlines managed to shred its wiring. Determined to get it in shape before Delta takes it and me to Tucson in October, I am in the repair shop on the morning of September 11. As each event is reported—second tower hit! the Pentagon!—we stop to say, "Good God!" and "It doesn't seem real!" In fact, it doesn't seem real, or not the kind of right-here reality we can do something about, so after the obligatory exclamations, we return to our discussion of my intermittently failing electric brakes. As the planes explode with all their contents (including, we learn later, one disability rights activist who is with those who fought back and crashed in Pennsylvania), we are swapping stories about airlines doing damage to wheelchairs. As I look back, I'm amazed. Everyone in the shop has a tale.

A few days later, as hopes of survivors are being abandoned, I am on the phone with the shop. My brakes are still misfiring. Delta will feel really righteous and patriotic next time it inspects my chair, I rant; they'll rip up my cables looking for terrorist weapons. The Marathon is too old for the abuse. For my next trip, I need a push chair with good brakes and a seat belt.

All right, they'll lend me a portable chair. While I'm away, they'll fix the Marathon and start the long-promised overhaul of a 1993 E&J X-caliber a friend gave me when he upgraded. Still, I fuss, "So, when I get home, I'll find two beautiful vintage power chairs in reliable working condition, right?"

I'm ashamed to admit to being so selfish, downright crass, impossibly insular. Maybe I can blame Charleston. It's an insular place, or, more precisely, peninsular. On our slim strip of city between two rivers on the edge of the ocean, we don't worry overmuch about what happens far away.

A big East Coast catastrophe does have an impact; some of us pass some frantic hours, donate to the victims' funds, or watch TV with horrid fascination—just as we do when there's a hurricane or earthquake. It's horrible, sure, but September 11 doesn't stir the same passions here that it seems to be rousing elsewhere. I don't know why. Maybe, living on a geological fault line and hurricane gateway, we've never felt invulnerable, and therefore can't experience shattered confidence now. Maybe we lack the energy for nationalistic fervor, given the force of our subnational allegiances to family, city, and region. Maybe our history is too vivid. Here, "the flag" means the stars and bars, not the stars and stripes. For many of us, often in opposing ways, the Civil War remains more real than any contemporary horror—more real than the fervid freelance terror of September 11, more real than the coolheaded government-sponsored terror that preceded it and now comes in its wake.

Or maybe I'm just making excuses.

◆

The October trip to Tucson is bad from the moment Beth sits on her airline seat and gets soaked with fluid or fluids unknown.

In the airport restaurant, I get food stuck in my throat. It's probably stress. In the confusion of the airport food court, eating under time pressure intensified by increased security, I probably failed to pay attention and swallowed a piece of dry white chicken meat no throat could handle. I tell myself it could happen to anyone. But it also happened—to me—two days ago, in the calm of my office as I ate a kind of soft pasta I have enjoyed many times without incident. That blockage lasted not quite two hours.

I'm still blocked when Beth and I again take off, strapped side by side and acting calm. The blockage isn't immediately dangerous, but until it clears, I can't swallow anything, even my saliva. I have to spit into a paper cup. When the cup gets full, Beth has to empty it. Swallowing has been difficult for many years, but this is different. Lately I've noticed a droop under my chin. This could suggest the failure of a muscle group, a progression of my neuromuscular disease. Or it could indicate that at age forty-four I'm getting flabby, as people do.

I try to force the thing down. I try to force it up. I try to relax. In my mind, I'm sweet-talking my throat, apologizing for so rudely shoving that big hunk of chicken down, asking it to forgive me, begging it to please open up and let the food pass.

On the last hour of the last leg of the flight, I swallow again, make one more attempt like all those countless others. The lump pops down. It's been seven hours. I am in tears, overcome, beyond happy to have this orifice back. Shaking for joy, I take in some ginger ale we get from the flight attendant, feel it flow wet and cold through an unobstructed muscle tube down to my stomach, where enzymes have been building up, waiting for some sugar to send to my blood. I'm nearly wrecked by hunger and thirst and frustration. That release. So easy, so fast, so lovely when it came. Why did it take so long?

I promise my throat that I won't give it anything the least

bit challenging until I am home again. Beth doesn't need the aggravation. Neither do I.

◆

"Aaron, you're out of your gourd," I say.

"Yes, I am, but what is your point?"

"My point is, even if we paper this whole convention with our cool yellow flyers, you're nuts if you think large numbers will come. People don't come out for this topic unless you kidnap them or something." Our Tucson convention workshop is on disability institutions. If this topic generally isn't considered sexy or even controversial, that's no accident. For over one hundred years, a powerful medical-industrial complex has trained us to think that people judged unable to care for themselves must, for their own good and the good of society, be consigned to government-funded lockup. Even forward-looking thinkers don't recognize the incarceration of some two million Americans in nursing homes, psychiatric facilities, and other institutions as a human rights violation. Our crowd ought to see it. We're the National Lawyers Guild, lawyers and legal workers organized, as our every publication says, to the end that human rights shall be held more sacred than property interests.

September 11 has turned our convention upside down. Originally, we planned to debate pushing for the impeachment of certain "justices" of the U.S. Supreme Court for unlawfully making George W. Bush president and for other high crimes against the possibility of democracy. Post–September 11, the "justices" deserve impeachment no less, but the times have us on the defensive against a new wave of militarism and repression. The Disability Rights Committee workshop must compete with the national emergency—urgent discussions of government spying on dissidents, mass arrests of demonstrators, suspension of civil rights, the illegal invasion of Afghanistan. Our workshop remains on the agenda only because Aaron fought for it like crazy.

"So what are we doing to MDA?" Aaron asks. "What's the plan?"

Tucson happens to be the site of the Muscular Dystrophy Association's corporate compound. My decision to attend this meeting came on the heels of a spectacular offensive from Jerry Lewis that sparked a fine counteroffensive. Back in May, Lewis told a TV interviewer, "You're a cripple in a wheelchair and you don't want pity? Stay in your house!" The audio clip, captured on Laura's Web site, has proven highly inflammatory—it gets Aaron, for one, in a lather, and gets more protesters out in more cities than ever before. But a week after our best-ever Labor Day, street protests go out of style and Lewis's remark no longer outrages. I ask MDA's corporate brass to meet with me while I'm in Tucson. They decline. A series of back-and-forth faxes culminates in their claim that their large public art collection will be packed up for travel just when I happen to be coming. This looks like fodder for a They-Refuse-to-Meet-with-Critics press conference. Even in these times, I figure, that might make Tucson local news. It's not much, but whatever I can organize in MDA's home turf will enhance my unmatched antitelethon stats; I could claim fourteen events in four cities in three states! Most miles traveled! But it is not to be.

"Sorry, Aaron. This morning I put in calls to the local papers, TV news, talk radio even. No producer or assignments editor would talk to me. No one would take a message. No one wants news tips. Not one newspaper. Not one station. It's the damnedest thing."

The anthrax scare has begun back east and everyone, everywhere, is modifying mail procedures, speculating about the transmission and effects, lining up cipro, spreading rumors, and otherwise getting in on the scare. Local news no longer exists. There is only one story and the disability rights movement isn't part of it.

◆

Even Aaron at full tilt couldn't get our workshop a good time slot. We convene at eight-thirty A.M., go for ninety minutes, then break for several hours before part two. The stellar panel we imagined we'd recruit doesn't want to travel post–9/11 so it's up to in-house talent: me (described in the yellow flyer as "hardcore crip"), Aaron ("crazy"), and our fellow committee pillar Brian ("not disabled yet") East.

We've put the chairs in a circle—it's a roundtable with no table. Brian, a "normal" public interest lawyer, is the natural moderator. Aaron and I are the panel. The audience is comprised of Aaron's wife and five or six people who are either kin or coworkers or former coworkers of Brian. As I am asking myself why we didn't do like the sane, nondisabled committees and yield up our time to the national crisis, two law students come in. Having chosen this discussion over all the concurrent demands on their attention, they look eager to go forth and change the world. Addressing the Guild tape recorder, Brian goes on the record and asks us to introduce ourselves and our connections to the issue.

"I'm Aaron Frishberg. The institutions to which I've been admitted—chronologically, not divided by type—are Spring Grove State Hospital, Maryland; Gracie Square Hospital, New York City; Hillside Hospital, New York City; Bellevue Psychiatric Center, New York City; Central Islip State Hospital, Long Island; Greystone State Psychiatric Hospital, New Jersey; City College of New York; Bellevue Psychiatric Hospital, again; New York Law School; Bellevue Psychiatric Center, again. I'm in solo practice in New York City, representing primarily people with psychiatric disabilities."

This is a hard introduction to follow. I've been behind the walls only as a visitor, and that's been enough to scare me into seeing this work as vital and urgent. "I'm Harriet Johnson. Throughout my life I have needed help from other people to bathe, dress, and get out of bed in the morning. Because of luck and privilege, I have people—paid and volunteer—to do that work for me in my home. Because of that help, I am free to run my own life. But my freedom hangs by a thread. A serious financial setback, one family catastrophe, one medical complication at the wrong time, and I could be locked up for life. It has happened to many people I know because they have needs exactly like mine. My solo practice in Charleston emphasizes disability and I'm currently serving on our governor's task force on home care."

With Brian's questioning, we talk through the politics and economics that got us where we are. Aaron describes the revolving door of psychiatric hospitals and the limbo of board-and-care homes for the chronically crazy, all following the ebb and flow of public funds. I lay out how old people with multiple, creeping disabilities, people with intellectual disabilities, and people like me wind up with a one-way ticket to nowhere. For all, "placement" is determined not by our needs, not by our desires, but by what the government will pay for. Public policies rob us of freedom and security just as surely as would a late-night knock on the door by the secret police. Part one ends with a teaser—a possibility that change is in the winds.

Weeks ago, I arranged for Brian and Aaron to take me to lunch—literally take me, pushing me there, so Beth could go off with a friend from Phoenix. Brian drops my papers into my bag, and I tell Aaron how to work those tight brakes and ease my casters over bumps. We're in a walkable university neighborhood with good sidewalks. The chair rides well, but it's like spending a few days in a borrowed body. The seat has a thick cushion. For pressure control and balance, I laid atop the cushion the strange collection of rags I normally sit on. Now, I'm taller than usual. I've moved from crotch-height to waist height. Interesting.

With some other Guild people, we find a table outdoors at a Middle Eastern restaurant. Hummus and babaghanoush are perfect. I ask Aaron to crumble up the falafel and drown it in yoghurt sauce, an abomination perhaps, but easy swallowing. I am grateful for a chance to refuel without time pressure. That throat blockage disrupted two meals and left me weak; I have some catching up to do.

I expect only the tape recorder to be there, but we return for part two of our workshop to find our remnant regathered, including those law students. We move to the good news: a landmark Supreme Court decision no one's heard of, *Olmstead v. L.C.* By establishing that disability institutions are segregation and that unnecessary segregation is discrimination under the ADA, this 1999 ruling gives force to the movement's demand for a world in which no one is ever locked up simply because that's what the government will pay for. Services must be offered at home; beyond that, we must root out the notion that needing help means needing to be controlled and supervised. Ultimately, we aim to build communities where people with disabilities get not only the help we need but the chance to contribute.

Since 1999, I've been deeply involved in the minutiae of in-home services, studying what's worked in communities around the nation. However, I'm rarely asked to think more generally about what kind of world I want. That's what the Guild does for me. Even for only a handful of people and a tape no one will hear, this discussion has been valuable.

✦

The hotel room I share with Beth is the first in my life that has both a view and a window low enough for me to see it. We can't believe it. On the horizon, mountains, jagged and rust-red like broken pots. Each night, a sunset, lurid purple, orange, crimson. Blue shadows. Then—even here in the city—bright stars on a black velvet sky. I've seen all this in innumerable cowboy movies but assumed I was looking at matte painting.

The meetings have been tense, but between them I've managed some lolling. I am beginning to feel rested, rare when I'm away from home. Yet getting out of bed is hard. The borrowed chair's seat belt buckle is in the wrong place and presses on a protruding rib. After hours strapped tight, not moving, the pressure goes from annoying to painful, like having a rock in your sock. But soon I'll be back in my maybe-fixed E&J Marathon. Back home.

Late on Sunday morning, the convention has closed and we're milling around. In high dudgeon, Aaron is remonstrating about the fact that the charter bus that took a Guild group to a meeting in Mexico yesterday had no wheelchair lift. I opted against the trip and now feel like saying "Oh well," but Aaron is abrim with righteousness and expects an outpouring from me. He seems to be low in whatever neurotransmitter allows most of us to shrug off injustices that aren't directly affecting us at the moment. I don't know the technical term, but whatever the diagnosis, our world will be a poorer place when they find a cure or effective treatment for it.

Beth appears as scheduled to take me away. A local Guild lawyer named Elizabeth stops us to thank me for a law practice tip I gave at a workshop last year. "I'm really glad it worked," I tell her. "Let me ask you for a tip in return. We want to do a little sightseeing this afternoon. Beth can lift me into a taxi. Can you think of an easy one-stop excursion?"

She offers better; she'll show us around in her SUV. From my speakers' bio, she knows I hold the World Endurance Record for Telethon Protesting; MDA's compound is a bit far, but we could ride by. There are interesting historical sites nearby. Sounds great.

Elizabeth drives around to the front of the hotel. I've never been in one of these tanks before. Beth stuffs me in the front seat, and I discover my floppy body has become unadapted to sitting in a car seat since the last time I tried it, when we took a taxi to the botanical gardens in Cuba. With improvised padding, I get stabilized, and finally we're off. Elizabeth proves to be a fine informant about the politics of scarce water, local voting trends, and the names of trees that are stiff and prickly even though to me they look like willows.

Our main stop is the Mission of San Javier. Beth lifts me into the borrowed chair. "Leave the seat belt off," I say, thinking of that tender spot on my rib. The church gleams white against the blueness of what is now midday, spectacularly placed on horizontal red emptiness, ringed by those distant red mountains. The site is familiar; it's represented Spanish America in scores of Hollywood movies. To my eyes, whose idea of landscape normality is the jungle of the Lowcountry, it looks like the moon.

We crunch over hard-packed gravel toward the church. Near the entrance, the gravel goes soft and a slope tilts me precariously forward. "Turn around!" I holler. It's a dumb power chair reaction; when I'm driving and a slope throws me off kilter, I turn hard against the slope to right myself. I'm about to say I'm not stable in my seat when I'm off my seat, tumbling, unable to catch myself, unable to break my fall, unable even to ball up. Body parts slam into the ground: foot, knee, knee, cheek, chin, shoulder, arms. It's more a splat than a thud. I'm a mess, sunny-side down, on hard red dirt.

"Harriet," Beth says, "tell me what you want me to do."

I don't know where my body parts are, though I know they're here somewhere. Her voice tells me which way is up.

"I guess—untangle me—straighten me out—on my back."

In a moment's stillness, I know she's using that dancer's ana-lytical mind, choreographing a way to move me without twist-ing, scraping, pinching, or breaking me. All the protocols would say leave me to paramedics, but the last thing I need is people who think they know what they're doing.

Beth crawls over my back. By reference to her body, I know my behind is up in the air and my spine is doubled up against itself. She slides her forearms around my trunk, encircles my arms, cradles my legs with hers, sets her head beside mine, and turns. In midturn, there is an instant of blinding pain that shoots through my right shoulder with a deep low pop, and then it's down to an ordinary knife stab, less intense than the pain I was too confused to feel when I was mashed against the ground. I think my shoulder was dislocated, and now it's back in.

Beth rolls onto her back and me on my back on top of her. She lets me have a deep breath and then slides out. She arranges my neck, then back, then arms, then legs. I hurt pretty bad in spots; I'm still confused about what spots, but now I know where my pieces are. I ask for padding on my bony edges. "I'm OK. I'll be OK, if I can just lie here."

I forget I have aspirin in my purse and ask Elizabeth to find some. A woman with a first-aid kit offers Tylenol. They taste like poison but I chew them up, two tablets, enough for a full-sized person. We use some salve and tissue. I've cut my face. A few people have gathered. Beth assures them she can get me up, in a minute, I'm fine. I tell Elizabeth, no, absolutely no, do not call an ambulance. No, I do not need to go to the hospital. If I can lie here awhile, I'll be fine.

I look at this amazing blue sky, empty of everything except this huge yellow sun straight over my head. It's just like the desert, I think, and maybe even say. Someone is standing over me in a big sombrero, no kidding, making a shadow for my face. On the rest of me, the sun's rays feel delicious.

"Harriet," Beth says, "we need to get you up. Do you want to try sitting up here?"

"No, just let me lie here awhile."

Elizabeth says she can bring the car over. I can lie down in the back.

"No, really. Once I pull myself together, I'll be OK. Let me lie here."

Beth is getting adamant. "We need to get you out of here. We're right in front of a church. It's full of people. Harriet, it's high mass. They're starting communion right now. In a few minutes, they're going to let out and we'll be in the middle of a couple hundred devout Spanish-speaking people wanting to help. Maybe looking for a miracle."

Damn. She's right. There's no time to waste. Elizabeth gets the car. The lift from the ground is excruciating but quick. My body fits neatly in the back compartment. I now perceive clearly that my right shoulder and left ankle are the injured spots. With the padding from my chair and stuff from my bag and our purses and a basket of clean laundry Elizabeth has in her SUV, we insulate the pressure points and build soft support for the parts that hurt to move. I make my muscles relax—when it comes to releasing tension, a neuromuscular disease is a great boon—until the pain is gone. When we get going—yes, back to the hotel, not the hospital!—the motion of this little chamber rocking on big rubber tires is profoundly soothing. Pointlessly, we regale one another with accounts of the little calamity we have just experienced and imagine what would have happened if all those good Catholics had come out to find me on the ground beside the empty chair.

I'm fine now. It'll hurt like hell to get me from this cozy spot to that hotel bed, but once it's done, I'll be fine again.

◆

All I need is some nausea medicine. Then I'll be fine. The shoulder hurts so much I can't sit up, but with Beth stretching the joint very slowly, following directions I give by rolling my eyeballs, I'm getting good passive movement with less and less pain. If I don't let the joint freeze up, maybe it'll be bearable tomorrow; I don't have enough muscle tone to get the usual day-after muscle strain. My left foot is excruciating and there's a disquieting creak somewhere above my ankle, but I don't have to walk on it, so it won't be hard to improvise a splint good enough to get me home. We won't know until tomorrow, but maybe tomorrow, maybe the day after that, I'm hoping I'll tolerate sitting up and getting carried in and out of airplanes all the way home.

Now comes this nausea. Like an idiot, I forgot about lunch, then on an empty stomach took four times more Tylenol than I usually take, then remembered I had aspirin and took that, too, and finally ate the only swallowable food on the room service dinner menu—guacamole and refried beans. Why didn't I ask for oatmeal? They could have made some. The shoulder pain has me stuck flat on my back. If I get sick I might aspirate. I want a Tigan suppository to knock out the nausea so Beth and I can sleep.

We ask the front desk if there's a house doctor. No, we should call 911 and go to the emergency room.

We call Elizabeth, hoping she has a doctor friend. She does, a good friend. He says we should call 911 and go to the emergency room.

We call my friend the nurse-attorney in Charleston. She knows dealing with medical people is the last thing I want to do when I'm feeling horrible, but it's not realistic to expect anyone to give me a prescription sight unseen. She means we should call 911 and go to the emergency room. I think about calling my brother the doctor in Minnesota, but he'd say the same thing.

Beth wants me to go to the emergency room. I am gagging and afraid of choking so I agree. Maybe I can get the medicine and get right back out. Beth promises to stay with me for as long as it takes.

Beth calls Elizabeth to tell her we're going, and within five minutes she is in our room, running interference with the paramedics. I'm rolled out on a stretcher down the hall and through the hotel lobby. As we head out, there's Aaron, apparently speechless at the sight of me, all pasty with worry. "She's fine," Beth tells him. "Sprained her shoulder and can't sit up and we're going to get some medicine." To me she mumbles, "I don't know whether to go with you or stay with him. Will he be OK?"

Of course she's joking, but there's a moment of unspoken panic when I think of putting my body under the control of people who aren't in the habit of following my instructions. Stay with me. You promised.

At the emergency room, they don't know what to make of me. The wheelchair—the paramount identity marker in most of my encounters with the nondisabled world—is back at the hotel. Laid out on a gurney, I take on nearly normal form, appear perhaps as a garden-variety anorexic. They've been told I've had a fall, that I cannot stand or sit up, and that I'm nauseated.

What they don't know is how those facts relate to one another and how they don't.

"The fall isn't why I can't walk. I hurt my foot, but probably it's nothing major. I have a neuromuscular disease. I've never walked. It was a fall from a wheelchair. I'm on the stretcher because I can't sit up. I can't sit up because I hurt my shoulder. But the reason I'm here is to get some nausea medicine."

"How long was she unconscious?" they ask.

"I wasn't unconscious. I was very, very conscious all the way through. This isn't concussion nausea. I took aspirin and Tylenol on an empty stomach and ate crazy. I just need something for the nausea. A Tigan suppository would be ideal. And you can splint my foot while I'm here. That would be good."

"First, we need to check you out." All I need is a Tigan suppository and a splint. What's to check out? If they're worried that I might misdiagnose myself, let Elizabeth cook up a legally binding release and I'll sign it. But here in the medical system, this body is no longer my responsibility to care for or neglect by giving directions to others' hands. Here, my body doesn't get what I want unless the medical people get what they want. I submit. I answer questions. I let them look at me, touch me, move me, X-ray me.

They say I have a hairline fracture of the left leg just above the ankle. I need a cast. On the right arm, the X ray shows a thickening of the bone near the shoulder. There is some debate but the consensus is that it's a compression fracture.

"We'll put it in a sling. You'll need to be non-weight-bearing with that shoulder for four to six weeks, but we can give you pain meds so you can fly home tomorrow."

"You said non-weight-bearing for four weeks?"

"Maybe six."

"I can't sit up without putting weight on that joint."

"The sling will carry the weight of your arm."

I try to make them understand it's not the weight of my arm hanging from my body that's the problem; it's the weight of my body hanging from my arm. I sit up by leaning on my elbows, mainly the right elbow. My right shoulder is what holds me up. They don't get it. They want me to sit up and try the sling. But they say the bone may break with weight-bearing; I'm not keen on any risky show-and-tell.

Beth tries to demonstrate my sitting technique. She's limber, but no contortionist. "I wish we had some pictures," she says.

We can get some, from the Internet. I tell them where to find some articles by me with photos of me sitting up.

In a few minutes, the team is huddled around my 1994 temporary campaign photo, which accompanies a funny piece I wrote about being called Doll Baby on the way to court. I'm thinner now, but that photo shows why I can't sit up. They compare it with photos Beth took to go with stories about Cuba and the Democratic convention.

"We're going to admit you," one of them says.

They want my Charleston doctor's name and contact information. Beth has been carrying a doctor's letter that tells the airlines to follow my exact instructions in handling my body, or, better yet, let my own personnel do it. She offers this for the doctor's contact information. "Make a copy of the whole letter," I say. "Read it. It explains all about moving me. It's a good letter," I add. "I wrote it."

The medical people laugh. I'm a little drunk from the shot they've given me.

They talk to one another more than to me. They need to bring in an orthopedist to tell us what to do with the bones, maybe an orthotist to build a brace so I can sit up. They will see how much pain medication I can tolerate. Work on a plan to get me back home.

Why do I need their plan? Why not follow my plan? Give me a Tigan suppository. Splint my foot. Send me back to the hotel. Let me do gentle stretches and go to sleep. Tomorrow I'll feel better. I'll be fine.

✦

It's a teaching hospital where professional types come in packs. Physical therapy and orthotics are cheerful, ready to get to work as soon as orthopedics gives the OK. The dietician pack asks about my food preferences. I've forgotten about my balky throat; Beth remembers to tell them I need soft food. The orthopod pack—the dominant species, it seems—is grim and full of certitude. They have no doubt that the thickened bone near the shoulder is a very fragile compression fracture. They confirm: no weight-bearing. Further orders: no movement.

My shoulder really, really wants to move—with someone's hands pulling slowly, carefully, at my exact direction, to work the kinks out. Even more, my whole body wants to move. At the base of my spine, I am feeling a spot of deep bone-tenderness that could quickly become a pressure sore. I can't turn to get weight off of it without moving my shoulder. Lying still is more dangerous, I think, than movement. Do they know how gently a person with dystrophic muscles can stretch? Have they ever seen a body quite like mine? Not likely.

But I am wiped out, not up to fighting with the pack of orthopods, here on turf where what they say goes. So instead of rejecting their advice—orders, they say!—I demand a pulsating air mattress. They say a special mattress is not considered medically necessary until after a pressure sore has developed. "The standard of care requires turning every two hours," I say. "You can't turn me. We need to do something else." They decide my tender spot might be a sore; because they can't turn me to look at it, they can justify the mattress.

An IV is giving me a steady flow of medicine, nourishment, and water. My saliva is as thin as water, maybe even normal; usually, I restrict my fluids to regulate my bathroom schedule. With all this effortless intake, I might gain weight here. This is good. Each drip—there's morphine in the bag—makes me a bit more placid. It's taking huge effort to fuss and inquire about the air mattress and keep them on their toes. Part of me no longer cares, is happy to drift. I close my eyes.

I am vaguely aware of Beth's presence, directing the handling of my body. The air mattress is here. They snatch the sheet I'm lying on and slide me onto another bed. There is pain. Sharp, stabbing. Right shoulder, left ankle. It's so startling I cry out, but it seems like someone else's pain, not mine. It is not felt so much as perceived, experienced at some remove, as though through telepathy. It causes no distress.

They power up the mattress. Almost imperceptibly, it inflates under me, raising my feet, then my hips, and then rolling up my curvy spine to my shoulders, neck, and head. It holds its breath for several seconds, then exhales in a slow wheeze under my body, taking me into its soft hollows, sinking and raising me with the rhythm of a giant animal lost in sleep.

It takes Beth and two nurse's aides working together to get a bedpan under me, clean me up, and give me a bath. Beth positions me and gives the directions I'd give if I weren't so blotto. One aide is tasked to keep my foot at the one angle that isn't agony. The other aide washes me. Despite all their care, it's painful. It's also as delicious as any pleasure I've ever known. The same drug that distances the pain makes the pleasure more keen. I always enjoy a warm bed bath, but this one, as I lie still under the hands of these three women—four strange hands, two hands I've known all my life—as I float in my opium haze over this billowing breathing mattress with its magical pumps. . . .

It's the kind of pleasure that could make a person give up the fight—whatever fight—for good.

The professional packs appear for the rituals of morning rounds. Through my haze, I hear the expected questions and imagine I'm giving the expected answers. Beth lets me know I'm being snide. Well, isn't that expected? Of course I'm snide when they're being so condescending and, even worse, treating me like a tragic case, someone in a horribly advanced state of deterioration, someone who's outlived any reasonable quality of life.

Wait a minute. That's not what I'm getting through my haze.

A woman doctor seems to be in charge. "Ms. Johnson," she says, "it's Monday morning, late morning in South Carolina. Has your office been called?"

"Yes, my sister called."

They turn to Beth. Is someone covering my deadlines? Has my calender been cleared? There should be another lawyer in charge. Beth explains that I have a good secretary and there are other lawyers in the office, not partners, but helpful colleagues.

This is something I've never encountered in a hospital: professional solicitude and respect. Other than my longtime primary care doctor, never has a medical provider acknowledged my responsibilities. In past hospitalizations, I've dealt with people who refer to my law practice in the past tense, give me Medicaid paperwork after I've presented my bar insurance card, show by every word and deed that they see my occupation as disabled and my life as nearing its end—and none too soon. They charge in to toss this or that piece of me here or there, denying me dominion over my own body.

Here, it's "We'd like to take your blood pressure. Can I get your arm here and lift it up?"

The blood pressure cuff tightens. "Ms. Johnson, we've been reading your Internet articles," the vital-statistics taker says.

"I've always wanted to go to Cuba. Is it hard to get them to let you in?" Loopily, I explain that Cuba is happy to have visitors from the United States; the problem is with our government.

Later a medical student is talking about the Democratic convention. Then the doctor in charge compliments my story about dressing up for court. She likes the nice linen dress I'm still wearing. It seems my collected Internet works are in my chart and being read by the entire treatment team. My stories tell them that, yes, I'm a crip in a dramatic state of decrepitude, but also, I have a life. The stories put my current predicament in context. I'm yanked from my natural habitat, helpless as a roach on its back, zonked on narcotics—and on another trip with my sister, a trip that has gone bad, but which, with luck, we'll survive with another story to tell.

Elizabeth, who has offered copious help and solidarity, brings our luggage from the hotel. She also brings food, talking books, back issues of *The Nation* and *In These Times* and a link to the world beyond the hospital. We are still just slight acquaintances, but the staff thinks she is another sister. She seems almost that way to us.

Elizabeth leaves with our dirty laundry, and I ask Beth to plug in a talking book by John le Carré. Zoomy, I deliver my oft-stated opinion that when the dust settles on the twentieth century, Le Carré's *A Perfect Spy* will be considered one of the greats. Alas, I discover, this one is one of the un-greats, less spy story than gangster story, written after the cold war has ended and there's no moral dichotomy for moral ambiguity to play against. I'm in no state to follow the pointless complicated plot. No matter. There is the pleasant sound of this voice reading to me, so unhurried, so relaxed, so full, and just as British as Winnie the Pooh. I let the lovely sounds wash around me, the lovely air mattress pulse under me, the lovely morphine drip through me, and it's a lovely afternoon.

Even when one of Le Carré's characters gets suddenly garrot-
ted, I am entirely undisturbed.

◆

I hear Beth through my haze. "She's getting too much. She's not
fussing, not throwing fits—not even carrying on. She's—gone."

The doctors discuss my dosage. My chart says I weigh
seventy-five pounds—the number I pulled from the air when
they asked me.

"Ms. Johnson, what do you usually take for pain?"

I have to think. "One baby aspirin."

"And that works?"

"Yes," I mumble from my spot on cloud nine.

Beth interjects. "She doesn't take medicine. She's drug-free.
I don't think she's ever been drunk or stoned in her life."

This would be a good time to tell them that I was drunk,
once, but it was an accident and I didn't like it. However, I
don't have the energy to tell a story or even give the teaser.
Maybe I am getting too much morphine. "Let me have some in
the morning," I say, "for the bath. Otherwise, I'll be OK."

I doze and the dope wears off. Without it, I'm comfortable
enough physically, at my ease on the moving mattress with Beth
periodically stretching my uninjured body parts. But emotionally, I'm suddenly a mess. John le Carré no longer lulls. We try
the TV. The endless anthrax talk is too distressing. We switch to
a nature documentary. That's too disconnected, out of time.

Nothing engages my mind—until it is overtaken by a
spreading fear that I'm on the cusp of my final decline. I imagine the official story. She was doing so well until she had that
fall. She didn't heal right. She was too weak to bounce back. She
never got out of bed. She never got out of the hospital. There
were complications . . . a sore, an infection. She needed total
nursing care. She had to go into a nursing home.

The time had come.

This is what happens. It might be fast—a wrong swallow goes to aspiration pneumonia, a blood clot borne of immobility goes to the heart. Or it might be slow, painfully bureaucratic. At the ER, I got diagnostic codes that call for a cast, a sling, and release. What if the bean counters decide I don't need to be in the hospital? Do I go back to the hotel? Beth can't deal with me in this condition, not all alone, not indefinitely. So add to my acute diagnostic codes my chronic ones. With them, the funders say I need long-term subacute care: nursing home placement. The nursing home's imperative is to keep you. They eat your money first, and when it's consumed, they feed on Medicaid. People like me don't get out. This is what I was explaining the other day, a lifetime ago, in that workshop with Aaron.

I need to get back home, where I can earn the money that pays for my life and freedom. If I don't get back soon, I might become one more person trapped in the disability gulag until I die.

✦

The hospital social worker is surprised that the bar medical plan hasn't yet rejected my continuing residence in this hospital. He warns me about my diagnostic codes and the arguable appropriateness of a nursing home. "If they start making any noises," I say, "tell me right away. I do know some lawyers."

I report truthfully that the pressure spot remains tender. They keep me on the expensive air mattress. The nausea has passed, but they have kept the IV running and put blood thinners in the mix. This acute treatment helps justify continuing acute hospital placement. Even so, the social worker says I should be prepared. He gives Beth a list of air ambulance companies so we can get quotes. He's contacted the medical plan about transporting me, but isn't hopeful. I might have to pay for it myself.

The packs of professionals visit and I'm my old self but desperate. They assure me that I'll be back to my life in no time. "Don't you get it?" I fuss. "I'm going to be laid up a long time. Maybe this is how it ends!" They validate my concerns, acknowledge that my injuries are serious for me and recovery will take time. "I don't have time!" I carry on. "I need to get back now! I can't afford to keep my office open if I'm not working. My secretary can only hold it together for so long. I've been hanging by a thread! I need to be back at work next week at the latest." No one can say anything right. Part of me knows that I'm being unreasonable, but I am powerless to stop.

"Should we call one of your lawyer friends?" Beth asks. "How about Susan?"

"I hate to bother her," I say. "A while back and for good reason, she gave written notice in a memo that she was done with rescuing all of us whenever we get into scrapes."

"Well, who else is there?"

"No one nearly so good."

"Let's call her. Harriet, this is serious. We need the best."

✦

The very sound of Susan's voice is comforting. It's a thing she has. I apologize for violating the terms of her memo. She cuts me off. "It's OK. You need help. And who is better than me?" She's heard the story from my secretary, who tells a story well. "Don't be afraid. You're not going into a nursing home. Not even for a minute. It won't happen."

"Susan, it happens all the time."

"I'll get on the insurance people right away. And if all else fails, I can borrow a hearse and go out there and get you."

"A hearse?"

"Yeah. I've driven a hearse, when I was in college to help out a friend. A hearse would work fine. Bernard would lend us one."

"I'm sure he would." I call him Judge, which is what he was until the 1994 election sent him back to law practice and the family funeral business. Remembering my cozy bed in the back of Elizabeth's SUV, rocking as the road rolled under me, I think a hearse odyssey with Beth and Susan might be fun, particularly if I can get a four-day supply of morphine to go. Renting an SUV would be simpler, but then the Judge wouldn't have the pleasure of complaining about getting sucked into Susan's scheme.

"But that's if all else fails," Susan says. "I'll start working on funding an air ambulance. Has the hospital started the process?"

She has a stream of lawyerly questions. Exhausted, I hand her over to Beth.

✦

It's been nearly a week, long enough to develop routines. I drug up for my morning bath, come down by lunchtime, and then dither, stew, and receive the continuing delegations of students and professionals. Sitters come to spell Beth. She has discovered places where she can get e-mail free and food cheap. Even when I'm paying expenses, she likes a deal and pretends that hanging out in her corner of my hospital room beats being at her job.

There are contacts with the world outside. Elizabeth phones and visits. About twice a day, my secretary calls for instructions and reports the news. Some long-awaited fees have come in. Good, I'll need them; the first air ambulance quotes have come in at $25,000 and $30,000. "Oh," I say, "forgive me. I haven't mentioned the flowers. They're astounding. The talk of the hospital. No one has ever seen anything like them. Tell everyone thank you."

"I told them you didn't want a fuss," she says, "but people wanted to do something. I figured one big one would be better than the funeral-in-progress look."

Definitely. Based on the size and the variety of exotic blooms I can't name, I figure most of my office mates gave two or three dollars and a couple of lawyers lacking social savvy dropped in twenties.

Beth has e-mailed Laura in Denver so cripdom will know where I am. I get a card she made on her speech-activated computer. There's a clip-art rodeo cowboy being dragged across the dirt and a message: "Sorry to hear you got thrown." It's another lifeline to the world I want to reenter.

Progress is being made on my behalf. Beth finds a local air ambulance company that's hungry for business. The price will be around $10,000, a bargain we now think and well within the limits of my National Lawyers Guild Mastercard ("Building socialism with every charge," I like to say). They will go whenever I'm ready, on short notice. On Friday, Susan is encouraging about coverage. It's not resolved, but looking good. "We'll have to transfer you to the hospital here, not straight home, maybe just for a day, because your policy covers medical transportation from out-of-network back into network. You're WAY out of network there." Meanwhile, she's checking into an air mattress at home. I may be stuck in my bed for a while, but at least I'll be back in my habitat, within reach of my office runner. I have new hope that I'll dodge the institutional bullet—this time.

Nothing wears me down like hope. I'm unsettled, discontented, frustrated. I'm crazy lying here while other people handle my phone calls and documentation.

I think I'm maintaining a good face, but Beth calls Susan again. "We need to go ahead and move her. She's hitting critical mass." Beth puts down the phone. "Susan says come on home. Put it on your Mastercard and she'll sort it out later."

OK. It's past time. Let's build some socialism with a $10,000 charge for the hungry, cut-rate air ambulance company. As my mother says, it's only money.

✦

By the time we work out the schedule, it's late Saturday night in Charleston. On Sunday morning, we locate Susan at church. She pulls my doctor out of the same church to arrange my admission. The hospital social worker is impressed.

An ambulance crew arrives and the jerk from bed to gurney is a jolting reminder that I'm still a mess. I'm drugged up again, but not with the stuff that disconnects me from pain; there's no doubt that the broken leg bone and ruined shoulder belong to me. I say good-bye to the air mattress, my dear friend and gentle comforter for the past week, and within minutes of landing on the gurney, the spot at the base of my spine is screaming at me to turn over. I can't. Beth tries to lift my hips to give me some relief but it's nearly impossible in the tight space of the ambulance.

At the airfield, we meet a plane whose insides are not as spacious as the ambulance I've just left. Another jolt and I'm switched to their gurney. They've been told about my pressure point and have promised padding, but all we get is a faded cotton quilt. We watch the boss peel off the crew's "spending money" from a fat roll of big bills ("I won it playing golf," he says) and wonder if we were wise to go with the cut-rate hungry company. Oh well. We've given up our hospital room and the ambulance that brought us here is gone.

While Beth signs my Mastercard authorization, I am again lying under the noonday sky. Here, the red ground is dressed in black asphalt, visually disguised as anywhere in the world. But the desert Southwest is still recognizable. The sky is as blue and empty as it was one week ago when I lay in front of the Mission Church of San Javier. The air is too dry to carry scents.

Beth goes on first and then I'm jammed into this capsule with a silent Mexican pilot and a cowgirl EMT, straight from some contemporary southwestern outlaw road movie. The last to board is the RN, a man who seems boyish, prepubescent, despite his gray hair. He's compact and lithe but still I don't see how he'll get to his seat; my gurney takes up the aisle. He crouches above me, puts his hands on the gurney, and in one continuous flip, he's in his place. Before my heart has had time to get pounding properly, he's grinning for all the world like a gymnast who's just nailed the perfect dismount. "My gymnastics training still comes in handy!" he says.

What the hell. I ask the gymnast for a suppository for the trip—the antinausea medicine that was all I wanted when I went to the hospital—and we're off. It's a rattling, shaking contraption, but we're in the air. Headed back east.

The hours wear on my tailbone. Beth tries to shift my weight, but turning over is still impossible. When we can, Beth and I close our eyes. When our eyes are open, they meet the unnaturally bright eyes of the gymnast RN.

"We're over jungle," Beth tells me. "It's gone from red and beige to green." Louisiana, I bet, some place where the ground is soft and spongy and the air is saturated with moisture, thick with smells, rich with life and death. A while after that, I can see for myself. Clouds. Pink. Lavender. Peach. The delicate pastels of a southeastern sunset. We're nearly home.

✦

After a week of respectful treatment at the Tucson hospital, the institutional smarminess of Southern medical culture comes as a shock. Against the assaults of medical officiousness, I truly need the constant attendance of someone familiar with my body and willing to do my bidding. Here, family and friends and paid workers are available to take turns; Beth goes home to her daughter and her job and I write another entry in my book of unpayable debts.

Charleston's orthopods order more X rays and decide I can try to move my shoulder, try to sit up, try to get back to my life. My brother Mac, the sound engineer, is the one who figures out how to get me up: when he has a night shift with me, he raises me slowly with one long arm and with the other stuffs my nooks and crannies with stabilizing towels. A day later, I am back home. There, a visiting physical therapist teaches me the same stretching exercises I was doing with Beth in the hotel right after I got thrown. A week later, I am back in a power chair—not my old Marathon, but the big black hand-me-down X-caliber the shop has overhauled in my absence.

My first trip to the office is on a Saturday. Sitting up hurts and the jostling in the van stresses my weight-bearing shoulder. Mac relocated my wheelchair controller to eliminate one especially painful movement, but still it's almost impossible to turn right. Never mind, I'll turn left until I've turned right. It's Saturday. No one will see my odd way of driving—or the pajamas I'm wearing.

I creep into the atrium of our building and am greeted by our boisterous pineapple fountain, bubbling and spurting welcome. But what's this? Just to the left of the fountain, they've placed an American flag, stars and stripes hanging limp and lifeless from a pole set on the floor. On the right, perhaps out of respect for differing views, is the palmetto state flag. I've been away for less than a month, and look what they do! The arrangement and proportions are all wrong: at not-quite-uniform height, they line up in one silly too-wide row.

Flag. Fountain. Flag.

9

Unspeakable Conversations

He insists he doesn't want to kill me. He simply thinks it would have been better, all things considered, to have given my parents the option of killing the baby I once was, and to let other parents kill similar babies as they come along, and thereby avoid the suffering that comes with lives like mine and satisfy the reasonable preferences of parents for a different kind of child. It has nothing to do with me. I should not feel threatened.

Whenever I try to wrap my head around his tight string of syllogisms, my brain gets so fried it's—almost fun. Mercy! It's like *Alice in Wonderland*. Now, having leapt down the rabbit hole and landed in this place, I find things becoming curiouser and curiouser.

It's a chilly Monday in late March 2002. I'm at Princeton University. My host is Professor Peter Singer, often called—and not only by his book publicist—the most influential philosopher of our time. He's the man who wants me dead. No, not me. Babies who might come to be like me if allowed to live. He also believes that in some circumstances it should be lawful to kill, at any age, individuals with cognitive impairments so severe that he doesn't consider them "persons." What does it take to be a person? Awareness of one's own existence in time. The capacity to harbor preferences as to the future, including the preference for continuing to live.

At this stage of my life, he says, I am a person. However, as an infant, I wasn't. I, like all infants, was born without self-awareness. And eventually, assuming my brain finally gets so fried that I fall into that wonderland where self and other and present and past and future blur into one boundless, formless all or nothing, then I'll lose my personhood and therefore my right to life. Then, he says, I might be put out of my misery, or out of my bliss or oblivion, and no one count it murder.

I am the token cripple with an opposing view.

◆

My reasons for accepting Singer's invitation are both political and personal. Politically, I see a rare opportunity to experiment with modes of discourse that might work with very tough audiences. Personally, I expect to get a great story, first for telling and then for writing down.

By now I've told the story to family and friends and colleagues on long car trips, over lunches and dinners, and in a couple of formal speeches. But it proves to be a story that won't settle down. It lacks structure; I'm miles away from a rational argument. The telling keeps getting interrupted by questions, like these, frequently asked:

Q: Was he totally grossed out by your physical appearance?
A: He gave no sign of it. None whatsoever.
Q: How did he handle having to interact with someone like you?
A: He behaved in every way appropriately, treated me as a re-

spected professional acquaintance, was a gracious and accommodating host.

Q: Was it emotionally difficult for you to take part in a public discussion of whether your life should ever have happened?

A: It was very difficult. And horribly easy.

Q: Did he get that job at Princeton because they like his ideas on killing disabled babies?

A: Those ideas apparently didn't hurt, but he's most famous for animal rights. He's the author of *Animal Liberation*.

Q: How can he put so much value on animal life and so little value on human life?

That last question is the only one I avoid. I used to say, I don't know; it doesn't make sense. But now I've read some of Singer's writing and I admit it does make sense—within the conceptual world of Peter Singer. But I don't want to go there, or at least not for long. It's only a place to visit.

✦

I first meet Singer in April 2001, when he is invited to the College of Charleston, not two blocks from my house, to lecture on "Rethinking Life and Death." I am dispatched by Not Dead Yet, the national organization that is leading the disability rights opposition to legalized assisted suicide and disability-based killing.

I arrive almost an hour early to reconnoiter, to take in the scene as the scene is forming. I mark key locations: security, media. The scene is entirely peaceful; even the boisterous display of South Carolina spring is muted by gray wisps of Spanish moss and mottled oak bark.

I roll around the corner of the building and am confronted with the unnerving sight of two people I know sitting on a park bench eating veggie pitas with Singer. Sharon is a veteran activist for human rights. Herb is South Carolina's most famous atheist. Good people, I've always thought—now sharing veggie pitas and conversation with a proponent of genocide. I try to beat a retreat, but Herb and Sharon have seen me. Sharon gets up, tosses her trash, and comes over. After we exchange the usual courtesies, she asks, "Would you like to meet Professor Singer?"

She clearly doesn't have a clue. She probably likes his book on animal rights. "I'll talk to him in the Q&A."

But Herb, with Singer at his side, is fast approaching. They are looking at me and Herb is talking, no doubt saying nice things about me. He'll be saying I gave a talk against assisted suicide at his secular humanist group a while back. He didn't agree with everything I said, he'll say, but I was brilliant. Singer appears interested, engaged. I sit where I'm parked. Herb makes an introduction. Singer extends his hand.

I hesitate. I shouldn't shake hands with the Evil One. But he is Herb's guest, and I simply can't snub Herb's guest at the college where Herb teaches. Hereabouts the rule is that if you're not prepared to shoot on sight, you have to be prepared to shake hands. I give Singer the three fingers on my right hand that still work. "Good afternoon, Mr. Singer. I'm here for Not Dead Yet."

I want to think he flinches just a little. Not Dead Yet disrupted his first week at Princeton University. I sent a check to the fund for the fourteen arrestees, who included a number of comrades in power chairs. But if Singer flinches, he instantly recovers. He answers my questions about the lecture format. When he says he looks forward to an interesting exchange, he seems entirely sincere. What stands out in memory about that first meeting is Singer's apparent immunity to my looks, his lack of the visible discombobulation I expect, his immediate ability to deal with me as a person with a particular point of view.

◆

I go into the hall with no plan. The flyer from Not Dead Yet has twenty good talking points, but they're secondhand. I know the people who wrote the flyer; they are scrupulously careful with their analysis. But if Singer claims he's been quoted out of context, I won't have much of a comeback. If he asks me which of his books or articles I've read in full, I'm in trouble. I'll have to say none. I need to glean something from the lecture itself, maybe some glint of disability prejudice, some whiff of the outrageous, that I can weave into the kind of withering cross-examination that happens in real life only when you're very lucky—and very well prepared.

Singer makes it easy. He lays everything out. The basic assumptions of Preference Utilitarianism. The illogic of allowing abortion but not infanticide, of allowing withdrawal of life support but not active killing. He weighs utilities and spins out his bone-chilling argument for killing disabled babies and replacing them with nondisabled babies who have a greater chance at happiness. It's all about allowing as many people as possible to fulfill as many of their preferences as possible.

As soon as he's done, I get the microphone. As a practicing lawyer, I disagree with his jurisprudential assumptions. Illogic is not a sufficient reason to change the law; law serves many competing needs and interests. As an atheist, I object to his using religious terms ("the doctrine of the sanctity of human life") to characterize his critics. Singer takes a notepad out of his pocket and jots down my points, apparently eager to take them on, and I proceed to what I see as the heart of my argument: that the presence or absence of a disability doesn't predict quality of life. I question his replacement-baby theory, with its assumption of "other things equal," arguing that people are not fungible. I draw out a comparison of myself and my nondisabled brother

206 · Too Late to Die Young

Mac (the next-born after me), each of us with a combination of
gifts and flaws so peculiar that we can't be measured on the
same scale.

He responds to each point with clear and lucid counterarguments. He proceeds with the assumption that I am one of the
people who might reasonably have been killed at birth. He
sticks to his guns, conceding just enough to show himself open-
minded and flexible. We go back and forth for ten long minutes. Even as I am horrified by what he says, and by the fact that
I have been sucked into a civil discussion of whether I ought to
exist, I can't help being dazzled by his verbal facility. He is so
respectful, so free of condescension, so focused on the argument,
that by the time the show is over, I'm not exactly angry with
him. Yes, I am shaking, furious, enraged—but it's with the big
room, two hundred of my fellow Charlestonians who have listened with polite interest, when in decency they should have
run him out of town on a rail.

✦

By the following December, a lot has happened—including
September 11 and my fall from my chair—but my Sunday afternoon chat with Peter Singer still merits a bullet point in my
annual canned December letter. But that causes a dilemma. It is
part of my personal honor code that anyone mentioned by name
in my canned letter gets a copy. The only exception is Jerry
Lewis; I am sure Lewis wouldn't want to hear from me. Should
the exception extend to Singer? I decide not. I write a brief note
on a beautiful card that is entirely free of religion, and put it on
the stack to mail.

✦

In mid-January, I get the nicest possible e-mail from Singer.
"Dear Harriet [if I may]." Just back from Australia, where he's

from. Glad to hear from me. Hopes I've fully recovered from my fall. Agrees with my comments on the world situation. Supports my work against institutionalization. And then—some pointed questions to clarify my views on selective infanticide.

I reply. Fine, call me Harriet, and I'll reciprocate in the interest of equality, though I'm accustomed to more formality. Skipping agreeable preambles, I answer his questions on disability-based infanticide and pose some of my own. Answers, and more questions come back. Back and forth over several weeks it proceeds, an engaging discussion of baby killing, disability prejudice, and related points of law and philosophy. Dear Harriet. Dear Peter.

Singer wants to understand how someone who is not a religious fanatic—who is, indeed, as good an atheist as he is—could disagree with his entirely reasonable views. At the same time, I'm trying to plumb his theories. What has him so convinced it would be best to allow parents to kill babies with severe disabilities, and not other kinds of babies, if no infant is a "person" with a right to life? I learn it's partly that both biological and adoptive parents prefer healthy babies. But I have trouble with basing life-and-death decisions on market considerations when the market is structured by prejudice. I offer a comparison hypothetical: "What about mixed-race babies, especially when the combination is entirely nonwhite, who I believe are about as unadoptable as babies with disabilities?" Wouldn't a law allowing the killing of these undervalued babies validate race prejudice? Singer agrees there is a problem. "It would be horrible," he says, "to see mixed race babies being killed because they can't be adopted, whereas white ones could be." What's the difference? Preferences based on race are unreasonable. Preferences based on ability are not. Why? To Singer, it's pretty simple: disability makes a person "worse off."

Are we "worse off"? I don't think so. Not in any meaningful

sense. There are too many variables. For those of us with congenital conditions, disability shapes all we are. Those disabled later in life adapt. We take constraints that no one would choose and build rich and satisfying lives within them. We enjoy pleasures other people enjoy, and pleasures peculiarly our own. We have something the world needs.

Pressing me to admit a negative correlation between disability and happiness, Singer presents a scenario: imagine a disabled child on the beach, watching the other children play.

It's right out of the telethon. I expected something more sophisticated from a professional thinker. I respond. "As a little girl playing on the beach, I was already aware that some people felt sorry for me, that I wasn't frolicking with the same level of frenzy as other children. This annoyed me, and still does." I take the time to write a detailed description of how I, in fact, had fun playing on the beach, without the need of standing, walking, or running. But, I've had enough. I suggest that we have exhausted our topic and I'll be back in touch when I get around to writing about him.

He responds by inviting me to Princeton. I fire off an immediate maybe.

Of course I'm flattered. Mama will be impressed. But there are things to consider. Not Dead Yet has declared—and I completely agree—that Singer's views are so far beyond the pale that we should not legitimate them with a forum. We should not make our own lives subject to debate. Moreover, any spokesman chosen by the opposition is by definition a token, not my favorite role. Yet I'm thinking about it. Even if I'm a token, I won't have to act like one. Also, I'm kind of stuck. If I decline, Singer can make some hay: "I offered them a platform, but they refuse rational discussion." I've laid myself wide open.

Singer proposes two exchanges of views, one during his ten A.M. undergraduate course on practical ethics and the other open to the whole university, later in the day. This sounds like debating my right to exist—and on my opponent's turf, with my opponent moderating. I offer a counterproposal, to which Singer proves amenable. I will give the class some comments on infanticide and related issues, and then Singer can grill me as hard as he likes before we open it up for the students. Later in the day, I might take part in a discussion of another disability issue in a neutral forum; I suggest the law school. Singer informs me Princeton has no law school, but I could introduce a topic and assign readings of my choice to a faculty/student discussion group sponsored by his department but with cross-departmental membership. I'm told it is a convivial dinner meeting. I accept and announce the topic: assisted suicide, disability rights, and the illusion of choice.

I inform a few movement colleagues of this turn of events, and advice starts rolling in. I decide to go with the advisers who counsel me to do the gig, lay low, and get out of Dodge.

+

I ask Singer to refer me to the person who arranges travel at Princeton. I imagine some capable and unflappable woman like Beth, whose varied job description at a state university includes handling visiting artists. Singer refers me to his own assistant, who certainly seems capable enough. However, almost immediately Singer jumps back in via e-mail. It seems the nearest hotel has only one wheelchair-accessible double room, a suite that rents for $600 per night. What to do? I know I shouldn't be so accommodating, but I say I can make do with an inaccessible room if it has certain features. Other logistical issues come up. We go back and forth. Questions and answers. Do I really need a lift-equipped vehicle at the airport? Can't my assistant assist me into a conventional car?

By the time we're done, Singer knows I'm twenty-eight

inches wide and don't fold up. I have trouble controlling my wheelchair if my hand gets cold. Even one step is too many. I can swallow purees, soft bread, and grapes. I use a bedpan, not a toilet. None of this is a secret, none of it cause for particular angst, but I wonder whether Singer is jotting down my specs in his little notepad, as evidence of how "bad off" people like me really are.

At some point, I realize I must put one more issue on the table: etiquette. I was criticized within the movement when I confessed to shaking Singer's hand in Charleston, and some are appalled that I have agreed to break bread with him in Princeton. I think they have a point, but, again, I'm stuck. I'm engaged for a day of discussion, not a picket line. It's not in my power to marginalize Singer at Princeton; nothing would be accomplished by displays of personal disrespect. However, chumminess is clearly inappropriate. I tell Singer that in the lecture hall it can't be Harriet and Peter; it must be Ms. Johnson and Mr. Singer.

He seems genuinely nettled. Shouldn't it be Ms. Johnson and Professor Singer, if I want to be formal? To counter, I invoke the ceremonial Lowcountry usage, Attorney Johnson and Professor Singer, but point out that Mr./Ms. is the custom in American political debates and might seem more normal in New Jersey. All right, he says. Ms./Mr. it will be.

At the office, I describe this awkward social situation to Tim. He gives forth a full-body shudder. "That poor, sorry son of a bitch! He has no idea what he's in for."

I feel like saying, Forget about Singer—I'm not headed into a forensic competition; I want to win hearts and minds, to connect with at least a student or two. But instead I accept a kind offer of solidarity. The Charleston bar takes pride in going for the jugular with courtly manners. I'm almost ready to go.

✦

Being a disability rights lawyer lecturing at Princeton does confer some cachet at the Newark airport. I need all the cachet I can get. Delta Airlines has torn up my power chair. Again.

When they inform me of the damage in Atlanta, I throw a monumental fit and demand that a repair person meet me in Newark with new batteries to replace the ones inexplicably destroyed. Then I am told no new batteries can be had until the morning. It's Sunday night. On arrival in Newark, I'm told of a plan to put me up there for the night and get me repaired and driven to Princeton by ten A.M.

"That won't work. I'm lecturing at ten. I need to get there tonight, go to sleep, and be in my right mind tomorrow."

"What? You're lecturing? They told us it was a conference. We need to get you fixed tonight!"

Carla the gate agent relieves me of the need to throw any further fits by undertaking on my behalf the fit of all fits. "Don't tell me," she shouts into a cell phone, "that you don't know somebody who knows somebody who has the key to a store where they sell batteries. Get somebody to get somebody to open up a store and sell you those batteries and get over here! She's lecturing at Princeton at ten in the morning and we got to get her there tonight!"

Soon there is a promise of batteries tonight, and I'm beginning to be charmed by the shouting manners of Newark. Carla barks an order to Princeton's lift-equipped contract driver to wait and provides food vouchers, phone cards, and the pass to the VIP lounge.

Carmen, the personal assistant I'm traveling with, pushes me in my disabled chair around the airport in search of a place to use the bedpan. However, instead of diaper-changing tables, which are functional though far from private, we find a flip-down plastic shelf that doesn't look like it would hold my seventy pounds of body weight. It's no big deal; I've restricted my fluids. But Carmen is a little freaked. It's her first adventure in power-chair air travel. I thought I prepared her for the trip, but I guess I neglected to warn her about the probability of wheelchair destruction. I keep forgetting that even people who know me well don't know much about my world.

We reach the hotel at ten-fifteen P.M., four hours late at the end of a very long day.

◆

I wake up tired. I slept better than I would have slept in Newark with an unrepaired chair, but any hotel bed is a near guarantee of morning crankiness. I tell Carmen to leave the TV off because I don't want to hear the temperature. Whatever it is, it's bound to fill me with dread. I hate to be cold.

With the help of Carmen's hands, I do the morning stretch. I let myself be propped up to eat oatmeal and drink tea. As the caffeine kicks in, silence gives way to conversation about practical things. Carmen lifts me into my chair and straps a rolled towel under my ribs for comfort and stability and to placate my shoulder, which has been creaky since Tucson. She tugs at my clothes to remove wrinkles that could cause pressure sores. She switches on my motors and gives me the means of moving without anyone's help. They don't call it a power chair for nothing.

I drive to the mirror. I undo yesterday's braid, fix the part, and comb the hair in front. Carmen combs where I can't reach. I divide the mass into three long hanks and start the braid behind my left ear. Section by section, I hand it over to her, and her unimpaired young fingers pull tight, crisscross, until the braid is fully formed. She binds the end with a rubber band and lets it fall past my knees. She hands me my earrings and I poke the wires in.

A big polyester scarf completes my costume. Carmen lays it over my back. I drape it the way I want it, but Carmen starts fussing with it, trying to tuck it down in the back. I tell her it's fine and she stops.

On top of the scarf, she wraps the two shawls that I hope will substitute for an overcoat. I don't own any real winter clothes. I stay out of the cold, such cold as we get in Charleston.

We review her instructions for the day. Keep me in view and earshot. Be instantly available but not intrusive. Be polite, but don't answer any questions about me. I'm glad she's agreed to come. She's strong, smart, adaptable, and very loyal. But now she's digging under the shawls, fussing with that scarf again.

"Carmen, what are you doing?"

"I thought I could hide this furry thing you sit on."

"Leave it," I say firmly. "Singer knows lots of people eat meat. Now he'll know some crips sit on sheep skin."

✦

The walk is cold but mercifully short. The hotel is across the street from Princeton's wrought-iron gate and a few blocks from the building where Singer's assistant shows us to the elevator. The elevator doubles as the janitor's closet—the cart with the big trash can and all the accoutrements is rolled aside so I can get in. Evidently there aren't many wheelchair users in this building.

We ride the broom closet down to the basement. We are led down a long passage way to a door that admits us into the well of a big lecture hall. As students drift in, I engage in light badinage with the sound technician. My brother Mac complains about people who act cute when they're being miked, so I always do it, to tweak him by proxy. My cute little prima donna act is natural enough. "Get that lectern away! It might make me look small!" The cordless lavaliere is my mike of choice. The technician is squeamish about touching me; I invite him to clip the mike to the big polyester scarf.

The students enter from the rear door, way up at ground level, and walk down stairs to their seats. By the time the hall is full, I feel like an animal in the zoo. In a way, I can't complain; unlike the zoo residents, I've voluntarily agreed to be displayed as a pedagogical tool. But I didn't reckon on the architecture, those tiers of steps that separate me from a human wall of apparent physical and mental perfection and keep me confined down here in my pit.

It's five minutes before ten. Singer is loping down the stairs. I feel like signaling to Carmen to open the door, summon the broom closet, and get me out of here. But Singer greets me pleasantly and hands me Princeton's check for $500, the fee he offered with apologies for its inadequacy.

So. On with the show.

✦

My talk to the students is pretty Southern. I've decided to pound them with heart, hammer them with narrative, and say y'all and folks. I give them peaks and valleys and play with the emotional tone, modulating three times in one forty-five-second patch. I talk about justice and even beauty and love. I figure they haven't been getting that kind of talk from Singer.

Of course, I give them some argument, too. I mean to honor my contractual obligations. I lead with the hypothetical about mixed-race nonwhite babies and build the ending around the question of who should have the burden of proof as to the quality of disabled lives. Woven throughout the talk is the presentation of myself as a representative of a minority group that has been rendered invisible by prejudice and oppression, a participant in a discussion that would not occur in a just world.

I let it go longer than I should; their faces show they're going where I'm leading and I don't want to let them go. But the clock on the wall behind them reminds me of promises I mean to keep, and I stop talking and submit myself to examination and inquiry.

Singer's response is surprisingly soft; maybe after hearing that this discussion is insulting and painful to me, he doesn't want to exacerbate my discomfort. His reframing of the issues is almost pro forma, abstract, entirely impersonal. The students' inquiries are fairly predictable: anencephaly, permanent unconsciousness, eugenic abortion. I respond to some with stories, but mostly I give answers I could have e-mailed in.

I call on a young man near the top of the room.

"Do you eat meat?"

"Yes, I do."

"Then how do you justify—"

"I haven't made any study of animal rights, so anything I could say on the subject wouldn't be worth everyone's time."

The next student wants to work the comparison of disability and race, and Singer joins the discussion until he elicits a comment from me that he can characterize as racist. He scores a point, but that's all right. I've never claimed to be free of prejudice, just struggling against it.

When the class ends, Singer proposes a walk around campus, unless I think it would be too cold. What the hell? "It's probably warmed up some. Let's go out and see how I do."

He doesn't know how to get out of the building without using the stairs, so this time it's my assistant leading the way. When we get out of the building, Carmen falls behind a couple of paces, like a respectful chaperone, and Singer and I continue the conversation.

In the classroom there was a question about keeping alive the unconscious. In response, I told a story about a family I knew as a child who took loving care of a nonresponsive teenaged girl, acting out their unconditional commitment to each other, making all the other children, and me as their visitor, feel safe. This doesn't satisfy Singer. "Let's assume we can prove, absolutely, that the individual is totally unconscious and that we can know, absolutely, that the individual will never regain consciousness."

I see no need to state an objection, with no stenographer present to record it; I'll play the game and let him continue.

"Assuming all that," he says, "don't you think continuing to take care of that individual would be a bit—weird?"

"No, done right, it could be profoundly beautiful."

"But what about the caregiver, a woman typically, who is forced to provide all this service to a family member, unable to work, unable to have a life of her own?"

"That's not the way it should be. Not the way it has to be. As a society we should pay workers to provide that care in the home. In some places, it's been done that way for years. That woman shouldn't be forced to do it, any more than my family should be forced to do my care."

Singer takes me around the architectural smorgasbord that is Princeton University by a route that includes not one step, unramped curb, or turn on a slope. In the distance, through an archway, I see what look like acres of colonnaded steps featured in the recent film, *A Beautiful Mind*. I cringe to think how this pleasant walk would look on film, perhaps in some flattering documentary about Singer; I can almost hear the voice-over, explaining that the docile American disability rights movement respects Singer's ideas, unlike the uncivilized rabble who ran him out of Germany a few years ago. Before I came, Singer asked about videotaping the class for an Australian filmmaker; I declined but didn't think to say no to photos generally. Would Carmen have the presence of mind to block the shot? I don't know. But I'm not worried. Within the strange limits of this strange assignment, it seems Singer is doing all he can to make me comfortable.

He asks what I thought of the students' questions.

"They were fine, about what I expected. I was a little surprised by the question about meat-eating."

"I apologize for that. That was out of left field."

"It's all right. I should have expected it."

"No, it wasn't your topic. But—I think what he wanted to know is how you can have such high respect for human life and so little respect for animal life."

"I'm sure that is what he wanted to know. People have lately been asking me the converse, how you can have so much respect for animal life and so little respect for human life."

"And what do you answer?"

"I say I don't know. It doesn't make a lot of sense to me."

"Well, in my view—"

"Look. I have lived in blissful ignorance all these years, and I'm not prepared to give that up today."

"Fair enough," he says, and proceeds to recount bits of Princeton history. He stops. "This will be of particular interest to you, I think. This is where your colleagues with Not Dead Yet set up their blockade." I'm grateful for the reminder. My brothers and sisters were here before me, and behaved far more appropriately than I am doing.

✦

Aaron, the coorganizer of the National Lawyers Guild Disability Rights Committee, has come by train from New York. At noon, we meet in the hotel lobby and go with Carmen to a restaurant nearby—my driving hand did get pretty frozen during the morning stroll. He asks about the class.

"It went fine, I suppose. They liked the talk, but I keep thinking of better things I could have said in the Q&A. I was tired."

Aaron assures me I was great, with all that confidence

lawyers so effectively convey when we have no knowledge of the facts. "I'm looking forward to seeing you take on the ghoul to-night."

"It's not like that. We are monstrously civil. And you need to fall in with the program and be civil, too." I hear an unpleasant stridency in my voice. I've invited a card-carrying lunatic into a delicate situation and now I wonder if I should have.

Our conversation turns to other topics. Our committee business. Our work. Fees we're hoping to collect any minute now. How cool that *A Beautiful Mind,* with its unstereotypical view of genius-in-madness, got the Academy Award. Our states' compliance—or noncompliance—with *Olmstead*'s civil rights challenge to disability institutions. I'm feeling better. Normally Aaron's big-city world seems far away from my life in a place that tourists call quaint. Here at Princeton University, Aaron seems like an old friend from my hometown: a place called Reality.

Heading back, Carmen and I tell Aaron about an interesting sign we've seen in the hotel. We decide to check it out. I roll up to the front desk, "Tell me about the Christopher Reeve Suite."

We learn that the actor has family in the area and often spends time at Princeton. After his injury, the hotel combined three rooms into one suite that is fully accessible. I ask if we can see it, and they give us the key.

There are two bedrooms, one with a king, one with two double beds. A sitting room with a Murphy bed, a dining area, a couch, chairs, and noncontroversial art books on the coffee table. A large ADA-compliant bathroom. I roll into the shower so I can say I've been in Christopher Reeve's shower. I invite Aaron to join me so I can say I've been in Christopher Reeve's shower with Aaron. Carmen pulls out a camera.

"Wait a second," Aaron says. He tidies his jacket and takes off his hat. "OK!"

✦

A van delivers Carmen and me to the evening forum about an hour early. Singer comes down from his office with a manilla envelope, "some reading material that may be of interest." He drops it in the floppy bag that hangs on the back of my chair. He hopes I had a pleasant afternoon.

Yes, indeed. I report a pleasant lunch and a very pleasant nap and tell him about the Christopher Reeve Suite.

"Do you suppose that's the six-hundred-dollar accessible suite they told me about?"

"Without doubt. And if I'd known it was the Christopher Reeve Suite, I would have held out for it."

"Of course you would have!" Singer laughs. "And we'd have had no choice, would we?"

I give him the short version of what it was like to be on the floor when Reeve spoke to the Democratic convention, and we talk about image and ritual in American politics, about Bill Clinton and the crew now in charge. Singer is easy to talk to, very good company. Such a pity that he regards lives like mine as avoidable mistakes.

The others arrive. I find I'm looking forward to the soft vegetarian meal that has been arranged; I'm hungry. Assisted suicide, as difficult as it is, doesn't cause the kind of agony I felt discussing disability-based infanticide. In this one, I understand and to some degree can sympathize with the opposing point of view—misguided though it is.

There are some awkward minutes when Aaron somehow sets off a frightening security alarm, but soon we settle into the conventions of an academic discussion. My opening sticks to the five-minute time limit. I introduce the issue as framed by academic articles Not Dead Yet recommended for my use. Law professor Andrew Batavia argues for assisted suicide based on autonomy, a principle generally held high in the disability rights movement. He says if we need assistance to effectuate our choices, we are entitled to that assistance, even if the choice is suicide. But psychology professor Carol Gill says it's disability discrimination to try to prevent most suicides while facilitating the suicides of ill and disabled people. She asks whether such discrimination is justified and makes a case from the empirical evidence that it is not. The case for assisted suicide rests on stereotypes that our lives are inherently so bad that it's entirely rational if we want to die.

In the discussion that follows, I argue that choice is illusory in a context of pervasive inequality. Choices are structured by oppression. We shouldn't offer assistance with suicide until we all have the assistance we need to get out of bed in the morning and live a good life. Common causes of suicidality—dependence, institutional confinement, being a burden—are entirely curable. I tell them about the *Olmstead* Supreme Court decision that declared unwanted, unneeded institutional confinement a form of illegal segregation. It is unknown to everyone in the room except Aaron and Carmen.

I struggle to give them a real-life perspective. When I talk about "the transformation to butt-wipee status," their reactions tell me I'm being more earthy than is customary among this herd of herbivores. But Aaron, the sanest person in the room, I'm thinking now, backs me up with dashes of reality from the psychiatric hospitals and courtrooms that he haunts, so I am emboldened to press on.

Singer, seated on my right, participates in the discussion but doesn't dominate it. During the meal, I occasionally ask him to put things within my reach and he competently complies.

I feel like I'm getting to a few of them when a student asks me a question. The words are all familiar, but they're strung together in a way so meaningless that I can't even retain them—

it's like a long sentence in Tagalog. I can only admit my limitations. "That question's too abstract for me to deal with. Can you rephrase it?"

He indicates that it's as clear as he can make it, so I move on.

Awhile later, my right elbow slips out from under me. This is awkward. Carmen is opposite me; to make the necessary adjustment, she'd need to stand up, walk around the table, and interrupt the flow of talk. Normally I get whoever is on my right hand to do this sort of thing. Why not now? I gesture to Singer. He leans over and I whisper. "Grasp this wrist and pull forward one inch, without lifting." He looks a little surprised but follows my instructions to the letter. He sees that now I can again reach my food with my fork. I get the idea that he may now understand what I was saying a minute ago, that most of the assistance disabled people need does not demand medical training.

A philosophy professor says, "It appears that your objections to assisted suicide are essentially tactical."

"Excuse me?"

"By that I mean, they are grounded in current conditions of political, social, and economic inequality."

"Exactly."

"What if we assume that such conditions do not exist?"

"Why would we want to do that?"

"I want to get to the real basis for the position you take."

"The real basis is that we're talking about making laws. Laws are made for societies. All societies have political, social, and economic conditions. Laws must be made with reference to those conditions. I don't see the point in assuming their nonexistence."

A few of the students seem to like this, but mostly I feel like I'm losing caste. It is becoming very clear that I'm not a philosopher. I'm like one of those old practitioners who used to visit my law school and bluster about life in the real world. Such a bore! A once-sharp mind gone muddy! That's how I regarded them then, but now I don't mind knowing I'm one of them. I've been changed by my years in the trenches.

The forum is ended and I've been able to eat very little of my pureed food. I ask Carmen to find the caterer and get me a container. Singer jumps up to take care of it. He returns with a box and obligingly packs my food to go.

✦

In the hotel room, I ask Carmen to check out the reading material Singer dropped in my bag. It's a copy of *Writings on an Ethical Life,* varied selections from his previously published work. The cover photo is startling. His disembodied head is encased in a graphic black bubble. His face is lit from beneath, a cinematographer's cliché for the spooky. I wonder if Singer, apparently as oblivious to visual image as I am image-conscious, has noticed that his publisher is trading on the public perception that he is, to use Aaron's term, a ghoul.

On the flyleaf, Singer has written, "For Harriet Johnson, So that you will have better answers to questions about animals. And thanks for coming to Princeton. Peter Singer. March 25, 2002."

Under the crazy circumstances, I think the inscription is entirely appropriate.

✦

When I get home, people are clamoring for the story. The lawyers want the blow by blow of my forensic triumph over the formidable foe; when I tell them it wasn't like that, they insist that it was. Within the disability rights community, the reaction is more tentative. It is generally assumed that I handled the substantive discussion well, but people worry that my civility may have given Singer a new kind of legitimacy. They're relieved that there were no photos and no press, but somewhat nervous when I say that one day I expect to write about the experience.

There is welcomed solidarity. I wouldn't have done it, says one comrade, but I'm glad you did. Thanks for putting your persona on the line. An elderly gent who tends to be a bit flirtatious, inquires, "Was your date with the professor consummated?" I reply, "Yes, if your definition of consummation includes civil academic discourse, pleasant strolling, and letting one's date pack one's doggie bag."

With others I can't be so flip. I hear from my movement sister Laura in Denver, who has written insightfully about power relationships and caregiving. She is appalled that I let Singer provide even minor physical assistance at the dinner. How could I put myself in a relationship with Singer that made him appear so human, even kind?

I struggle to explain. I didn't feel disempowered; quite the contrary, it seemed a good thing to make him do some useful work. And then, the hard part: I've come to believe that Singer actually is human, even kind in his way. The prejudice he represents isn't limited to monsters and ghouls. There ensues a discussion of good and evil and personal assistance and power and philosophy and tactics for which I'm profoundly grateful.

I e-mail Laura again. This time I inform her that I've changed my will—she'll get the book Singer gave me, with its peculiar inscription. "It will make a fine addition to your collection of books on disability, or nice fuel for a bonfire—whichever you prefer." She responds that she's changing her will, too. I'll get the autographed photo of Jerry Lewis she received as an MDA poster child. We joke that each of us has given the other a "reason to live."

I've had a nice e-mail from Singer, hoping Carmen and I and the chair got home without injury, relaying positive feedback from my audiences—and taking me to task for a statement that isn't supported by a relevant legal authority, which he looked up. I report that we got home exhausted but unharmed, and concede that he's caught me in a generalization that should have been qualified. It's clear that the conversation will continue.

I am sucked into the daily demands of law practice, family, community, and politics. In the closing days of the state legislative session, I help get a bill passed that might move us one small step toward a world in which killing won't be such an appealing solution to the "problem" of disability. It's good to focus on this kind of work. But the conversations with and about Singer continue. Unable to muster the appropriate moral judgments, I ask myself a tough question: Am I in fact a silly little lady whose head is easily turned by a man who gives her a kind of attention she enjoys? I ask Laura, but in somewhat different terms: "Do you think I've been taken in by a sure-enough sociopath?"

"I don't think so," she answers, "but I wonder if your Southern politeness has dulled your righteous anger."

I have to confess—something about Laura draws me toward confession—that I can't seem to sustain righteous anger for more than about thirty minutes at a time. My view of life tends more toward tragedy.

◆

The tragic view comes closest to describing how I now look at Peter Singer. He is a man of unusual gifts, reaching for the heights. As he has written, he wants a system of ethics derived from fact and reason, that largely throws off the perspectives of religion, place, family, tribe, community, maybe even species— to assume "the point of view of the universe." His is a grand, heroic undertaking.

But like the protagonist in a classical drama, Singer has his flaw, that unexamined prejudice—that all-too-common belief that disabled people are inherently "worse off," that we "suffer," that we "have a lesser chance of happiness." Because of this prejudice, and his rare courage in taking it to its logical conclusion, catastrophe looms. Here in the midpoint of the play, I can't look at him without fellow-feeling.

I am regularly confronted by people who tell me Singer doesn't deserve my human sympathy. I should take the role of Nemesis and make him an object to be cut off, silenced, destroyed absolutely. And I find myself lacking a logical argument to the contrary.

I am talking to Beth on the phone and Singer's name comes up. "You kind of like the monster, don't you?"

I find myself unable to evade, certainly unwilling to lie. "Yeah, in a way. And he's not exactly a monster."

"You know, Harriet, there were some very pleasant Nazis. They say the SS guards went home and played on the rug with their children every night."

"I suppose that's true."

Her harshness has come as a surprise. She isn't inclined to moralizing; in our family, I'm the one who always sets people straight. She can tell I'm chastened; she changes the topic, lets me off the hook.

When I put the phone down, my argumentative nature feels frustrated. In my mind, I replay the conversation, but this time defend my position.

"He's not exactly a monster."

"He's advocating genocide."

"That's the thing. In his mind, he isn't. He thinks the humans he is talking about aren't people, aren't 'persons.'"

"But that's the way it always works, isn't it? They're always objects, not persons. He's repackaging old ideas. Making them acceptable."

"I think his ideas are new, in a way. It's not old-fashioned hate. It's a twisted, misinformed, warped kind of beneficence. His motive is to do good."

"What do you care about motives?" she asks. "Doesn't this beneficent killing make your disabled brothers and sisters just as dead?"

"But he isn't killing anyone. It's just talk."

"Just talk? It's talk aimed at policy and law. Talk that's getting a receptive audience. You of all people know the power of that kind of talk."

"Well, sure, but—"

"If talk didn't matter, would you make it your life's work?"

"But," I say, "his talk won't matter in the end. He won't succeed in reinventing morality. He stirs the pot, brings things out into the open. But my side will win out. We'll make a world that's fit to live in, a society that has room for all its flawed creatures. If Singer is remembered by history, it will be as a curious example of the bizarre things that can happen when paradigms collide."

"What if you're wrong?"

"I'm not."

"But what if? Assume, arguendo—"

"Since when do you say arguendo?"

"Assume," she continues, "he convinces people that there's no morally significant difference between a fetus and a newborn. Assume that just as disabled fetuses are routinely aborted now, so disabled babies are routinely killed. Assume, further, that some future decade takes it further than Singer wants to go. Might some say there's no morally significant line between a newborn and a three-year-old?"

"Sure. Singer concedes that a logical bright line cannot be drawn. But Singer wouldn't propose killing anyone who prefers to live."

"Ah yes," she says, "that overarching respect for the individual's preference for life. Do you really think it holds up? Isn't it a bit naive?"

"Yes. I'd call it a fiction or a quasi-religious belief. I think, logically, once you kill someone all preferences are moot."

"So what if you can't break disability prejudice? What if you wind up in a world where the disabled person's 'irrational' preference to live must yield to society's 'rational' interest in reducing the incidence of disability? Doesn't horror kick in somewhere? Maybe as you watch the door close behind whoever has wheeled you into the gas chamber?"

"That's not going to happen."

"How do you know?"

"It's just not going to happen."

"Do you have empirical evidence?" she asks. "A logical argument?"

"Of course not. And I know it's happened before, in what was considered the most progressive medical community in the world. But it won't happen. I have to believe that."

Belief. Is that what it comes down to? Am I a person of faith after all? Or is this just wishful thinking? Am I clinging to foolish hope that the tragic protagonist, this time, will shift course before it's too late—even though I know that's not how these dramas play out?

I don't think so. It's less about belief, less about hope, than about a practical need for definitions I can live with.

If I define Singer's kind of disability prejudice as an ultimate evil, and him as a monster, then I must so define all who believe disabled lives are inherently likely to be less happy, or that a life without a certain kind of consciousness lacks value. That would make monsters of many of the people with whom I move on the sidewalks, do business, break bread, swap stories, and share the grunt work of politics. The definition would reach some of my family and most of my nondisabled friends, people who show me enormous kindness and who somehow, sometimes manage to love me through their ignorance. I can't live with a definition of ultimate evil that encompasses all of them. I can't refuse the monster-majority basic courtesy, respect, and human sympathy. It's not in my heart to deny every single one of them, categorically, my affection and my love.

The peculiar drama of my life has placed me in a world that by and large thinks it would be better if people like me did not exist. My fight has been for accommodation, the world to me, and me to the world.

As a disability-pariah, I have had to struggle for a place, for kinship, for community, for connection. I am still seeking acceptance of my humanity; Singer's call to get past species seems a luxury way beyond my reach. My goal isn't to shed the perspective that comes from my particular experience, but to give voice to it. I want to be engaged in the tribal fury that rages when opposing perspectives are let loose.

I can only trust in the fact that, while we struggle, we must also live with our theories and with one another. As a shield from the terrible purity of Singer's vision, I'll look to the corruption that comes from interconnectedness. To justify my hopes that Peter Singer's theoretical world—and its entirely logical extensions—won't become real, I'll invoke the muck and mess and undeniable reality of disabled lives well lived. That's the best I can do right now.

10

Art Object

When the e-mail comes in, I spend a solid two minutes in drop-jawed amazement and the next fifteen combing the codes on the Internet header for a sign that it's a practical joke, some telltale trace of Beth, maybe, or whoever put me on Oral Roberts's mailing list when I was in law school. The header betrays nothing. The post sure seems to be from a.real.person @nytimes.com, offering to publish my long narrative of my day in Princeton and piling on the praise—in fact, carrying on like someone from the small-town South. New Yorkers are blasé, aren't they? Well. I dial the putative sender's ostensible number, with its apparent Manhattan area code. I'll ride this prank where it goes.

Goodness. It's no prank. They love the story. Furthermore, they love me. At least they love the Internet-searchable me, the occasional contributor to various small publications, what Southerners call a bit of a bird, what they at the *New York Times Magazine* call a "unique voice"—with, they say with some delicacy, an "interesting visual image." Google has given them the same photos it delivered to the ER in Tucson. "Your story includes a powerful visual description of your body," I'm told. "We see some of your other writings are accompanied by a portrait. We presume you'll have no objection to being photographed?"

For any lawyer, the answer to a question beginning, "We presume you'll have no objection," must be, "It depends." I hem and haw and I guess that makes the point.

"Of course it depends. You need to know how it will be done. We'll work with you on that. We have really wonderful photographers and we'll need your ideas. We want you to be pleased. You will be pleased."

The conversation ends with more praise and mention of a sum more than ten times higher than any payment I've ever received for writing, higher even than my two biggest uncollectible legal fees of the year combined. The other details can wait.

◆

It's December 2002, weeks since I've heard from anyone at the magazine. The editorial process has been complicated by the unknown timing of the seemingly inevitable invasion of Iraq; they can't figure out how to fit my story around the coming catastrophe. Now the photography department is asking if I'm available for a shoot at the end of the week. They're ready to send a photographer to Charleston.

"Before we schedule anything," I say, "we need to discuss the plan. Is this a little picture of the author, or what?"

The scheduler wants to schedule and be done, but I can't seem to get my hands on my calendar until I know more. Finally I get some information. They plan, at this stage, to put me on the cover. Inside the magazine, they want a big photo-documentary spread showing the details of a typical day in my life.

"I don't think so," I say. "I don't know who I need to talk to, but before y'all send anyone down, I need to have a conversation with the person who makes these decisions to come up with a plan that works for me and for the magazine. I'd hate for y'all to send someone down here with an assignment that won't work."

There is a momentary frisson. Maybe it's because I said y'all. Twice. The photography department assures me the photodocumentary will be wonderful. I'll love it. It will be done appropriately.

"It doesn't matter how it's done," I say. "It's just not something that I want to do. Certainly not with this story."

My editor calls, then someone else, and I spend a good chunk of the day going back, forth, and around with the magazine. I don't like deprecating a plan they think exciting and interesting, but finally I have to say I think the daily life documentary idea is trite. It's also beside the point. The story isn't about a typical day, but a series of events that are highly unusual. I don't want this unusual story diluted with a distracting visual narrative about the Amazing Crippled Attorney! Need another reason? My daily life is such that one photo is about as good as ten. It's one position in one power chair. I could be in my office at the computer or on the phone, in my van or on the street, have my chin on or off fist, but visually it's pretty samey. I don't play golf or climb rocks or wash windows or cook breakfast or do anything to support an action shot. Most of my action is verbal and cognitive. Let's come up with something better.

At the end of the day of nay-saying, my understanding is that a photographer is coming to shoot a cover portrait and to discuss other ideas with me. I am confident that we can come up with something that will work.

◆

I invite photographer Katy Grannan into my office with her brown-eyed assistant, John. Katy loves the story. She also loves my cheekbones. Very sculptural. She is very impressed that I don't wear makeup. Ever. "You were so right," she says, "about that daily life photodocumentary concept. That's so trite. Let me explain what I do. I am not a documentary photographer. I am a portrait photographer. I don't do daily life. What I will do is an interesting series of beautiful portraits in content-rich daily life environments."

"Like?"

"The environments you encounter in the course of your day, from the time you wake up in the morning." Her eyes drift, visualizing things unseen. "What do you use? Maybe a bathtub. It could be beautiful."

Her gaze suggests she sees me draped, half-recumbent like Saint Teresa in her ecstacy or party chair Anne Frances getting bad news on the telephone, but nude. "I'm sorry. From my point of view, this sounds pretty identical to what I said no to. I told them I'd pose for the cover and talk to you about what else. I'm sorry if you didn't get the word. You might want to call New York. Meanwhile, we can go ahead and do the cover. Tell me what you have in mind for that."

She wants to sell me on the content-rich daily life environments concept. "Adam Moss—the editor in chief, you know—wants daily life environments."

"Well, he needs to know that won't be possible. Can we get him on the phone?"

Instead of answering, she asks if she and John can go to my house and look around. "No," I say. "I live with aged parents and don't do business at home."

"But the home is your personal space."

"Exactly."

"That's why I need to photograph you in it."

"No," I say. "How about the office? This is where I spend most of my waking hours."

She looks around. It's a big sunny room with old brick and

eclectic furnishings and art, plants, political mementos, and lots of little animals people have given me because other people have given me little animals to such an extent that it looks like I collect them, which I don't. There are also stacks of files and piles of paper.

"No, the office isn't good. Too much—" She pauses to find the right word. "Stuff!"

I might have called it content, but you can call it stuff. "Well, sure, it would look busy in a photo, so we could clear some of the stuff out and . . ."

Katy's thin face says no about the office. She turns to John. "Maybe we could do something—I don't know—green? Vegetation?" John likes it.

There is a copious amount of green vegetation in the immediate neighborhood, so I give them walking directions and ask them to call with the location. After an hour, they're back.

"There's not a lot out there," Katy says, pushing her hair away from her face, "but we found a stucco wall covered with vines with pretty nice leaves on the sidewalk."

She gives the location just as my secretary comes in. "Hey, that's the same block as your house!" She doesn't know I'd like to kill her for letting them know my content-rich daily life will be within such easy reach.

We're about to get going and an old friend drops in to borrow money. I introduce him to the photographers from New York. He falls on his knees as he often does. "Damn!" he says, "that magazine must have money to burn! Aren't there any Southern photographers good enough to take Harriet's picture?"

By the time I reach the vine-covered wall with the pretty good leafy sidewalk, Katy has spoken to New York. The word is evidently that she must secure my voluntary cooperation. She desperately wants to get in the house, which is so content-rich the health department would shut it down if they had jurisdiction.

To Katy, no means maybe. She makes tentative insinuations about getting into my house while John sets up the equipment. It's a state-of-the-art Victorian-style camera. Katy twists sideways and hangs her head batlike behind a cloth to get the view and tells me that I will need to be very still. She's chosen this spot partly, she says, for the terrific natural light. John brings out reflectors and shades and big big lights and makes adjustments until both natural and unnatural light fall with absolute perfection on my cheekbones and the high dome of my forehead.

For each shot, John puts film in a frame that pops into the camera. A different frame holds Polaroid film so they can get a quick idea of how things are looking. Katy directs me to tilt my head, move my eyes, adjust a finger, and stop smiling.

"What do you want me to do? Frown?"

"No, don't frown. Just don't smile."

Just not smiling isn't something I know how to do. It's not part of Southern culture. I try, but I know I'm not not smiling right. I don't want to look sad and pitiful. I don't want to look dead. I pretend I'm a fashion model and do that vacant gaze.

"Beautiful!" Katy says. "John, isn't that beautiful?"

"She's got it. Beautiful!" he says.

There are about fifty shots, each requiring new film, light measurements, light adjustments, camera change, head tilting, eye movements. We're opposite my neighborhood corner grocery store. People are coming in and out and I feel irretrievably silly surrounded by all these lights with this thin upside-down woman and this rather charming Hispanic man saying Beautiful, Beautiful. An old Gullah man rides by on his bicycle and nearly falls off. "Hey naah, Attorney! I know her!" I'm sure every movement of the Good Luck Lady is being reported to the Egyptian people who run the store.

It's been dank and misty all day. The breeze picks up and the mist is getting thicker. "It's going to rain," I say. "We better knock off."

It seems Katy is right on the verge of the perfection that her whole life has sought. She's working on lighting my shoe buckle. She can't stop.

It's raining sure enough. "Three more!" Katy says.

No way. I zoom around the corner, up the ramp, onto my porch. Of course Katy and John follow.

Dad opens the door to let us all in. He knows I have no tolerance for rainwater. "We're going to be talking on the porch," I say. Dad retreats. Katy is obviously much annoyed, but John has me thinking he's pulling for me.

We have a protracted discussion that goes in several different directions. Just let us look around in the house, let us just discuss it, we won't shoot without your permission, we won't use anything you disapprove. No No No. I say we've done the portrait. If they need more pictures, there must be something else. The story is about talking, I suggest. Maybe she could take pictures of my mouth talking. Or how about my hands gesturing? My hands, I point out, are interesting. I have thin tapered fingers that make weird shapes when they move, long perfect fingernails—I don't polish them! ever!—all very sculptural. Katy's face goes dark. Her camera doesn't do action shots, doesn't do close-ups. It's a specialized portrait camera. If Katy does the spread, it must be the Harriet full-body portrait collection. I'm not doing that. I'm sorry she has been sent on an impossible assignment. I will be glad to tell Adam Moss she has done everything possible to make it happen, but the subject does not consent.

"So, then," I ask, "are we done? Do we have the cover portrait, or can you think of anything else?"

She says she'd like to get a second portrait, to give the

magazine a choice for the cover, or maybe to open the article inside the magazine. Fine, I say, but we'll need to go to the office
or somewhere indoors. It's raining hard now.

"You have that wonderful description of your back in the
story. I want this one to show your back."

I spin around. "Here it is. Do you want to set up here?"

"Not good. The dark dress makes it blend into the wheelchair."

"Can we hang a light-colored shawl on the back of the chair
for contrast?"

"No," Katy says, "we really need to get you out of the wheelchair. How about in your bed, undressed? It would be really, really sculptural, really beautiful."

"No. Remember? We're not going in the house."

Katy accuses me of maidenly modesty, but I don't think I'm
as modest as the average maiden. She assures me she'll make me
look beautiful, but I'm not worried about looking bad. To me,
it's more about the story. Just as the story isn't about my daily
life, so it isn't—or shouldn't be—about me. It's from me, sub-
jective not objective, and multiple images of me, dressed or undressed, beautiful or not, would draw readers out of the story,
make them distance themselves from my experience, and invite
them to stare at me the way they usually do. I'm not cooperat-
ing with that.

Katy is convinced I'll like it if I give her a chance. "We don't
have to go into your house," she says. "There are other beds in
this town. John and I have hotel rooms. Why don't you let us
get you in bed with your clothes on and try some things and see
how it feels and take some pictures if you're comfortable and
anything you don't like won't be used."

I can't believe it. Get me in bed. Try some things. Anything
I don't like. . . .

It's the classic pornographer's come-on line. Here I am,

forty-five years old at this time, extremely decrepit, and I'm hearing the classic pornographer's come-on line, directed at *moi*. It is so surprising, so outrageous, so funny—I can't say no. So I say yes.

They are staying at a hotel just up the street from my office, in the zone where my daily comings and goings are known to all the locals. Katy drives me in my van. Despite having all the equipment to cope with, John gets there first and, in my honor, switches Katy to the accessible room. Now the hotel staff know that Attorney Harriet will pass a few hours in a room that has one king-sized bed in the company of a Yankee woman in army pants and boots and a good-looking young Cuban-or-something man who is toting lots of lights and camera equipment and says they're with the *New York Times*. Oh well. What good has my blameless reputation ever done me?

The so-called accessible room is laid out so there's no wheelchair clearance on the side of the bed from which I must be lifted. "It's a one-person job," I say. "I don't care who. It requires a good back and the ability to follow exact instructions." John raises his hand to volunteer.

I instruct John to grope in my crevasses to release the seat belt, then put one arm around my back and the other under my knees and quickly shift my weight onto his body. I explain how he will carry me two steps back to the bed, do a half-turn, and lay me upside down, feet at headboard. During this process, John doesn't speak. Katy asks the questions he might be expected to ask: "Does he need to support your head? Are your feet OK hanging?" I answer Katy, and John carries out the instructions. This is odd. I wonder whether this is an interpersonal dynamic they've worked out between themselves or some New York union rule whereby the assistant does the heavy work but doesn't talk to the model.

I am directing the slow pivoting of my body from upside

down to right side up. "John. Wait." Katy says. "I think I like her like that. What do you think, John?"

John backs up and appraises me. "Beautiful."

"I think so. Yes. Interesting. Beautiful. Harriet, do you mind if we take some pictures of you like that?"

What the hell. It's not a bad mattress and it's been an exhausting day—I haven't even mentioned, I think, that we had a sniper scare at the office right before Katy and John arrived— and I'm finding the vacant model's gaze isn't so difficult when there's a ceiling to stare at instead of neighbors coming in and out of the corner store to be ignored.

They set up the lights and the reflectors and the shades as I practice my stare and almost fall asleep it takes so long. They strip the bed of the patterned bedspread, remove all "stuff" that can be removed, and shoot me on pristine white sheets in dark gray dress, gray-stocking feet oriented toward pillows and headboard but a bit askew because the pivoting toward right-side-upness was under way when Katy decided she likes me upside down.

"Harriet," Katy asks, "can you turn your head?"

I try, but I can't. Too much drag from the sheets. "No, not at this angle."

"Can John turn it for you?"

"Sure."

We do about forty shots of Crip Venus in Charcoal Gray Jersey Dress. As they go along, they take Polaroids intermittently. Then John sets me up, cross-legged, like Contemplative Buddha with Collapsed Spine. And more and more and more. Beautiful. Beautiful. Beautiful.

I stare my stare and try to remember when my body has ever had positive attention from nondisabled people. Probably when I was a normal-looking baby; quite likely a change occurred when I graduated from a baby stroller to a wheelchair. Since then, nondisabled people have sometimes complimented my clothes or hair or dangly earrings, but polite people generally ignore my body, regard it as something to look past on their way to appreciating my "good" qualities. What's outside doesn't matter, is the message I get from polite people; what matters is my brain, my character, my inner self. That history tells me to tune out these photographers, see this attention as fake flattery, manipulation aimed at getting the exotic back shot or the content-richness they want, but I don't think that's it. Right now they're entirely focused on what's before them. My body. They are staring at me in a way that's entirely new to me. I am an art object. Being under that gaze, beautiful beautiful beautiful, feels odd and interesting and still yet overwhelmingly silly.

After three hours or so, they join me on the bed and lay out the Polaroids. I must say, truly, they are marvelous. Sculptural. Interesting. Beautiful. I have never seen myself this way. Strange. A very odd little shape—a big head atop a twisted torso, squat and squashed and very thin, simultaneously enchanted frog and middle-aged princess. Such skin as shows is luminous. There's unusual intensity, maybe a hint of irony, behind the model's stare. Good cheekbones, too, just like Beth's. And, in the pages of the *New York Times Magazine,* an irrelevant freak show.

I give sincere compliments. "If I ever do a nekked coffee table book like Madonna, you are the people I'd want to shoot it. These are beautiful." But I won't authorize these pictures to accompany the Princeton story. Simply impossible. And I'm not baring a shoulder, unzipping an inch or two, or whatever the next step would be. No means no.

Whereupon Katy surrenders. She told the editors I would not yield! She agrees the assignment wasn't right. There should be no narrative content in the photos. The narrative should be in the story. She was on my side all along.

✦

I have agreed to a second portrait, outdoors, with clothes on. The next morning it's raining again so I grudgingly let them set up on my porch. The porch unavoidably has Deep South color—white columns and run-amok vegetation—so Katy gets a content-rich daily life environment after all. Katy has offered to select my clothes but I still won't let her in my house, let alone give her the run of my clothes rack. I have complied with her request to create a color contrast with the chair and show off my back. It's a soft clingy turquoise knit.

Now we are congenial. All is in harmony. The dress is good. The porch is perfect, much better than inside. I am an excellent sculptural subject.

Katy scrutinizes the Polaroids. "John! Look!"

"Her feet!"

"Beautiful, aren't they?"

"Amazing," John says.

"Harriet, look! Your feet!"

"Beautiful." I've never paid them much attention, but yes, dangling in small round-toed cotton Chinese shoes, they are beautiful.

Geneva peeps through the door to see if we're still here. "Come on out," I say. She scowls big and I make formal introductions. I tell them she's been working with me for twenty-three years.

"No pictures of me, now," she says.

"No, don't worry," I say. I ask them to show Geneva the Polaroids. She studies them with an entirely unreadable face. "What do you think?"

"These all they got?"

"Yes," I say. "What do you think?"

"Well, if these the best they got, I reckon they got to use these." Having been seen, Geneva takes off to go home.

"Is she always so negative?" Katy asks.

"Oh, no!" I say. "She is one of the most genuinely positive people I have ever known."

"Then why—"

"It's just a little thing with her. She probably thinks she's supposed to have an attitude about New York people taking my picture."

They want a head-and-shoulders shot. At Katy's request, I have brought out a number of shawls. Katy selects one crocheted in natural cotton and wraps me up. She designates a spot in front of the white stucco wall and John goes about moving the equipment. He has been going back and forth to the truck and somewhere along the way got dog mess on his shoes and tracked it over the porch. I don't want to get it in the deep treads of my tires and it's difficult to get in the right spot while maneuvering around the equipment and steering clear of the dog mess.

"We need paper towels," Katy says. "Can John go into the house just to get paper towels?"

"We don't use paper towels," I say, "and Geneva has left for the day and I don't know where she keeps the rags. We'll have to work around the dog shit." So working around the dog shit, we do frame after frame, with minute adjustments of head tilt, hand position, lights, and camera.

At length they pull out the Polaroids. Katy gasps. "John. Look."

"Amazing."

"You see it, don't you?"

"Of course I see it."

Katy brings the picture to me and squats down to share the moment. "Look."

"What?" I see white Harriet in white shawl against white wall.

"You don't see it?" she asks.

"What?"

John answers. "It's Frida Kahlo."

Hmmm. In this shot, the wheelchair isn't recognizable as such. The shawl could have come from New England or Appalachia but as it happens I got it in Cuba. So I've got dark eyes and slick dark hair, parted in the middle and braided. Oh. Here we go. I've never noticed it, but Katy's extreme camera shows it clearly: on my upper lip, the tiniest whisper of dark fuzz.

They've taken 180 pictures all together. I ask as they're packing up. They expect two will be used; no more, I think and hope, because they're all pretty samey. As we make our adieus, I shake hands and apologize for being such a difficult subject. Katy does not say I was a delight to work with and it was a pleasure meeting me, but John does.

I am moved to apologize to Katy again. I'm sure there's no one better at what she does, and I've fouled things up. "I mean, from your point of view, what could be worse? A small-town prima donna!"

They laugh a bit too hard, but that's all right. We're done. My modeling career is at an end, and none too soon.

◆

Or not. Within the week, Katy phones to say that, due to a defect in the frame that houses the film, the pictures didn't come out. All they have are the Polaroids in all three locations. The good news is, based on the Polaroids, the editors loved the pictures I authorized. Contritely, she asks please, will I let them reshoot? My contract doesn't require me to pose for pictures—I checked long ago—but I want to cooperate. Getting the cover is a big deal. If it's done right, it will mean something in the disability community. "OK," I say, "and I guess this time it'll

be easier since we'll just be redoing the ones I approved, right?"
Right. We pick a day in January.

The e-mail confirming the appointment is troubling. "The
Times loved the Polaroids I showed them. This time, I will bring
a muslin backdrop for the cover shot and we can easily do this
picture outside again, weather permitting. (The backdrop is a
solid dark gray and black. Very simple.) Adam Moss especially
loved the portrait of you sitting upright on the bed. I know you
liked this picture but did not want the story filled with too
many portraits of you, and the editors agreed. They also understood your refusal to do any 'day in the life' stuff." It sounds a
bit like she's expecting a second bite at the apple.

I write back in part: "I trust you let Adam Moss know I
won't reshoot the pictures in bed! Apart from the problem of
numerosity, they're counter to what I want to do with this particular story. The backdrop sounds fine, and I'm game to redo
the wall/porch stuff—whatever is needed."

The next I hear from Katy is a phone call after she has arrived in Charleston. She wants me to come to the hotel. She has
told Mr. Moss that I loved the picture of me sitting in bed but
didn't think it was right for the story, and he says they, the magazine editors, decide what's right for the story, and they want me
on the cover, no less, out of my wheelchair, in contemplative-
Buddha-with-collapsed-spine position. She says it really is much
more "powerful" than me in my chair. In the chair, she says, I
look "frail." Everyone agrees.

I hit the roof. I let them shoot me out of my chair with the
agreement that I could decide what can and cannot be used and
my decision stands. They are nuts if they think I look more
"powerful" in bed, when in fact I need my chair to do anything
or go anywhere on my own. I do happen to be "frail," in or out
of my chair. If the wheelchair seems so negative to everyone,
they need to get over it. I am not shooting any pictures out of

my wheelchair. Get Mr. Moss on the phone and I'll tell him myself.

Katy argues from multiple angles. She accuses me of "hiding" behind my wheelchair, of "dishonesty." Then she tries again to sell me on the idea that I'll look beautiful and powerful out of the chair. She commends the example of a "brave" woman who allowed herself to be photographed naked with burns all over her body. She thinks I am more "real" without my wheelchair. It's incomprehensible to me. But I guess my relationship to my chair—my sense that appearing without it would be an unpardonable betrayal of my community—is equally incomprehensible to her. I say we don't need to continue discussing it. I am willing to reshoot the pictures in my chair that I have approved. Let's do that.

We meet at the viney wall. Even though I'm furious—actually because I'm furious—I greet them with a nice Dixie smile. As before, Katy wants a face free of expression. Whatever. To the viney wall they fasten a black velvet curtain that folds over to cover the still-leafy sidewalk. Clipping cloth to a neighbor's ivy strikes me as a real invasion of his space, but I guess it is a city, and his wall abuts a public sidewalk.

The Polaroids come off, and it's "Alas poor Yorick": white bony head floating against blackness of shawl and background. I don't object. This isn't about making me look pretty. I let them remove the raggy bag from the back of my chair. I let them drape a shawl over the rolled-up rag that protrudes from either side of my knees. Losing the raggy bag, hiding my unique approach to leg support, I've lowered my cool-crip factor by five or six points, but that's relatively unimportant.

I agree to meet them on my porch tomorrow noon. We'll reshoot exactly what we did before. Except, Katy says, "Instead of the turquoise, could you wear something white?"

"All my white dresses are packed up for the winter."

"Well, try to find something white."

"But you loved the turquoise. Mr. Moss loved the turquoise. I think the turquoise shows off my back very nicely. Why don't we just reshoot in the turquoise?"

"If white is absolutely impossible, do you have ivory? Beige? Maybe a very pale gray?"

✦

They want to shoot at noon to get "good light" on the porch. I don't tell them this will interfere with my difficult eating schedule. I can make it work.

At the office at eleven, I eat a yoghurt and drink a third of a cup of tea. I'm worried about having fluid at an unusual time of day, but I can't possibly deal with Katy without caffeine. At eleven-thirty, I roll home, knowing I'll be slowed by students walking to their twelve o'clock classes and by the early lunch traffic downtown. I get to the porch, expecting them to be set up. They're not there. I wait. I go inside and phone the office. No messages. I get someone to look on my desk for Katy's cell number and I call her.

"Katy. This is Harriet."

"Yeah, Harriet."

"I'm here waiting for you."

"I've been sick. Violently ill. We're in the truck, just around the corner."

I go back outside and soon they arrive, thirty minutes late. It takes forever for them to get from the truck to the porch. There is a prolonged discussion outside the truck, apparently involving the reflectors and shades. Finally John comes up, then Katy.

"No white dress."

"No."

"And why is that?"

I'm tired of this. "Is an explanation really needed?"

"What's with you? I just asked a question."

"White dresses are packed up. This is January. You liked this one last time. We're redoing the pictures that didn't come out. This was what I wore in the pictures that didn't come out."

Katy tells me she has been vomiting. I do not chastise her for being late and not getting word to me.

They set up to shoot head and shoulders in front of the white wall. As before, I let them wrap me in the crocheted white shawl. Then Katy takes an opaque white shawl from among the white options I have obligingly provided and spreads it over the back of my chair. She stands back, hangs upside down behind the camera, and tells John, "We might be able to make the chair fade into the wall."

I want to say no, but it's a head-and-shoulders shot, and lots of crips' wheelchairs don't show at that level so maybe no one will know I let them hide my chair. I don't nix it, but I must fuss. "Oh, the hideous wheelchair must be concealed."

Katy bristles. "What is this obsession you have with always showing your wheelchair?"

"It's not an obsession. It's part of how I look, and—"

"Well aesthetically, it doesn't look good."

"Not to you, which to me is kind of insulting, like if you said aesthetically, your boobs don't look good or your color isn't right or something like that. But anyway we can do this head-and-shoulders shot this way. I'm just annoyed and I'm the kind of person who will get less annoyed if I'm allowed to express it just a little bit."

"You are the most difficult subject I've ever worked with!" Katy says. I'm amazed; I understand she's photographed people like Meg Ryan. "You have to make absolutely everything into a big battle, and it's not JUST because you're in a wheelchair; it's your whole way of thinking."

"I don't make everything into a battle," I insist. "We have a disagreement. I do have a different way of thinking. That's true. And, you're right, it's not just because I'm in a wheelchair. I'm not like every other person in a wheelchair, just like you're not like every other photographer, I'm sure. Each person is unique."

John interjects, "And thank God for that, right?" He might on some level enjoy the cat fight, but now he's ready to get down to work. Yes, so are Katy and I.

We take a zillion photos of white me, in white shawl, in front of white stucco. The Polaroids demonstrate that the chair does indeed vanish.

We set up on the porch, and Katy seems surprised that they've lost the perfect light they would have had at noon. The sun moves fast down here in equatorial Carolina, I almost tell them, and no Joshua is here to make the sun stand still so I can get my picture taken. I sit and wait while reflectors and shades are adjusted and ever-changing light is metered and remetered and further adjustments are made.

Katy makes conspicuous reference to the Polaroids from the last time, removes shawl to show dreaded happy turquoise dress, and ostentatiously sets me up in the same spot, same angle, same pose. But the light's all wrong. Last time it was a rainy morning. This time it's a sunny afternoon. The sun won't go where she wants it, but I position myself from place to place. Finally, she's satisfied.

Katy is hanging upside down, looking through the camera. "You'll be glad to know your chair is out front and center and your dark controller is in really sharp focus against that white column."

"Terrific. I've always dreamed of seeing a really gorgeous picture of a power chair controller in something like the *New York Times Magazine*."

John, whose job is presently to be affable, chats me up about legal topics. What do I think of all these people on death row who keep getting found innocent by DNA? Can they sue the state? What do they have to prove? What kind of damages can they get?

Meanwhile, photos proceed. Slowly, carefully, in vast numbers.

We're about done, but Katy wants me to move over a couple of inches to catch the new light. She's making me do tight tiny turns and my spindly fingers are working hard on the joy stick. A shaft of sunlight squeezes over the main bough of the pecan tree and illuminates my hand.

"Wait! Just like that! Your hand! It's beautiful. Keep it out there. On that controller."

At last. Three shots of full-body me with gleaming sunlit controller and they're packing up. I tell Katy and John I'm not shaking hands in case there's a stomach virus going around and John says, "You're right, please don't. I feel kind of queasy, to tell you the truth." But I wish them a safe trip back and hope they will be reasonably happy with the results.

"Oh yes," says Katy, "the pictures are good!"

I go into the house and luckily there are personnel inside who can enable me to enjoy an unscheduled pee, the first in many a year—the eleven A.M. tea passed right through me. I sit cross-legged on bed, in princess frog pose, and do the long-delayed phase two of lunch. My swallowing problems are not getting any better. I am still getting frequent blockages. My current theory is that I need to relearn how to swallow different textures using my surviving musculature. This week I'm working on raw oysters and white bread.

I give Dad a report of the day so far. "Am I really the kind of person who makes everything into a big battle? Am I so difficult?"

"Oh no," he says. "You're easy to deal with. As long as you get exactly what you want and no one gives you any shit."

✦

The pictures are gorgeous.

The *New York Times Magazine* cover has been described as beautifully disturbing, and most nondisabled people seem to see it that way. I'd prefer to call it disturbingly beautiful, but I'll take it the other way around if I must. The disturbing part happens inside people's heads; this unconventional body, draped and lit and posed like a fashion model, apparently floating in space in a power chair, disturbs preconceived notions, makes people question what they think they know. The beautiful part? Well, that's me. Objectively seen by Katy Grannan.

Inside the magazine, page one of the story has only a little text and a huge picture of me on the porch, framed by classical columns, shaded by dense green vegetation, wearing a soft dress I commonly wear to work, joy stick gleaming in the sun, almost an image from daily life. Then you turn the page, and I'm gone. There's nothing to stare at, only words, and more words, the story the way I tell it, the way I have lived it, from the inside out.

11

Good Morning—An Ending

It is dark when Geneva's hands turn me over. It's dark as night, but my bones tell me it's morning, they are so eager to be moved. I lie curled on my side as hints of sun push through thick low clouds and then through my window shades and I hear a mourning dove making that coo that every Southern boy learns to make when he's eleven by blowing into his hands. The dove's moaning call provokes a tittering response from his prospective mate. I eavesdrop on the doves' back-and-forth conversation and think of my beloved and of my cooing and of his tittering and of the impossibility of our mating and of his great love of natural beauty—and, perhaps improbably, I smile.

From the next room, there is the unnatural beauty of a domesticated dog snoring and the crackle of Geneva leafing through the *Post and Courier;* as always, I know she's looking to see who died yesterday and what the horoscope promises for those living today. The dog whimpers in her sleep. Geneva speaks, quietly so as not to awaken me if I'm still asleep, but gruffly. "Dog. What you dreaming of?"

When Geneva gets gruff with the dog, it's usually for the

benefit of whatever Johnsons are in earshot. Reflexively, I take her question to my heart.

What am I dreaming of? The sweet untouchable man who sent me one red rose this Valentine's Day, who loves me in most of the ways that I love him, who will be happy for me to tell him about this ordinary everyday awakening, who reminds me that there's more to touching and being touched, more to moving and being moved, than what bodies can do for bodies—and, also, yes, without doubt, who agrees with me that what bodies can do for bodies can be very very good.

Geneva brings my breakfast and then gives me a bedpan and then washes me, starting with the nighttime crusts in my eyes, all the way down to the spaces between my toes, and everything in between. If it's not Geneva, it's someone else, someone I've chosen, someone following my instructions. It's a daily necessity, entirely practical and matter-of-fact. I sometimes think how strange it would be to do these morning things in solitude as nondisabled people do, and to regard, as many of them do, a life like mine as a dreadful and unnatural thing. To me it is so natural to feel the touch of washcloth-covered hands on flesh that is glad to be flesh, to rejoice that other hands are here to do what I'd do for myself if I could.

Those hands get me in the clothes I want to wear, get me in my power chair, get me positioned for the day, and set me out. On my own, on the streets and sidewalks in an ordinary morning at home, I roll to the office.

Driving the chair is far more difficult now than in years past. That period of immobility after I fell from my wheelchair left my right hand and arm significantly weaker; it took time to learn to drive again, using my left hand for support. I've lost a lot of flesh with the result that I'm vaguely tottery. As the sidewalks irregularly slant toward the street, as I zoom up and down curb cuts, slam over rough slate, my body strains against the seat belt and the rolled towel underneath it. It's all I can do to keep myself upright. It's all about balance and compensation, resisting gravity and going with the movement. If I'm either too stiff or too relaxed, my head will fall back or my weight-bearing elbow will shift and bounce my hand off the controller. Now driving the chair requires real concentration and skill, and the harder it gets, the more I love doing it. As my limits press closer, I begin to understand what athletes mean when they talk about being in the zone. When driving the chair demanded less from me, I got less from it. It's the same with other hard-won things.

Some days, my morning roll is in some way eventful. There is an encounter with a stranger, a chance meeting with a friend, some unfolding drama that doesn't involve me but provides material for interpretation and narrative. On uneventful days, when nothing is happening, there is the simple delight of movement, of jostling and bouncing and shaking, of controlling what can be controlled, flowing with what can't. I make up little games. Some days the game is No Brakes! The object is to cover as much ground as possible before I have to stop and hear those electronic brakes click on. I look way up the street to gauge the traffic patterns and figure when I need to start creeping, how slowly, to hit the intersection exactly when the walk sign comes on. Some days the game is a simple headlong rush to the destination. I zoom through chaotic swarms of tourists, zip around the raggedy sidewalks I know so well, loop around every inconveniently placed garbage can, with maximum speed and also with style and grace.

At times, the movement is only incidental. What engages me then is being here, in this city. I rarely stray from my standard route, a route where I know the terrain intimately and the local people imagine they know me. My path is constrained but endlessly varied. I watch the sun move up in the morning sky and in and out of clouds, take in the changing light that constantly reinvents the city's classic, composed beauty. I feel the moist air roll over my just-washed skin, breathe in the odors of sea and flowering trees and restaurant grease. Some of the best mornings are the mornings when nothing happens, when there is no story but the continuing relationship of this old city with the ocean that roars just out of sight and with the living jungle that tentatively tolerates our existence here.

◆

How is it possible that nondisabled people tend to feel sorry for me? It still takes me by surprise. Peter Singer couldn't imagine a disabled child enjoying a day at the beach and he's hardly alone. The widespread assumption that disability means suffering feeds a fear of difference and a social order that doesn't know what to do with us if it can't make us fit its idea of normal. When we seek what we need to live good lives as we are, we come against that wall. Why bother? the thinking runs; all they can do is suffer. When nondisabled people start learning about disability, what seems most startling, most difficult to accept, is the possibility of pleasure.

For decades, little noticed by the larger world, the disability rights movement has been mobilizing people from the back rooms and back wards, along with more privileged people like me, to speak plainly about our needs. We make demands. We litigate. Run for office. Seize the streets. Sit through the meetings. Mark up the drafts. That kind of work has changed the world and we need to continue to do it.

But we need to do something else besides, something that may be difficult but is, I think, vital. We need to confront the life-killing stereotype that says we're all about suffering. We need to bear witness to our pleasures.

I'm talking in part about the pleasures we share with nondisabled people. For me, those include social engagement of all kinds: swapping stories, arguing hard, getting and giving a listening ear. A challenging professional life. Going to movies, concerts, and exhibits. Wearing a new pair of earrings. Savoring the afternoon hit of Dove dark chocolate. I enjoy those pleasures the same way nondisabled people do. There's no impairment; disability makes no difference.

But I'm also talking about those pleasures that are peculiarly our own, that are so bound up with our disabilities that we wouldn't experience them, or wouldn't experience them the same way, without our disabilities. I'm talking about pleasures that may seem a bit odd.

Let me give some examples.

John Hockenberry rolls across the Brooklyn Bridge self-propelled in a manual wheelchair. As he describes it, it's a high no one but a hotshot para can really know.

A nation within a nation, of Deaf people, capitalizes its name to demand recognition as a language group, equal to any other in dignity and ferocious beauty.

Barry Corbet, a hotshot para now falling apart, is stuck in bed for several weeks with a pressure sore. As he lives with one marvelous view, he says life doesn't go away; where would it go? He says life has never been richer or more juicy.

In an essay on smell, Helen Keller wrote that she could never warm up to another person who did not have a distinct and recognizable body odor.

After decades of torment, Professor John Nash recognizes his delusions for what they are and lets voices and visions and mathematical creativity cohabit in a mind unlike any the world has ever known.

My friend Kermit, a quad on a budget, goes out to lobby the legislature and finds a coffee under way. He can't grasp with his hands so he makes a legislator feed him a donut. The last lobbyist out removes his clip-on tie.

At a summer camp, a mentally retarded boy badgers a girl in a wheelchair to teach him to play checkers. He knows he's slow and she's bored, but he won't give up. Then something clicks and her explanations make sense at last and he sees the patterns and wins the game. For the smart girl in the chair—for me—it's a humorous, humbling lesson. For the slow boy, there's joy in pushing his intellectual limits. The peculiar pleasure is unique to each of us, but it's also shared; the sharing makes a bridge across our differences.

Throughout my life, the nondisabled world has told me my pleasures must be only mental, never physical. Thinking to help me, it has said my body is unimportant. I respectfully disagree. For me, the body—imperfect, impermanent, falling apart—is all there is. Through this body that needs the help of hands and machines to move, that is wired to sense and perceive, comes all pleasure, all life. My brain is only one among many body parts, all of which work through one another and cooperate as best they can.

Some people, disabled and otherwise, conceptualize a self distinct and apart from the body. I may at one time have done so. I'm not sure. I know it is somehow possible for me to talk about me and my body as though separate, even though my mind and heart say we are one. At this stage in my life, my body constantly makes its presence known as needed, telling me with an urgent pain to deal with a wrinkle under my seat belt, or reminding me with a tremble or ache or flutter of its desire for food or rest or some other pleasure. Now the body I live in doesn't only affect me. It is me.

The nondisabled world tells disabled people generally that our lot is unavoidably tragic, and if we're smiling, we're smiling through tears and despite suffering. In the face of these powerful social forces, I believe that living our strange and different lives, however we choose and manage to live them, is a contribution to the struggle. Living our lives openly and without shame is a revolutionary act.

◆

I might stop there, but before I close I think I owe you an apology. You probably want to know about my Valentine. If you've come this far with me, you're a curious person, and it's a natural thing to be curious about. You want the whole story—who he is, how we met, what happened when, and why I call him untouchable and our mating impossible.

You wonder. Is it a disability thing? Not mine surely! So maybe his or some combination?

You know, or you should know by now, everything's not always about disability. It could be a simple issue of geographical distance. Or any number of other things. A taboo. A hang-up. A code of honor. A fetish. He might be married, in prison, or a monk. He could be in hiding—a fugitive from justice or the spy who loves me. One of us, maybe both, might be gay. All these things happen, right?

Wait. You might be overinterpreting. You might consider whether the untouchability and impossibility might be temporary. You know how I carry on. I could be playing around, pining my way through a short-term separation. Could he be on a hop out of town, for example, or have a case of the flu?

Maybe, just maybe, we're dwelling on sex when what's important is love.

So what about that, you may ask, this love I mention—is it a sweet safe harbor from life's tempests? Or is it in itself a hurricane, all sturm-und-drangful? Does it give strength or drain energy? Upset equilibrium or restore balance? Are my love and I earnest, deeply serious, or do we joke and tease and flirt? Does he bring out the silly girl in me or draw out something like wisdom?

Mercy! Could it be Abelard and Heloise all over again?

The answer is yes. To some of those questions—certainly not all. Which? I am sorry, but I'm not telling.

The story's not for publication. In truth, there's no story. What they call love stories are actually about conflicts. A story needs some series of obstacles leading to some crisis. This one may be just beginning, in the setup before events play out. If so, I hope the ending is a long way away; these preliminaries are so delightful as to deserve dragging out. Or, better yet, the story might have happened real quick when we weren't paying attention. I dare to hope this is the happily-ever-after that is insufferably boring to everyone but the happy lovers themselves.

Much as I might enjoy relating the details of our billing and cooing, much as I might like to show off each little love token like that law school roommate who taped all those love-ly cards to our dorm room wall, I'll spare you. Be grateful. I'm doing you a kindness. Love, in its real and pleasant form, is best lyrical, not narrative. It's most enjoyed not as a diversion, but woven into the fabric of the routine.

So, lacking a tellable story, withholding the blow by blow, I'll try to give you the benefit of my experience in terms more politic and general. I know a juicy romance might be more fun, but this is what I have to offer you.

My experience so far has taught me that love and sex and intimacy are like so many other things.

The barriers are formidable. The constraints are by definition insurmountable.

No doubt. And yet—

In love as in life, every impossibility opens a door to some surprise. However many things may be entirely foreclosed or more trouble than they're worth, the possibilities that remain are so numerous, so varied, so far beyond the capacity of one person to experience, so marvelous—that they might just as well be infinite.

At dawn, it's usually impossible to predict whether the day will bring strange events fit for narration or the routine lyricism of life and love. Either way, it's good to meet each morning's sun awakened to all the possibilities.

Author's Note
and Acknowledgments

Here, I might be tempted to thank everyone who has made a significant and valuable contribution to my work and life, but I know the list would be unbearably long—even if I were to limit myself to contributions made within the past two or three weeks. This book gives a hint, but only a hint, of how beholden I am, day to day, to friends, family, professional colleagues, movement comrades, paid and volunteer assistants, casual acquaintances, and strangers who help me to do what I do. So I will say a few words on how this book came to be, and leave vast legions unacknowledged.

I learned to tell stories mainly from my mother, Ada Austin Johnson, who happens to have a Ph.D. in comparative literature with an emphasis in short prose narrative, but who acquired storytelling skill from her family and the air we breathe. My writing the way I do owes a great deal to Barry Corbet. As editor of *New Mobility,* Barry somehow got me doing, just for fun, a kind of writing I never imagined I'd do; portions or versions of chapters 1, 5, 6, and 7 originally appeared in *New Mobility,* greatly improved by his editing. Since his retirement, he has been a constant source of the best kind of criticism and unfailing encouragement in all things. Along with Paul and Kelly Timmons, he was first reader of this manuscript.

Barry was also first reader of "Unspeakable Conversations," whose publication in the *New York Times Magazine* catapulted my tales into a book. I wrote that piece imagining Barry would tear it apart and help me make it coherent, but instead he passed it on to his friend, a kind stranger to me, James Salter, who got it to the *Times* magazine. I remain amazed, not only that my story found such a forum, but also that it touched readers—many of whom wrote, e-mailed, and phoned—in ways I don't understand but deeply appreciate.

And there would have been no Unspeakable Conversations, but for Laura Hershey and Diane Coleman of Not Dead Yet, who chased me down one Saturday and told me to go to Peter Singer's lecture at the College of Charleston the next day. I thank them for issuing that challenge, for their friendship and solidarity before and since, and for their contributions to a movement that has opened doors for me and for millions of others and promises to transform the world in fundamental ways. Hoping as I do that the disability rights movement will prevail and disabled lives will no longer be a subject of debate, I can't thank Professor Singer for a lively discussion, but I can and do thank him for his hospitality and grace in the face of unintended consequences. At the *New York Times Magazine*, I honor Katherine Bouton for a beautiful edit and Katy Grannan for stunning photography that unquestionably drew readers to the story.

With a brilliant soft sell, Sam Stoloff of the Frances Goldin Literary Agency convinced me to undertake this book and has ably shepherded it and me over unfamiliar terrain. I am delighted that he led me to editor Jennifer Barth and Henry Holt and Company, whose faith in me and my writing is sometimes almost terrifying.

Five people spent long hours sitting in my office suite on weekends as I clattered at the keyboard to fulfill my contractual obligations to Holt: Carmen Polito, Beth Mevers, Kurt Schumacher, Karen Moldovan, and my father, David Johnson. Finally, I thank the listeners over many years who gave these tales their first reason to be.

About the Author

HARRIET MCBRYDE JOHNSON has been a lawyer in Charleston, South Carolina, since 1985. Her solo practice emphasizes benefits and civil rights claims for poor and working people with disabilities. For over twenty-five years, she has been active in the struggle for social justice, especially disability rights. She holds the world endurance record (fourteen years without interruption) for protesting the Jerry Lewis telethon for the Muscular Dystrophy Association. She served the City of Charleston Democratic Party for eleven years, first as secretary, then as chair.